For Andrew Brook

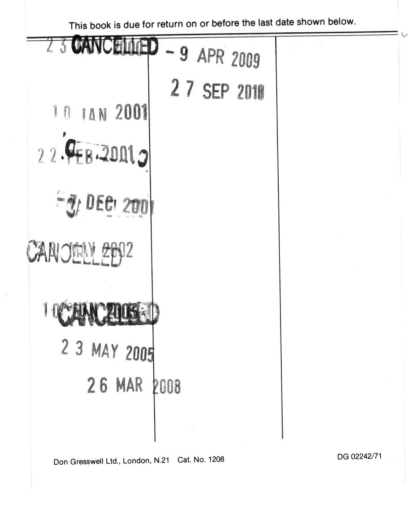

Perspectives on Equality

Constructing a Relational Theory

Christine M. Koggel

ROWMAN & LITTLEFIELD PUBLISHERS, INC.
Lanham • Boulder • New York • Oxford

ROWMAN & LITTLEFIELD PUBLISHERS, INC.

Published in the United States of America
by Rowman & Littlefield Publishers, Inc.
4720 Boston Way, Lanham, Maryland 20706

12 Hid's Copse Road
Cummor Hill, Oxford OX2 9JJ, England

British Library Cataloguing in Publication Information Available

Library of Congress Cataloging-in-Publication Data
Koggel, Christine M., 1955—
    Perspectives on equality : constructing a relational theory /
Christine M. Koggel.
      p.   cm.
    Includes bibliographical references and index.
    ISBN 0-8476-8805-4 (cloth : alk. paper).—ISBN 0-8476-8806-2
(pbk. : alk. paper)
    1. Equality.   I. Title.
HM146.K64   1998
305—dc21   97-35810
                                          CIP

ISBN 0-8476-8805-4 (cloth : alk. paper)
ISBN 0-8476-8806-2 (pbk. : alk. paper)

Printed in the United States of America

♾ ™ The paper used in this publication meets the minimum requirements of
American National Standard for Information Sciences—Permanence of Paper
for Printed Library Materials, ANSI Z39.48—1984.

Contents

Preface

Each of us is situated in a complex network of relationships that structures our lives, experiences, and perspectives in diverse ways. It would seem, then, that an account of relationships and the perspectives of those who are in oppressive relationships would be relevant to an analysis of the conditions needed to achieve equality. Yet liberal theory, which has been the focal point around which theorists have examined equality as a concept and as a goal, has not paid much attention to relationships. A central aim of this book is to change that. By taking the sociality and interdependence of human beings as the starting point for theorizing about conditions for treating people with equal concern and respect, relational theory challenges traditional liberal conceptions of personhood and of what is needed to achieve equality. Instead of limiting itself to an account of what individuals need to flourish as independent autonomous agents, a relational approach to equality asks what moral persons embedded and interacting in relationships of interdependency need to flourish and develop. Attending to the details of the lives of those who are affected by unequal and oppressive relationships shaped by particular social practices and political contexts reveals the significance of diverse perspectives. We need to take them into account in an analysis of equality. Those who are on the margins of society have distinctive perspectives, ones that reveal inequalities that tend to go unnoticed in practice and also in theory. After a careful and extended examination of the real strengths and the equally real limitations of liberalism, *Perspectives on Equality* puts an analysis of the role of relationships in language, people's lives,

and communities to work, drawing out the relevance of relationships and the perspectives of those in oppressive relationships to
an account of what is needed to treat all people with equal concern and respect. Room is then made for exploring innovative
proposals for addressing the inequalities of those whose difference
continues to matter to life prospects.

The project of studying relationships in order to reconceive
liberal conceptions of equality represents an intersection of long-
standing interests in Wittgenstein, equality, theories of justice, and
feminist work on care ethics. I am grateful to the Social Sciences
and Humanities Research Council of Canada for a doctoral and a
postdoctoral fellowship and to Queen's and York Universities
where I took up the fellowships. I would like to thank commen-
tators and audiences at the Canadian Philosophical Association,
the Canadian Society for Women in Philosophy, Carleton, York,
Queen's, Bryn Mawr, Haverford, and the University of Peking at
which earlier versions of much of this book have been presented.
I have learned an enormous amount from the increasing number
of theorists who are putting relational insights to work in various
areas of inquiry. The names of scholars whose writings have influenced my thinking appear throughout this work. Others have
been directly involved in the project and I would like to thank
them by name.

I owe an enormous debt of gratitude to Christine Overall and
Christine Sypnowich, who supervised the project in its very early
stages as a doctoral dissertation. The project benefited from Christine Sypnowich's extensive knowledge of liberal and socialist theory and from her critical acumen. I relied on Christine Overall
not only for her depth of knowledge of the feminist literature,
but also because she has been a role model in every sense. I would
like to thank Jerry Bickenbach for comments on an early version
of the chapter on affirmative action, which appeared in a special
volume on equality that he edited for *The Canadian Journal of Law
and Jurisprudence*, and Naomi Scheman for comments on an early
version of Chapter 2 on the language of equality, which will appear in a volume on Wittgenstein in the Penn State *Rereading the
Canon Series* that she is editing. Claudia Card and Mary Jeanne
Larrabee read the whole work and made many valuable sugges-
tions. I hope I have succeeded in incorporating all of them.

Susan Sherwin and Lorraine Code are central to my research,

both as feminist theorists whose work on relational theory is important and as mentors whose encouragement, advice, and support are greatly appreciated. Susan Babbitt, Sue Campbell and graduate students in the Philosophy Department at Queen's University prodded and probed at crucial stages and helped me organize and clarify my ideas. Discussions with students in seminars on equality theory and on feminism at Bryn Mawr College and moral and financial support from the college were enormously important in the final stages of the project. Special thanks goes to Michael Krausz. His support as chair of the philosophy department at Bryn Mawr and as a colleague and friend have been invaluable. I would also like to thank Noella Chamberlin and my sister, Maureen Koggel, who in very different ways made an enormous contribution to the completion of this project. Most important, I want to thank Andrew Brook. He has been there at all stages in this journey of constructing a relational theory of equality. In particular, he has read and provided extensive feedback on numerous drafts. This project has benefited enormously from his keen philosophical and editorial skills, but it would not have appeared at all without his tireless support and encouragement. All these people helped to bring this project to fruition in more ways than they know or I can express. Finally, the professionalism of all those at Rowman & Littlefield who were involved in the production process has been exemplary. Special thanks goes to Christa Davis Acampora, Robin Adler, Deirdre Mullervy, Lynn Weber, and freelancers Linda Carlson and Lynn Gemmell.

1

❦ ❦ ❦

An Overview: Steps toward Reconceiving Equality

Liberal theory has had an enormous impact on our understanding both of equality and of people. The fundamental teaching of classical liberalism that each human being has equal moral value and deserves equal concern and respect has become the foundation for various liberal accounts of how societies need to be structured to ensure equal treatment. Within the liberal tradition, theorists have provided ever-more substantive interpretations of what people need in order to flourish in social relations marred by a legacy of discrimination and inequality. Yet the view that relationships are of primary significance in people's lives and that people are essentially interdependent beings has played a limited role in equality theory. If anything, liberals have perceived these features of people to be inimical to equality, aspects of human lives that need not be taken into account in theories of justice.

In this book, I pose a seemingly simple question for liberal conceptions of equality. What happens when we take the inherent sociality and interdependence of human beings as the starting point for theorizing about conditions for treating people with equal concern and respect? The answers to that question will radically alter our understanding of equal concern and respect and of what is needed to satisfy the principle. To begin to understand the difficulties in meshing ideas about the significance of relationships with arguments central to traditional equality theory, think about how liberal theory's cherished notions of self-determination, autonomy, moral agency, and responsibility are heavily vested in accounts of individual interests, individual life plans, and individual liberty rights. The idea that relationships are relevant to an understanding of equality will need careful unpacking. In particular, we will need to examine arguments from a wide range of theorists who put social relations more generally in the foreground.

Chapter 2 takes the first steps toward reconceiving equality by showing how relationships are relevant to equality analysis in the most basic way: they underlie the very language of equality. When I say that people are equal, my description relies on a relationship I draw between a standard of comparison and the people I am identifying as equal. When I endorse equality as a worthy moral goal and proclaim how people ought to be treated, my prescription rests on a comparison between some state of affairs I conceive and the actual conditions of people who are treated unequally. Differences, inequalities, and cases of unequal treatment are determined relationally in the sense that they are judged as deviations from a presumed standard or norm. This seemingly simple strategy of describing how we in fact use concepts like "equality" is drawn from Wittgenstein's account of meaning as use, an account central to the discussion in Chapter 2.

Wittgenstein's work is not generally taken to be either relevant to moral and political theory or instructive for understanding the meaning of moral concepts like equality. Yet, his method of imagining simple language games in which people communicate and interact with others can be used for more radical purposes than he would have imagined. His account of how words function in language games is ideal for focusing attention where I think it needs to be: on the social contexts within which people interact in purposive ways. When we focus on human interaction and social practices, the function and relevance of certain kinds of relationships become apparent: relationships of similarity and difference are shaped in social practices and political contexts; standards and rules are established in relationships with others and for particular purposes; and learning the standards and following the rules are conditions for being understood by others and accepted in relationships in communities. I call this complex of relationships relational features of language and of people. We now have a space for examining how judgments of difference, inequality, and unequal treatment emerge through human interaction in purposive social practices and for shaping a conception of people as fundamentally social and interdependent beings. These insights about the relational features of language and of people and the interconnectedness of the two then form the backdrop against which I begin the critical examination of liberal and pre-liberal conceptions of equality in Chapters 3, 4, and 5.

Chapter 3 starts with a discussion of procedural equality, in particular of its historical application prior to the advent of liberal theory. An application of the relational insights from Chapter 2 teaches us that the procedure of treating like cases alike is central to all rule-following activity. When applied to people, however, identifying properties and grouping people accordingly gives those properties immediate moral significance. Prescriptions for treatment closely follow descriptions of people. Grouping people into unequal categories circumscribes the very activities, roles, life plans, and relationships of all those taken to share certain properties. Classical liberalism's decisive contribution to our understanding of equality is to undermine the notion that people can be justifiably grouped into unequal categories and to argue that procedural equality needs to be grounded by the principle of treating all people with equal concern and respect. Examining classical liberal arguments for what makes people equal serves several purposes. It allows me to reconceive liberalism's understanding of equal concern and respect in relational terms and then to give it a foundational place in the relational approach to equality that I advance. It also highlights the gap between the classical liberal theory of equal concern and respect for all and the entrenched practices of unequal treatment for many. It is these entrenched practices that we need to understand, and relational insights into the role played by unstated norms in social practices can help.

The relational features of language and of people illuminate the significance of norms in our social practices and political contexts, norms that are often hidden in the background, function to perpetuate beliefs about the inferiority of differences, and continue to make those differences significant to the way people are treated. Feminist theory has been instrumental in uncovering these norms and revealing their effects on people. I turn to Gilligan's work and her basic insight that traditional psychological theories of moral development judge women's moral reasoning capacities by measuring them against norms that fit men's experiences and lives. This insight allows me to take my analysis in a different direction: to highlight the unequal and oppressive relationships that get shaped by the taken-for-granted norms that are in place in social practices and political contexts. It also allows me to introduce the idea that examining the perspectives of those who are in these relationships is important to an account of what equal concern and respect demands, a complex idea that plays a vital role in the critique of liberal theories of equality in Chapters 4 and 5.

Extracting from classical liberalism the foundational principle of equal concern and respect does not yet tell us what is required to satisfy the principle. Two main theories have emerged in the liberal tradition with answers to the question about the conditions for equal concern and respect: formal and substantive equality of opportunity. All liberal theorists agree that treating people with equal concern and respect means providing each person with an equal opportunity to pursue the goals he or she values. Formal theorists argue that people are treated with equal concern and respect when there are no formal barriers that prevent them from pursuing life plans and goals and that the mere removal of those barriers is both necessary and sufficient for meeting the demands for equality. Nozick presents a well-known defense of formal equality. Chapter 4 critically evaluates this account of what is needed to treat people with equal concern and respect.

The inadequacies of Nozick's purely formal conception of equality become apparent when relational insights as described so far are employed and when new ones from Marxist political theory, generally thought to be hostile to equality analysis, are brought in. Critiques of Nozick by G. A. Cohen and Kai Nielsen begin with a thesis central to Marxism: "[t]he human essence is no abstraction inherent in each single individual. In its reality it is the ensemble of the social relations" (Marx 1845, 423).[1] The thesis plays a central role in the argument that the individual abstracted from political contexts and protected by rights of noninterference is an illusion. Social practices and political contexts shape people's lives in ways that determine life prospects and levels of freedom. Such an analysis goes a long way toward demonstrating the inadequacy of the Nozickean account of individuals who have their freedom enhanced and are best able to flourish when there is no state interference in their lives.

Yet Marxists tend to focus on one sort of relationship that limits life prospects and well-being; that between capitalists and workers. I argue that we need to examine oppressive power relationships of all kinds as a way of challenging even further liberal theory's resistance to the idea that relationships are relevant to an understanding of equality. On the surface, that resistance may be less evident in liberal substantive equality theory, the most influential of which is that associated with John Rawls's theory of justice. In allowing our considered judgments about fairness to enter into assessments of equal opportunity, Rawls acknowledges that inequalities emerge in social and political contexts of discrimination in which some people through no fault of their own do not have equal opportunities. In Chapter 5, Rawls's theory of justice becomes the focal point for delineating what is distinctive about a relational approach to equality.

Rawls takes it to be a positive feature of his method for arriving at principles of justice that any moral person can enter the thought experiment of the original position, stand apart from his or her own particular ends, and obtain a point of view that is impartial and unbiased about all perspectives. Susan Moller Okin, Seyla Benhabib, and Marilyn Friedman have all raised objections to this sort of account of a "thin" liberal self. I expand on these critiques and argue that we need people with all their encumbrances and in all their embeddedness in social and political contexts engaged in critical thinking about difference and perspectives to know what equality is and requires. Impartiality, in the sense of the ability to treat each person with equal concern and respect, is achieved not through the monological thinking of a solitary and isolated moral reasoner, but through a communicative process of an ongoing dialogue among different points of view.

What emerges from the critical examination of Rawls and the use of a wide range of ideas of various critics of Rawls is a radically revised original position and a new understanding of what is needed to treat people with equal concern and respect. Knowledge about the details of people's lives as they experience them and as they are affected by unequal and oppressive relationships shaped by social practices and political contexts leads to an acknowledgment of the significance of diverse perspectives and the need to take them into account in an analysis of equality. In my account, two principles emerge from this dialogical process: we ought to treat people with equal concern and respect, and we ought to respect human diversity and ways of being. To put the principles into effect, the dialogue will need certain methodological procedures for strengthening and expanding the function of reflective equilibrium, procedures such as mechanisms for ensuring that all perspectives are taken into account and that all current and proposed policies are tested by procedures that allow people to demand and assess justifications for them.

The dialogic process not only emphasizes the moral significance of our inherent sociality and interdependency, it also emphasizes its ontological significance. I turn to ontological questions about personhood in Chapter 6, where I confront familiar questions about the liberal self and then the communitarian self that is proposed in its stead. A prevalent criticism is that in liberal theory, selves are atomistic, individualistic, competitive, and possessive beings. This may be true of libertarian accounts of negative liberty rights of noninterference, but liberal substantive theorists who defend positive rights to welfare, for example, would not seem to fall prey to this criticism. But, as communitarians point out, there are other problems with the liberal self as Rawls conceives it. In contrast with the Rawlsian self, who can stand apart from his or her ends and attachments, communitarians argue that people are embedded and encumbered beings who are shaped by attachments and community values. I need to distinguish my account of a relational self from this well-known and, at least on the surface, similar communitarian self. My goal differs from communitarian ones. I want to expose the norms in a community and make their effects on the lives of all members of that community apparent. I want to draw out the full implications of a social relations view of the self for a theory of equality. To that end, the relational self implicit in Gilligan and explicit in some of the rich and varied feminist literature on and about the ethic of care provides a better model of the self than does communitarianism.

As interpreted through Gilligan's work, care is an approach that focuses on interpersonal relationships and our responsiveness to the needs of others as a legitimate foundation for reasoning about morality and moral problems in general. But Gilligan's focus on dyadic personal relationships has resulted in a characterization of care as a moral approach associated with women and applicable only to personal relationships in a private realm, not to issues of justice. I avoid the debates about whether women are more caring than men and whether care constitutes a legitimate approach to morality, and focus on an aspect of the ethic of care that has received less attention: the basic insight that the "different voice" realizes the significance of being in a "web of relationships" and reasons about moral problems in terms of connection with rather than separation from others. I then focus on the web of relationships within which we are situated to expand feminist insights into the significance of care and caring relationships in people's lives.

We are in multiple relationships situated in a constantly changing web of relationships embedded in various social practices and political contexts. Grasping the ontological and moral significance of relationships of all kinds on identity and self-concepts sheds new light on the care perspective and its function in relationships. Expanding the network of relationships beyond those considered by Gilligan shows the multiplicity of ways in which relationships can be oppressive, discriminatory, and damaging to the freedom and flourishing of some members of communities. By highlighting the effects of relationships of power, authority, and oppression on those who are identified as different and unequal, I begin to draw out the full implications of both personal and public relationships for an understanding of what is needed to treat people with equal concern and respect.

We discover that it is those who are perceived as different and inferior who tend to adopt the ethic of care. Once this becomes clear, "care" neither accurately describes an orientation particular to women nor adequately captures the processes involved or the interactions that take place between the powerful and powerless, the oppressor and the oppressed. The orientation that is described as care in the literature on the ethic of care is more appropriately described as an orientation to other, a perspective that emerges in structures of power that force those who are oppressed to situate themselves in relation to their oppressors. The notion of orientation to other is intended neither to replace nor exclude care in its general sense of concern for others. The idea of orientation to other switches the focus from care in and of itself to relationships in general, of which relationships of care are but one kind. Be-

cause the notion of orientation to other presents a critical perspective on relationships of all kinds and on caring for others in them,
it broadens the scope of an ethic of care from a theory of moral
responses in personal relationships to a political theory concerned
about equality and justice.

Those who are oppressed need to be sensitive to the effects and
implications of all relationships, both those at the personal level
and those in broader social and political contexts. They need to
know about the laws and decisions made by those in power because their lives and relationships are adversely affected by them.
As a result, those who are oppressed have particular vantage points
that can contribute to a greater understanding of how social and
legal structures maintain and perpetuate oppression. The notion
of orientation to other begins as a descriptive point about power
relations, but it has prescriptive potential. The idea that the perspectives of people who are detrimentally affected by the power
relations they are in are valid and valuable responses to structures
of power allows us to grasp that these are vantage points for identifying what is needed for equality and beginning the process of
change to current oppressive structures. Relational theory draws
attention to the interactive relations between those who are oppressed and those who oppress as potential sites for challenging
and changing oppressive structures.

A relational conception of the self as situated in a network of
complex and ever-changing relationships provides a richer account of moral agents and agency than is evident in either liberal
theory or care ethics. Applying relational insights about the significance of our embeddedness in a network of complex and
ever-changing relationships results in a critique of care that em-
beds the notion in the broader one of an orientation to other and
a critique of justice that elucidates the importance of taking diverse perspectives into account as a way of understanding what is
needed for equality. In the final two chapters, I draw out some of
the implications of all these relational insights for theories of
equality and justice and for practical policy issues.

In Chapter 7, the distinction between formal and substantive
equality is reintroduced, and Martha Minow's phrase "dilemma
of difference" is used to describe how liberal conceptions of
equality are structured by a framework that allows only two options for those who are oppressed: either they assert their similar-

ity to those in power and demand equal treatment, or they claim their difference from those in power, request special treatment, and risk being further stigmatized and disadvantaged. Within this liberal framework of policy options, feminist criticisms of equality sometimes misrepresent liberal theory, but are often themselves misappropriated and misunderstood. Relational insights once again provide a base first for revealing the underlying structure of a liberal framework that casts difference as a dilemma and then for opening the door to reconceiving the supposed tension between care and justice.

We will learn that justice as it is conceived in the Rawlsian sort of substantive equality theory is, among other things, a care perspective and that care embodies key principles of the justice perspective. We will also learn that justice needs to pay more attention to the kinds of relationships that are at the center of the care perspective more specifically and of the orientation to other more generally. Finally, we will learn that an account of our responsibilities to others requires that we place care in a framework of justice. The result of this examination is that the tension between justice and care perspectives is resolved neither by prioritizing one or the other nor by assimilating care into justice, as liberal theorists currently conceive justice, or justice into care, as feminist ethicists currently conceive care. Each can inform the other and transform the whole.

Justice is not jettisoned by a relational approach; rather, a critical perspective on relationships tells us what justice requires by revealing what is needed for treating people in all kinds of relationships with equal concern and respect. One focus of such a theory will be the impact of relationships of power, of oppression, and of authority on the people who are in them and the inequalities such relationships generate. The perspectives of those who are oppressed offer valid and valuable vantage points for imagining new ways of being, for bringing new social relations into being, and for challenging and changing oppressive structures. At the end of Chapter 7, I use relational insights to reconceive the function of rights discourse and to extend the range of positive rights to include rights to present perspectives and to have current and proposed policies tested through justificatory procedures. Lastly, relational insights are drawn together into a coherent and persuasive whole when we apply them to the practical policy issue of affirmative action. This is the topic of Chapter 8.

Affirmative action measures literally place members of disadvantaged groups into positions from which they were formerly excluded and in which they are currently underrepresented. Affirmative action is an ideal policy issue for highlighting the distinction between formal and substantive equality, for depicting the pitfalls of the dilemma of difference, and for testing and applying relational insights. A relational approach provides a new perspective on and defense of affirmative action by showing how the presence of members of disadvantaged groups in structures of power can change entrenched stereotypes of difference as inferiority, alter institutional and workplace structures that perpetuate inequalities, and challenge the assumptions underlying the liberal ideal of equality as an equal opportunity to compete for positions awarded on the basis of merit. Here we learn in concrete detail how relational theory can expand our understanding of the conditions needed for treating all people with equal concern and respect.

Relational theory holds that we are essentially and fundamentally social and interdependent beings and that who we are and what we become is constituted by "the ensemble of the social relations" in which we are situated. The main thesis in this book is that taking the relational self as the starting point for theory has far-reaching implications for theories of equality and justice and for policy issues. While a relational approach may appear to undermine the liberal view that the individual is the unit of moral worth, what it really does is highlight the complexity of freedom and agency in social practices and political contexts. Rather than simplify descriptions by focusing on individuals, a relational approach calls for a reconception of liberalism's cherished notions of autonomy, rights, and justice in terms that take unequal and oppressive relationships and the perspectives of people who are in them into account.

I consider the complexity of relational theory to be a positive feature of it. However, as Martha Minow remarks, the complexity of relational approaches has its disadvantages too. "Relational approaches are risky. . . . What happens to individualism? What happens to confident claims of right and wrong, to knowing assertions of distinctions and differences? Moreover, relational ideas seem complicated and diffuse. And finally, relational ideas seem to require too many changes, changes in basic vocabulary as well as world view, changes in social structure and architecture. For all these reasons, relational ideas trigger resistance" (Minow 1990a, 228). Our "knowing assertions of distinctions and differences" need to be undermined in a context in which "knowing" judgments of difference continue to have a detrimental impact on people and on relationships. This book is about giving precedence to relationships in political theory. The results of the inquiry identify some of the shortcomings of liberal conceptions of equality and reveal some of the conditions needed for treating all people with equal concern and respect by truly respecting human diversity and ways of being.

2

❧ ❧ ❧

Relational Features of the Language of Equality

Introduction

The prescriptive statement "Equality for all people!" seems unambiguous enough. It suggests that inequality still exists for some, and it expounds equality as a worthy goal. Yet, from the time of Aristotle, political theorists have given different accounts of what makes people equal, and they have come up with conflicting and controversial prescriptions for achieving equality. In this chapter, I shall use the seemingly simple strategy of examining how the concept "equality" functions in ordinary cases in which we describe things as equal to explore whether this sheds light on more complex cases in which "equality" is used to prescribe treatment. In what is probably the best-known conceptual work on equality, Peter Westen thinks that "the advantage of conceptual analysis is that, being grounded in ordinary language, it rests on matters on which each of us is already an authority" (Westen 1990, xix). But he then draws the disappointing conclusion that a conceptual analysis has "nothing to say about what many people above all wish to know—nothing about what equalities actually exist or ought to exist" (Westen 1990, xix). While it is true that an examination of the ordinary use of "equality" will not give substantive answers to what sorts of inequalities are unjust or how a state of equality can be obtained, I think it can provide a framework for those answers.

What I do when I examine how "equality" is used is different from what ordinary language philosophers who study our moral concepts do. Rather than engage in the project of determining the necessary and sufficient conditions for applying a term like "equality," I shall argue that we need to think ourselves into the contexts in which determinations of equality are made and speech acts prescribing equality are used. This is precisely the central feature of Wittgenstein's method for explaining meaning, imagining simple language games in which people communicate with one another. By using Wittgenstein's famous example of the builders and adding increasingly sophisticated kinds of speech acts to their simple language, ones that Wittgenstein did not himself imagine, the complex and taken-for-granted background activities that go into making determinations of equality come into sharp relief. In describing what people *do* when they learn to communicate and interact with others in moral contexts, the assumptions and structures underlying prescriptive statements of equality become apparent. In terms of the overall project of showing how relationships are relevant to equality analysis, I shall use Wittgensteinian methodology for several ends: to draw out relational features of language and of people, to highlight the real complexity of moral arguments for equality, and to begin to reveal particular inequalities not recognized by traditional equality theorists. Despite Wittgenstein's own conservatism, his method can have radical implications.

The Framework: Wittgenstein's Theory of Meaning

In his later work, Wittgenstein attempted to undermine previous theories of meaning (including his own earlier account) that took words to be just labels for objects—whether those objects were things in the world or ideas in the head.[1] Wittgenstein's method of illuminating what words mean is "to study the phenomena of language in primitive kinds of application in which one can command a clear view of the aim and functioning of the words" (Wittgenstein 1953, §5). He asks us to think of words as having their home in language games, the context of human activity and purpose. He uses the method of describing language games both as a critique of traditional theories of meaning and as a way to develop his own positive account of meaning as use. Words have functions in purposeful activity in the same way that particular objects have functions. "Think of the tools in a tool-box: there is a hammer, pliers, a saw, a screw-driver, a rule, a glue-pot, glue, nails and screws.—The functions of words are as diverse as the functions of these objects. (And in both cases there are similarities.) Of course, what confuses us is the uniform appearance of words when we hear them spoken or meet them in script and print. For their *application* is not presented to us so clearly. Especially when we are doing philosophy!" (Wittgenstein 1953, §11, his emphasis).

By paring down the description of a language to such simple language games as what builders *do* when they identify different kinds of building stones and learn to fetch them when asked, Wittgenstein has us focus on purposive activity as central to an account of the meaning of words. Consider Wittgenstein's example of the simple language of the builders. "The language is meant to serve for communication between a builder A and an assistant B. A is building with building-stones: there are blocks, pillars, slabs and beams. B has to pass the stones, and that in the order in which A needs them. For this purpose they use a language consisting of the words 'block', 'pillar', 'slab', 'beam'. A calls them out;—B brings the stone which he has learnt to bring at such-and-such a call.—Conceive this as a complete primitive language" (Wittgenstein 1953, §2).

The first observation to make about Wittgenstein's description of the language of the builders is that the successful application of such simple concepts as "slab" points to a basic underlying human capacity to recognize relationships of similarity and difference, a capacity that is vital to being able to identify kinds of building blocks correctly.[2] For each order "slab," builder B fetches that stone by identifying the slabs in the pile that she has learned to differentiate from other kinds of stones.[3] But by immediately placing the capacity to identify similarities and differences into the context of the activity of building, Wittgenstein moves us away from the idea that the meaning of a word is given in the connection between word and object to the whole context of activity and purpose in which the word has its use.

Part of learning what a word means is learning to connect word and object, but there is more than one way to do this (think about connecting "gray" with the object slab) and for more than one purpose. The builders build, but we could just as easily imagine a language in which people were taught to perform some religious ritual when presented with the word "slab." Perhaps in that language, people would be taught to interpret the way the stones are placed as different messages from the gods. Here, the word "slab" would refer to the same object, but the placement of the object would be relevant and result in different rules for the use of "slab." "With different training the same ostensive teaching of these words would have effected a quite different understanding" (Wittgenstein 1953, §6). Words do refer to things in the world and, in this sense, Wittgenstein is a realist. But to know the meaning of words is to be familiar with the standards, rules, and practices of a community of language users. The builders learn their language in the context of responding to the speech acts of others engaged in the activity of building. The rules of the language involving religious rituals represent social practices that result in different sorts of interactions and relationships among the language users than those that we find in the builders' language.

Things in the world are categorized for particular purposes, and people learn what counts as similar and different at the same time as they learn how to interact and communicate with others in purposive activity. They learn the standards and rules for use in a community and behave accordingly. So far in our description of the meaning of concepts like slab, we are dealing with standards of comparison and rules for use that are widely known and agreed-upon. Yet even in the context of such a simple language, Wittgenstein's account of meaning as use can already handle more complicated kinds of speech acts in which disagreements arise or mistakes are made: an appeal to the agreed-upon and established standards and rules for application could be made. A builder who brings a slab when asked to bring a pillar can be shown how slabs differ from pillars. An inability to apply the concepts and follow the rules may be corrected by training the builder to focus on the relevant similarities and differences for purposes of classifying things.

In anticipation of what is to come, we can extend the idea of the importance of rule-following in our social contexts and begin to illustrate the complexity of different types of judgments by imagining cases that neither the builders' game nor Wittgenstein allow. Builders who are incapable of following the rules because of some cognitive or physical disability might be excluded from building activities, and rules for their exclusion could be provided. If the incapacity is intermittent (say a builder is debilitated by depression), we could imagine the judgments and the rules for treatment that accompany perceptions of this kind of incapacity. The person, for example, could be judged to be lazy or unwilling to build. People judged to have similar incapacities might all be subjected to the same rules for treatment. These examples begin to reveal part of what happens when people are themselves subjected to judgments of similarity and difference.

For now, I want to build a case for the central role of standards and rules in a community of language users and to do so by expanding the simple language of the builders to incorporate other kinds of speech acts and language games. Wittgenstein imagines an expansion of the builders' game that introduces just such possibilities. Notice that purpose and use are still central to his account of what the new speech acts mean: "[b]ut now it looks as if when someone says 'Bring me a slab' he could mean this expression as *one* long word corresponding to the single word 'Slab'—Then can one mean it sometimes as one word and sometimes as four? And how does one usually mean it?—I think we shall be inclined to say: we mean the sentence as *four* words when we use it in contrast with other sentences such as, '*Hand* me a slab', 'Bring *him* a slab', 'Bring *two* slabs', etc.: that is, in contrast with sentences containing the separate words of our command in other combinations. . . . We say that we use the command in contrast with other sentences because *our language* contains the possibility of those other sentences" (Wittgenstein 1953, §20, his emphasis). As I take it, Wittgenstein's point is that purposes dictate the need for new distinctions, which in turn create new concepts and multiply the possibilities for different language games. The meaning of words is not to be found in analyzing the separate units, but in understanding how the words are used in language games.

In this expanded language, speech acts such as questions and doubts are possible. Now we can say such things as "No, bring *me* a slab, not *him*" or "I asked for *two* slabs, not *three*." We can now even imagine the builders creating a language game in which orders are filled randomly or in which they sometimes bring any number of slabs when asked to bring "two slabs." But we cannot imagine that they could play this language game unless they already knew their way around the language in which orders were followed in a consistent and predictable way. It is only against the backdrop of clarity, certainty, consistency, and predictability in the application of rules that they can play a game where these elements are not present or not important. In these imagined cases of following the orders randomly or purposely getting the orders wrong, we understand this as a game in the ordinary sense of the word "game." When language users learn the rules and practices of their community, they become virtually unaware of the activities of comparing, judging, and following rules. They just know what to do.[4]

The background of consistency and predictability in the following of rules is assumed and counted on in cases of doubt and disagreement about the application of rules, a background to which we appeal in cases from the use of the simplest concepts to the application of the procedural rule of treating like cases alike in complex legislation. We will discover at the beginning of the next chapter, when I begin the examination of traditional conceptions of equality, that the taken-for-granted background of consistency and predictability in rule-following sheds light on the appeal and importance of an understanding of prescriptive equality as the purely procedural "treating like cases alike."

I have concentrated on what Wittgenstein tells us about the use of words in order to highlight elements that are not always clearly in view, ones that form the background conditions for learning a language. Wittgenstein draws our attention to the mundane things we fail to notice when we try to say what a word means. We are beings with such basic capacities as noticing similarities and differences and fitting what we perceive when confronted with a new case under concepts that are already established for particular purposes. Judging things as equal is basic to learning a language at all. We also live in social contexts in which those judgments assume background agreements about the rules to follow in order to make what are taken to be correct comparisons and judgments. Language grows out of the interactive and purposeful activity of people in relationships in communities.

Wittgenstein uses the idea of a language game, describing the

meaning of words as they are used by people in contexts, to highlight the taken-for-granted background of purposeful *activity* that
is integral to creating standards and following rules. While his aim
is to undermine accounts that take the meaning of words to be
mere labels for objects or for ideas, I want to use these descriptions
of background activity to highlight certain relationships that are
central to an understanding of how moral concepts function: relationships of similarity and difference are shaped in social practices
by community members; standards and rules are established in
relationships with others and for particular purposes; and learning
the standards and following the rules are conditions for being understood by others and accepted in relationships in communities.
Aspects of "equality" in its prescriptive sense as an element in
how we ought to treat people come into sharper focus when we
keep these relational features of language and of people in mind.

Describing Features and Prescribing Treatment

As complex as the expanded language of the builders has become,
the determinations of equality that are made in these language
games are fairly simple and easy to understand. They involve becoming familiar with the established standards of comparison and
identifying the things that share the same descriptive features.
These kinds of determination are generally referred to as statements or judgments of "descriptive equality." When the builders
note the relevant similarities and differences and classify building
blocks accordingly, they determine what things are equal. When
they respond to orders at the appropriate time and in the appropriate context, they apply the rules of treatment for similar cases.
Notice, however, that unlike describing what "slab" means, in
describing what "equality" means, we no longer describe how to
use one word, but capture what is involved in using all words. To
pin down what equality means in general terms is to describe the
background conditions of being familiar with the standards and
applying the rules in various language games. Each meaningful
speech act assumes the background activities of subjecting some
thing, person, or event to an agreed-upon standard of measurement and then judging the particular case to be the same as or

different from the standard. "Equal" is the word used to describe the outcome of determining relationships of similarity.

The statement that opened this chapter, "Equality for all people," is an example of a prescriptive statement of equality in that it prescribes treating all people equally. But notice that this rallying cry implies a number of equality claims: the claim that all people are equal (they all share some relevant descriptive feature(s), the claim that these equals ought to be treated equally (they ought to have the same treatment because they share those features), and the claim that achieving a state of equality is a morally worthy goal (we ought to provide conditions that remove inequalities for some people). Once we try to imagine applying standards of comparison first for identifying people as descriptively equal and then for prescribing treatment to those descriptive equals, we quickly notice why the kinds of statements that prescribe equality are "more elusive and problematic" (Westen 1990, 10) than statements that describe what things, events, and states of affairs are equal. When we try to say what "equality" means when it is used in the context of moral arguments for equality, it seems as though Wittgenstein is right to say of ethical judgments in general that "[a]nything—and nothing—is right" (Wittgenstein 1953, §77). Wittgenstein's comments on ethics and ethical concepts are notoriously confusing and perplexing. Nevertheless, his method of describing what people *do* in contexts in which they interact with others can shed light on the function of "equality" when it is used prescriptively.

As we learned in the last section, imagining new language games and the various uses and functions that words and speech acts can have not only emphasizes the endless possibility and variety of language games but also demonstrates just how complicated the descriptions of some activities can become.[5] This also happens when we add moral concepts and behavior to the language of the builders, an addition that Wittgenstein himself did not work out. In fact, in his rather obscure remarks about morality in the early work of the *Tractatus*, Wittgenstein takes ethics to lie beyond the realm of what can be expressed in language. Some of these remarks suggest that he held a mystical view of ethics as ultimately a personal outlook on the world, one that frames a way of being in the world and about which we ought to remain silent. "We feel that even when *all possible* scientific questions have been answered, the problems of life remain completely untouched. Of course, there are no questions left, and this itself is the answer" (Wittgenstein 1961, 6.52, his emphasis). Wittgenstein then has this to say about ethics and its place in his work in a letter about the *Tractatus*: "the book's point is an ethical one. . . . My work consists of two parts: the one presented here plus all that I have *not* written. And it is precisely the second part that is the important one" (Engelmann 1967, 143).

In *Ludwig Wittgenstein: The Duty of Genius*, Ray Monk succeeds perhaps more than any other Wittgenstein scholar not only in making sense of the relationship between the two parts of the *Tractatus* but also in showing that in the transition from his early to his later work, Wittgenstein maintained a view of ethics as a kind of outlook that frames one's actions and interactions in the world.[6] I want to defend Monk's interpretation that throughout his life Wittgenstein consistently held a view of ethics as a kind of "outlook" or "framework" and to do so in the context of explaining the apparent lack of fit between this view of ethics and the later Wittgenstein's account of meaning as use, a lack of fit that is evident in the tensions present in Susan Hekman's account of ethics in Wittgenstein's later work.

Hekman points out that even though Wittgenstein advances a "rigorous social concept of language" in his later work, he excludes ethics from this conception. "For the later Wittgenstein, language is exclusively a social activity: meanings are defined by use; justification is conventional and relative to language games; private languages are impossible. Yet ethics does not seem to have any place in this social world" (Hekman 1995, 120). Hekman finds a place for ethics in Wittgenstein and in the social world he describes by making a case for viewing moral discourse as a language game and by arguing for a multiplicity of language games representing kinds of moral discourses and outlooks. Yet, Hekman also wants to argue that moral behavior and beliefs are integral to what it is to be a member of a community: "moral voices are central—even integral—aspects of what it means to be a subject, that becoming a subject and developing a moral voice are inseparable" (Hekman 1995, 113). The latter point seems to speak against treating morality as a kind of language game distinct from other language games. It would seem instead to support the view that morality reflects persons acting and interacting in all language games. As Seyla Benhabib puts it, "[t]he domain of the moral is so deeply enmeshed with those interactions that constitute our lifeworld that to withdraw from moral judgment is tantamount to ceasing to interact, to talk and act in the human community" (Benhabib 1992, 125–126).[7]

I think a better strategy for discussing morality in the context of Wittgenstein's later work is to use the advice he gives in one of the few references to moral concepts that he makes in the *Philosophical Investigations* and then to expand on this in a way that Wittgenstein did not (and perhaps would not): "[a]nything—and nothing—is right.—And this is the position you are in if you look for definitions corresponding to our concepts in aesthetics or ethics. In such a difficulty always ask yourself: How did we *learn* the meaning of this word ('good' for instance)? From what sort of examples? in what language-games? Then it will be easier for you to see that the word must have a family of meanings" (Wittgenstein 1953, §77, his emphasis). Not only does this advice fit with Wittgenstein's description of the meaning of concepts as intersecting, crisscrossing, and weaving through various language games, it also lends support to the view that ethics is a whole outlook, the participation and interaction of moral agents in a community.

Wittgenstein tells us that in the more complicated case of defining our moral concepts we should still follow the same procedure of examining the contexts in which the concepts and statements are used. His advice can be implemented by revisiting the builders' community and adding the more complex language and activity associated with the making of prescriptive statements of equality to their language. What happens when the builders learn to group people on the basis of features they are judged to have in common and to follow rules that prescribe treatment for members of those groups highlights the relational features I have identified thus far—only this time, people are themselves the objects of classification. Think of the complex of relationships identified earlier, only now in the context of concepts that group people: relationships of similarity and difference are shaped in social practices by community members; standards and rules are established in relationships with others and for particular purposes; and learning the standards and following the rules are conditions for being understood by others and accepted in relationships in communities.

Suppose that when builder B fetches two slabs after builder A gives the order "two slabs," builder A refuses to take them. Builder B shows that she understood the meaning of builder A's order by telling him that she brought "two," not "three," and "slabs," not "pillars." He agrees that she understood the meaning of "two slabs," but explains that the order was intended for builder C, a man, and that he is following the rule "only males give and receive orders to build." We can provide a purely descriptive account of the use and meaning of equality for builder A in his interaction with builder B (who, for now, is more appropriately called aspiring builder B). He learns what "pillar" means by learning to identify the features that differentiate pillars from other building blocks and by understanding the place given to pillars in the activity of building. We can say that he learns what "woman" means by being able to identify the features that differentiate women from men and by understanding their role with respect to building. If the rule is "only males give and receive orders to build," he is not making a mistake in this language when he refuses to interact with aspiring builder B. But notice that he is following a very different sort of rule from the one he follows when he gives the order "two slabs" instead of "three pillars." The rule he follows in relation to aspiring builder B is one that takes the information about *who* responds to his orders to be relevant to the activity of building. When a woman responds to his orders, he takes the case to be different from when a man brings the stones. In other words, he operates with the rule that women are not like men and ought to be treated differently.

When we describe the meaning of "equality" in prescriptive statements about equality of the sort exemplified in the builders' new rule, the same features basic to our application of other concepts reappear: the basic background capacities of comparing and judging cases and following the rules of a community of language users in applying the concept to particular cases. Builder A knows how he ought to treat aspiring builder B because he exhibits the ability to identify cases that fall under the descriptive class "woman" and to follow the rule that excludes women from building. But describing the activity in the way we have done so far may make it seem as though similarities and differences are merely discovered, classifications capture real and essential features in the world apart from our interpretations, and judgments are neutral reflections about how the world is actually ordered. These are features characteristic of an essentialist view of the world and a realist picture of language. Certainly, builder A's immersion in the practices supporting his perceptions of and interactions with women would have him believe that the world is structured in this way and that "woman" means nonbuilding person.

What can we say about the descriptive features of people that form the base for prescriptions? Are they "real" in the sense that they describe the way the world is structured outside of human interpretation and interaction? Statements that prescribe treatment need descriptions as their base—features that can identify and classify people as similar in relevant respects. Even at the basic level of identifying features, however, prescriptive statements can be made. We can argue that some people ought not to be described in a particular way or that all people ought to be described differently. This already reveals something about the fixity of descriptions that is at odds with realism as traditionally understood. The realist holds that there are real essences of things that are discoverable and identifiable through investigation of the world. The descriptive features that are constitutive of a given person or thing are taken to determine the universal categories under which particulars fall independently of human interpretation. We will need to question this realist account of categories and descriptions.

Are the descriptions "nominal" in the sense that they are just interpretations that represent arbitrary conventions? A nominalist account of meaning takes the categories that people assign to things that share descriptive features to be purely a matter of convention and convenience. But this does not seem to be an accurate depiction of categories and descriptions either. We will discover that disagreements about descriptions matter to us because prescriptions for treatment closely follow descriptions. The features that people are taken to share are used as the base for prescribing treatment for those who are identified as descriptively equal and this activity of categorizing and describing is embedded in *concrete* social practices and political contexts.

Debates about realism versus nominalism and essentialism versus constructionism are notoriously complex and raise big topics in philosophy of language and metaphysics, for example. I intend to discuss only some of the issues for the purpose of defending the claim that descriptions are neither real nor nominal *in the senses just outlined.* A relational approach as captured thus far in insights about the relational features of language and of people supports rather than undermines the idea that categories that group objects capture features in and facts about the world, but those features and facts reflect and rely on human interpretation and interaction. Weighing the arguments on each side of realism and nominalism tips the scale on the side of realism, but only when care is taken to clarify what is meant by realism. Perhaps there is no better way to articulate the kind of realism I shall defend than to turn to Aristotle's, or what might be better described as an "Aristotelian," understanding of equality.

Descriptive Similarities: Facts or Social Constructions?

Consider the following comments from Aristotle about equality and justice: "All men think justice to be a sort of equality . . . [T]hey admit that justice is a thing and has a relation to persons, and that equals ought to have equality" (Aristotle. *Politics,* 1282b18–22). Out of Aristotle's comments about equality *as* justice and justice *as* treating equals equally has emerged the well-established idea that equality as a prescription for how people ought to be treated means that "like cases ought to be treated alike." This sense of equality is what we now refer to as "procedural equality." However, in remarks from the *Politics* that immediately follow the prescription that equals ought to have equality, Aristotle asks a question of which, in the end, he seems not to realize the full significance: "[b]ut there still remains a question: equality or inequality of what? here is a difficulty which calls for political speculation" (Aristotle. *Politics,* 1282b22–24). The question and answer indicate that determinations of equality presuppose comparison to some standard—equal or unequal with respect to some descriptive feature or features. In other words, treating like cases alike requires that judgments about what cases are alike be made according to what are determined to be relevant criteria of likeness or similarity for purposes of treatment. This account may seem to be compatible with the descriptions of the builders' community in which language users construct categories by determining relevant criteria of similarity and do so for particular social purposes. As is well known, however, Aristotle took differences among people to be inherent and natural and not socially determined in this sense.

The standard interpretation of Aristotle is that he based his conception of applying rules for treating like cases alike on the view that real or essential descriptive properties determine the categories under which people could be identified and classified. The Greek conception of essence was of the "whatness" of a thing, its irreducible, unchanging, and sometimes unknowable "form." The idea in this conception is that "there is some one determinate structure to the way things are, *independent of all human interpretation*" (Nussbaum 1995, 68, my emphasis). Martha Nussbaum refers to this kind of essentialism as "metaphysical realism" (Nussbaum 1995, 67–68), a useful term for clarifying a sense of realism that most realists no longer defend. She goes on to argue, however, that Aristotle was not a metaphysical realist.[8]

In the domain of moral and political arguments for equality, once the metaphysical realist "discovers" the descriptive facts that sort people into categories, there is little room left for prescription except to exhort people to discover their "station" in life and perform its "duties."[9] Rosemarie Tong cites the historical legacy of this kind of essentialist argument. "Essentialist claims about what makes certain groups of people the way they are . . . are the political-philosophical constructs of conservatism. The history of essentialist arguments is one of oppressors telling the oppressed to accept their lot in life because 'that's just the way it is.' Essentialist arguments were used to justify slavery, to resist the Nineteenth Amendment (which gave women the vote), and to sustain colonialism by arguing 'altruistically' that 'the natives are unable to run their own governments' " (Tong 1989, 135). Whether Nussbaum is correct in suggesting that Aristotle rejected this sort of essentialism, his account of the ends or purposes inherent in things and people had the same conservative effect of prescribing treatment for women and slaves, for example, that merely reflected their social status and roles at the time, status and roles that in turn were taken to be dictated by nature.

I think the first step to resolving the complexities underlying the activity of describing people is to reject metaphysical realism and thereby undermine the idea that the descriptions are secure and fixed outside of human activity and purpose. In other words, we focus on the "activity" and reject the notion that categories reflect the structure of the world apart from human interpretation. This raises the question of whether and what sort of realism is left to defend, a question for which we can begin to find answers by returning to a discussion of Wittgenstein.

In highlighting the background activity involved in identifying difference and determining what the difference will mean, it may *seem* as though Wittgenstein shifts the focus from a realist account of differences as objectively determined and discoverable to a nominalist account of language users classifying things as a matter of "arbitrary definitional conventions" (Babbitt 1992, 150). Yet, Wittgenstein himself distinguishes his theory from nominalism. "[I]t may look as if what we were doing were Nominalism. Nominalists make the mistake of interpreting all words as *names*, and so of not really describing their use, but only, so to speak, giving a paper draft on such a description" (Wittgenstein 1953, §383, his emphasis). When we describe the activity of the builders as though we ourselves might be there in those relationships in which the standards and rules are established, we begin to discover that neither a realist emphasis on descriptive and factual differences nor a nominalist emphasis on arbitrary conventions captures the builders' background activity of learning to identify relevant similarities and differences in the purposive context of language games. Wittgenstein's account of meaning can be understood as a rejection of both realism and nominalism in their strict and stripped-down versions.

Nominalism as traditionally formulated cannot explain why some categories assigned on the basis of arbitrary conventions, as they put it, have universal or widespread connections with social arrangements, for example, a point captured by Jane Flax when she writes, "physically male and female humans resemble each other in many more ways than we differ. Our similarities are even more striking if we compare humans to, say, toads or trees. So why ought the anatomical differences between male and female humans assume such significance in our sense of selves as persons?" (Flax 1990, 51). The key difference between nominalism and a theory of meaning as use is the role of social and communal practices in the determination of meaning. Actual purposeful activity determines how we categorize things in even the simplest cases in which we name objects in the world. "Slab" can mean "object of religious worship" as well as "object for building" and in the two cases, different features of slabs are noticed and taken as relevant, and different interactions and relationships are thereby created. This may appear to correspond with arbitrary conventions for labeling objects in the sense that it is "arbitrary" whether slabs are objects for building or for religious worship. However, as the expanded examination of Wittgenstein's account of meaning as use illustrates, it is the social context of purposeful activity that determines the use and this makes it nonarbitrary.

The Wittgensteinian view of meaning as use need not be a rejection of the realist insistence that there are facts. The realist "finds it amazing that the world could so kindly sort itself into our categories. He protests that there are definite sorts of objects in it . . . which we have painstakingly come to recognize and classify correctly" (Hacking 1986, 227). With respect to the real features of people, the "robust realist does not have to argue very hard that people also come sorted. Some are thick, some thin, some dead, some alive" (Hacking 1986, 227). Yet, a realist account that emphasizes the discovery and description of facts in a world that comes already sorted does not adequately explain the close connection that obtains between categories and the purposeful functions for which people create and use categories, purposes which lead them to focus on some features and to ignore others. Slabs have real features that we notice, classify, and categorize, but what features we decide to focus on are determined by the function that slabs have in our language. As Martha Minow puts it, "[o]f course, there are 'real' differences in the world. . . . But when we simplify and sort, we focus on some traits rather than others" (Minow 1990a, 3).

We respond differently to the case of builder A refusing to interact with aspiring builder B from the way we would react if he told her she had brought "three slabs," not "two." Her gender may be a difference that is real, but when that biological difference is identified as the basis for describing, defining, and circumscribing her activities, the inadequacy of both a realist account of independent facts and a nominalist account of arbitrary categories is more obvious and intense than when we are dealing with concepts like "slab." When applied to people, judgments of similarity and difference are laden with prescriptive force. When people are identified, compared, and judged on the basis of descriptive differences, these practices have consequences for determining who can engage in what activities and how the activities function in communities. These practices determine the meaning given to the very actions and behavior of people, practices that are different from those involved in describing and defining slabs or stars. As we notice from the description of the builders who exclude women from building, the practices also determine the kinds of relationships and interactions that can and do take place between community members.

I have gone well beyond Wittgenstein in connecting speech acts with social and communal practices to explain what equality means when it is used in moral prescriptions. Prescriptive statements of equality are made in social and political contexts where standards that measure inequalities and rules that apply treatment for unequals matter to the lived lives of people. Wittgenstein focuses on the implications of meaning as use for language. His methodology can also be used to draw out the importance of examining the relationships formed in and through social practices and affected by the standards and rules of a community. We can learn about the meaning of "equality," its use and function in political contexts, by highlighting the underlying relational features, both of language and of people. Focusing on the relational aspects of language and of people allows us to grasp what is at stake in an Aristotelian account of equality.

Aristotle established a close connection between descriptions and prescriptions in his "discovery" of particular properties that then served as justifications for circumscribing the activities and roles of all people who shared those properties, justifications that restricted the realm of moral and political agents by denying membership in the political community to some people. The descriptions work to define the categories and then to justify the roles and functions of those who fit the categories. Minow provides an apt description of the effects of an Aristotelian conception of equality when she writes, "society assigns individuals to categories and, on that basis, determines whom to include in and whom to exclude from political, social, and economic activities. Because the activities are designed, in turn, with only the in-

cluded participants in mind, the excluded seem not to fit because
of something in their own nature" (Minow 1990a, 21). The discussion of the realism/nominalism debate teaches us that the categories we use to group people describe features in the world that
people have and share, and in this sense our categories are not
arbitrary. However, categories are constructed in social contexts
for particular purposes and this requires attentiveness to the moral
and political implications of "describing people."

The expansion of the builders' language to include the moral
concept of equality highlights the relational features of language
and of people that I have been emphasizing thus far: relationships
of similarity and difference are shaped in social practices by community members; standards and rules are established in relationships with others and for particular purposes; and learning the
standards and following the rules are conditions for being understood by others and accepted in relationships in communities.
With a better understanding of the use and function of prescriptive statements of equality, it becomes clear that the whole background complex of standards, rules, and practices in a community
has an impact on relationships in that community. We learn to
identify similarities and differences in relationships in which such
factors as authority and power play a role in the establishment and
maintenance of the standards and rules, factors that are particularly
deep-running when we identify differences and categorize people
accordingly.

These descriptions of how relationships of similarity and difference are established in interactive and purposeful social contexts,
which in turn shape relationships among people in a community,
undermine both a simplified realist view of categories as merely
read off from the world and a nominalist view of categories as
mere arbitrary social constructions. An examination of the relationships that underlie our categories and of the people who make
or are subjected to them generates an account that is neither
strictly realist nor nominalist, neither purely essentialist nor con-
structionist. I now want to go well beyond Wittgenstein by analyzing the role of relationships in the creation of standards and
rules through a critical examination of Ian Hacking's account of
"dynamic nominalism," an account he also describes as neither
strictly nominalist nor strictly realist. Hacking's account takes us
in the direction of examining the role of relationships of authority

and power in the social construction of categories. We will discover, however, that while Hacking raises the important point that categories that describe people are constructed in social relations, he fails to acknowledge the moral and political implications of this fact, implications that he takes to be tangential to his main project of describing kinds of categories. It will become clear that attention to relationships—in particular moral and political contexts—generates an account better described as "dynamic realism" than as "dynamic nominalism."

Making Up Difference

In "Making Up People," Hacking describes his account in this way: "[t]he claim of dynamic nominalism is not that there was a kind of person who came increasingly to be recognized by bureaucrats or by students of human nature but rather that a kind of person came into being at the same time as the kind itself was being invented" (Hacking 1986, 228). To use one of Hacking's examples, dynamic nominalism explains that until descriptions of homosexuals and homosexual activity appeared, the concept "homosexual" and the person we now describe as homosexual did not exist. While their sexual activity and practices existed and could be described prior to the creation of the category "homosexual," the particular identification and description of those practices as a way of marking the difference between homosexuality and heterosexuality happened when the concept came into being. Current descriptions of what homosexuals do and who they are got their meaning at the same time as the category "homosexual" was created. "[A] kind of person came into being at the same time as the kind itself was being invented" (Hacking 1986, 228). According to the sources cited by Hacking, the concept "homosexual" first appeared "only toward the end of the nineteenth century" (Hacking 1986, 225–226).

David Halperin's discussion of homosexuality in the context of classical Greek civilization lends support to Hacking's argument that categories and the people they describe come into existence at the same time. Halperin argues that sexual practices in ancient Greece were conceptualized mainly in terms of relations between citizens with differential power and status and not on the basis of a gendered sexual orientation. He uses this account of the ancient Greek understanding of sexual relations to argue that because same-sex relations did not have the meaning for ancient Greeks that they have for us in our understanding of "homosexual," neither the category "homosexual" nor the kind of person existed in ancient Greece (Halperin 1989). As Susan Babbitt puts it, "[I]n advance of the coming about of a certain kind of society, one couldn't be understood as a homosexual, be treated as one and deliberate about one's life as one" (Babbitt 1995b, 313).

Hacking next argues that unlike objects such as slabs, which remain unaffected by the labels given to them, what happens to people who are labeled does depend on our descriptions.[10] In other words, at the same time as we identify descriptive features as the basis for categorizing people, rules are set in place for treatment of those people. But more importantly for the purpose of highlighting relationships, Hacking then makes the point that the people so labeled can and sometimes do respond to the labeling and to the treatment. This is captured in Hacking's description of the "two vectors of influence," vectors that represent the "dynamic" interaction between people who do the labeling and people who are labeled. "One is the vector of labeling from above, from a community of experts who create a 'reality' that some people make their own. Different from this is the vector of the autonomous behavior of the person so labeled, which presses from below, creating a reality every expert must face" (Hacking 1986, 234).

Hacking describes a process whereby "experts" do the labeling and those who are labeled are thereby described. In addition, Hacking's model of the two vectors of influence suggests that sometimes people change to fit the descriptions of them and sometimes they are able to challenge and change those descriptions. In his article, Hacking provides two sorts of examples that show how the two vectors can have different strengths in different circumstances. In the case of the split personality labeled by medical experts, there is very little that those who are labeled as "splits" can do to change the meaning of the category they are put into, and, according to Hacking, this tells us something about the power and authority of the medical profession. Hacking tells us that in the case of the category "homosexual," on the other hand, "the labeling did not occur in a social vacuum, in which those

identified as homosexual people passively accepted the format.
. . . It is quite clear that the internal life of innumerable clubs
and associations interacted with the medico-forensic-journalistic
labeling" (Hacking 1986, 233). Here, the vector of influence
pressing from below by those labeled as homosexual was and is a
force affecting the labeling and the description. Already, this account of the interaction between those who do the labeling and
those who are labeled in terms of relations of power and of possibilities for agency and for change suggests moral and political consequences, ones that Hacking does not follow out.

Hacking's main concern is with language, with making up people as a linguistic phenomenon, and not with the impact that
determinations of difference have on those who fall under a classification of difference. He tells us that his "concern is philosophical
and abstract" (Hacking 1986, 222) and that his account of dynamic nominalism and the two vectors of influence provides only
a "partial framework." He further admits that his "scheme at best
highlights what the dispute is about. It provides no answers"
(Hacking 1986, 234) and that he "reflect[s] too little on the ordinary dynamics of human interaction" (Hacking 1986, 222).
Hacking does not work out what I take to be the most important
implications of his account: the moral and political consequences
of the power relations and the interdynamics between the persons
doing the labeling and those who are labeled. But we can begin
this work by bringing in features of the relational insights I have
been describing thus far, applying them to aspects of Hacking's
account of dynamic nominalism, and then moving beyond Hacking's skeletal account of the two vectors of influence.

I have been focusing throughout on speech acts as interactive
communicative processes in purposive contexts and this means
that, unlike Hacking, one of my main concerns is precisely to
reflect on the ordinary dynamics of human interaction. What
happens to people assigned to categories of disability, for example,
affects in advance how their behavior and speech acts are understood, what relationships they can enter into with other people,
and what level of influence they have for changing the meaning
of the categories to which they are assigned. These relational features not only point to the complexity of language games and our
interconnectedness in a "network of relationships," but they also
highlight the underlying moral and political implications of

"making up difference." The activities of describing people and circumscribing their activities are situated in concrete political contexts and shaped by entrenched social practices and in this sense the relationships are dynamic and *real*.

The second aspect I want to discuss emerges from a logical point about language. Categories identifying people on the basis of some descriptive feature or features assume a standard of comparison from which differences are identified and made relevant for particular purposes. For example, homosexuals are defined as different from the standard of comparison, heterosexuals. Hand in hand with the identification and categorization of particular people as different go descriptions of appropriate activity for those who are different from the norm, activities determined by people in concrete social practices and political contexts. These features again point us to an account of dynamic *realism*. In the next section, I will use these relational insights about human interaction and the role of standards of comparison as well as other relational insights to explore precisely that territory that Hacking avoids: the moral and political implications of the categories we use to describe people.

Moral and Political Implications
of Assigned Difference

The descriptions of the various language games capture the relational features of interaction and cooperation among community members. Not only do members reach agreements about how to identify, compare, and judge items, but it is a feature of language that the agreements they reach are integral to their day-to-day engagement with others in purposeful activity. Such interaction also involves disagreements, doubts, and challenges about standards and rules and it is through this kind of interaction that changes to the meaning of our concepts and speech acts occur.

When we classify things and use them for particular purposes, we can imagine what might happen when cases of disagreement arise concerning the standards and rules. In the simplest version of the language of the builders, we could imagine that a builder engaged in the activity of building suddenly claims that slabs do not function as useful building materials. We can also imagine various resolutions to this kind of disagreement: the builders decide to eliminate slabs as building materials, they decide that slabs can be used for other purposes, they decide that the builder is wrong about slabs and continue to make the same distinctions and follow the same rules, and so on. No consequences more severe than perhaps a period of readjustment to new standards or rules and a need for some retraining follow from this kind of disagreement or conflict. When discourse about objects in the world is involved, this kind of interaction, cooperation, interpretation, and changing of standards is a reflection of ordinary purposive human activity. We need to keep these relational features in mind and then get inside the language of the builders who perceive women as different in order to understand what happens to relationships when that kind of determination is made.

What is disturbing about the builder who identifies women for the purpose of excluding them from the activity of building is that the category, "woman," and the rule, "only males give and receive orders to build," determine the meaning of difference in ways that specify and circumscribe activities, roles, and relationships. For example, the sentence "women can build too" would be a false statement or perhaps be understood as a joke in a social context in which the rules that exclude women are settled and fixed. Women are just not perceived as having building capacities. If we assume the rule to be not only well-understood and accepted but backed by relations of power or entrenched in tradition, then two kinds of consequences result for aspiring builder B: she may accept descriptions of what her difference means, not perceive herself as a builder, and never challenge the description of her as a nonbuilder, or she may perceive herself as having the capacity to build and even aspire to be a builder, but have no power to change the meaning of her difference in the context of an established practice that excludes her from building. The agreement about the meaning of her difference in relation to the norm of male builder has consequences that limit the choices she has for interacting, participating, and acting in this social context that excludes descriptions of her as a builder.

Other consequences flowing from labeling and describing women as nonbuilders can be imagined. Women are excluded from building altogether and from contexts in which building skills and practices are learned and discussed. We can imagine that "work" is defined as engaging in building activities and that "workers" are builders. In defining some kinds of human activity as "work" and in determining that some kinds of "work" are appropriate for certain people, all sorts of repercussions with respect to circumscribing, evaluating, and valuing human activities emerge. Who takes care of children and those who are unable to build, who gets paid, who makes meals, who runs for office, and the different values given to these activities go along with the identification and labeling of people. Another example illustrates a similar point. If we go back to the example of the builder who is told that he is wrong to consider slabs as useless building materials, we can imagine that a number of judgments about his ideas being "off" would result in his being ostracized or identified as mentally incompetent. Various purposes or social conditions determine the value placed on possessing the right skills and making the correct judgments.

All of these valuations and judgments happen in the context of social practices in communities. Judgments about the value and worth of various kinds of activity go with the practice of labeling people as different. "[I]t is difficult to say 'different' without saying 'better' or 'worse' " (Gilligan 1982, 14). There are two things I would like to clarify to forestall possible objections, objections that I cannot address fully here. First, I am not suggesting that all inferences from descriptions of difference to prescriptions for treatment are morally reprehensible. An example of describing people that we might not condemn is using builder C's physical weakness and inability to carry slabs as a reason for exempting him from the activity of building. But even in this example, the need for a heightened awareness of and sensitivity to the moral and political implications of constructing a category like "disability" and establishing rules of treatment for those fitted into the category is apparent when we examine the relationships that are thereby formed. Second, I am not suggesting that only descriptions of *people* lead directly to moral prescriptions. Our treatment of animals depends on how we classify and describe them, and these actions have moral implications. The point I will make for now is that in both cases the weight needs to rest on an examination of the social context and an evaluation of the moral arguments rather than on an appeal to facts about descriptive properties of things in the world in abstraction from facts about the social practices and political contexts that give those properties meaning.

Focusing on the activity of identifying descriptive features and of defining the meaning of the features emphasizes that categories are created from a particular perspective and for a particular purpose. This is the second point that I identified as missing in Hacking's account of "two vectors of influence." The builders learn a language by learning what *others* know and by being trained to perform speech acts in the context of purposeful activity. Those others are language users who already know the standards and rules and are in a position to teach those who do not yet know and who need to learn in order to become participating members of communities. Parents teach children, teachers instruct students, employers train employees, politicians convince citizens, and builders teach nonbuilders. While relations of power and authority are implicated in the activity of establishing and maintaining standards and rules in general, they are particularly evident when the standards and rules apply to people.

The notion of a perspective from which to compare and judge is necessary to the activity of determining who is equal to whom. "A reference point for comparison purposes is central to a notion of equality. Equality asks, equal compared with whom?" (Minow 1990a, 51). That difference is identified as difference in comparison to a standard is a fact of logic. Identifying difference assumes a standard of comparison, a norm, from which the difference is identifiable and defined as meaningful. Standards are created and maintained by members who have the power to identify and assign meaning to difference and the authority to apply and maintain the rules for use. When language learning is successful, norms and purposes become so much a part of the background that they are taken for granted and hidden. This point about norms will be developed in the latter half of the next chapter and will be central to the critique of liberal theory.

Focusing on the purposive activity underlying the creation of standards of comparison and the setting up of rules allows us to examine the dynamics of relationships out of which difference and the meaning given to difference emerge. When people are classified according to some descriptive feature or features, this has consequences for who can participate in the activities of creating and changing meaning and who can be a contributing mem-

ber in the purposeful activities of a community. As we discovered
with the builders, categorizing people raises questions of inclusion
and exclusion. When we describe the processes involved in
"making up people" in terms of relationships, we create a space
for perceiving those categorized as different differently. "Difference, after all, is a comparative term. It implies a reference: different from whom? I am no more different from you than you are
from me" (Minow 1990a, 22). We also create a space for examining the inequalities that emerge in and through the relationships
between the powerful and the powerless, those who constitute
the norm and those who are excluded.

While he does not develop the point sufficiently, Hacking is
correct in another way to differentiate human and nonhuman categories: categories that group people need not be fixed and unchanging in the way that a concept of measurement such as meter,
for example, is. People have the features that identify them as
different, but because they communicate and interact in relationships, their behavior and speech can have an effect on the meaning of the category into which they are placed. An account of
actual and potential relationships between those taken as the standard and those who deviate from the standard begins to explain
how the degree of influence from each of the vectors can vary
from context to context. It can also begin to describe opportunities for challenge and change not covered by Hacking's model of
two vectors of influence, a vector of power that creates categories
and one that reacts. For now, I will just sketch some of the possibilities and develop the points in greater detail in the chapters that
follow.

Contexts of severe oppression obtain when total power resides
with those who establish and maintain the rules and where genuine interaction is forbidden or restricted, as in rules of segregation
or apartheid, for example. In less-restrictive contexts, where there
are interactive relationships between those who are oppressed and
the oppressors, the oppressed are able "to press from below" to
influence and change the meaning of their assigned difference.
These relationships of interaction and communication explain
how those perceived as different can become effective agents for
changing the meaning of their difference as inferiority and inequality. A key point in this book is that relationships between
those understood as the standard and those viewed as different

from the standard contain the potential for changing the meaning of difference and the social practices that make differences significant to how people are treated. It is also in contexts of relationships that those who are different from the norm not only challenge current norms but imagine and bring into being new possibilities for moral personhood and agency to which the dominant are forced to react. This last possibility is an example of what Susan Babbitt calls "moral imagination," a possibility that shows how categories can also be created "from below" in a way not covered by Hacking's model of "two vectors of influence."[11]

Drawing Conclusions and Looking Ahead: Implications for Equality Theory

The account of the builders' language and of the impact of their discourse on others when prescriptive statements of equality are added to their language makes what started as a very simple language much more complicated and complex than Wittgenstein ever imagined. Noticing similarities and differences and judging items to be the same as or different from standards is a logical feature of language. Yet, these human capacities of comparing and judging are so inextricably intertwined with the activities of communicating and interacting with others that descriptive accounts of relationships of similarity and difference removed from accounts of people in purposive relationships miss important elements of moral concepts. We can now understand what underlies the kind of account of morality provided by Hekman and Benhabib, namely the embeddedness of moral judgments and behavior in all aspects of a person's life. People are social beings whose actions and interactions take place, are shaped by, and have meaning in particular social practices and political contexts. People deliberate and make decisions in the context of planning a life in response to and in relationships with members of a community. Thus, moral beliefs, moral judgments, and moral behavior are not incidental aspects of people's lives, but are embedded in being a person in a community. To return to a point made in the context of interpreting Wittgenstein on ethics, morality forms the kind of personal outlook that frames our actions in the world and our interactions with others. I will end this chapter by indicating very briefly some of the ways in which relational insights about language and about people are relevant to a theory of equality.

Prescriptive statements of equality need to be understood in the broader context of a variety of many different language games, how these speech acts function in relationships in communities. When we are dealing with people, descriptions of them affect how they can be, to whom they can relate, and what they are understood to contribute or are permitted to communicate. It will be important to an analysis of equality to be aware of relations of power and of who is excluded from participating in particular social and political contexts. The kinds of inequalities that emerge when we look at the details of how and why people are identified on the basis of distinctive features, what effect this has on the possibilities for interactive and purposeful activity, and what implications and consequences for identity and self-concepts emerge from the activity of labeling are not recognized by traditional equality theorists. These inequalities manifest themselves when we focus on the relational features of language and of people.

To be complete, a theory of equality must take on the task of uncovering and evaluating who or what counts as equal, for what purposes, and in what sorts of relationships. Together, in their interconnectedness and inseparability, the relational features of language and of people in communities can contribute to an understanding of the meaning of difference and its relevance to a theory of equality in a way not dealt with by traditional equality theory. When aspiring builder B is subjected to the agreements reached about what her particular features will mean in particular social contexts, this has consequences for how and who she can be. Aspiring builder B is herself the object of the activity of identifying similarities and differences. Perceptions of her and of the roles appropriate for someone like her will affect the range of choices available to her, including opportunities for her to participate in the activity of changing or challenging meaning, for her to enter into and develop particular kinds of relationships, and for her to acquire the kind of confidence and self-respect that allow her to develop her talents and pursue her goals. As we will discover in the next few chapters, these are some of the things rejected in an Aristotelian conception of equality and not dealt with by equality theorists within the liberal tradition.

3

❦ ❦ ❦

From Aristotelian Procedural Equality to Classical Liberalism

Introduction

I have used Wittgenstein's method of describing language games to highlight the relational features of language and of people who interact in purposive contexts. In describing the activity underlying speech acts and extending this activity to builders who use moral concepts, I suggested that the activity of classifying people has immediate moral consequences because it defines and circumscribes the activities and roles understood as appropriate for people identified as members of that category. These kinds of determinations of difference affect the range of choices available both for interacting with others and for participating in particular activities. Even if aspiring builder B demonstrates her ability to identify and fetch building blocks, the difference of gender is taken to justify her exclusion from that language game. Aspiring builder B and all others "like her" are treated equally in the sense that they are all excluded from building activities. This is the kind of exclusion permitted in a conception of equality as the purely procedural "treating like cases alike," a conception introduced in the previous chapter in connection with Aristotle.

Liberal theory's decisive contribution to our understanding of

equality is to argue that certain similarities trump virtually all differences, at least as far as a justification of equal treatment is concerned. Classical liberal theory has been responsible for
expounding the idea that all people have equal moral worth and
deserve equal concern and respect simply because they are autonomous agents with self-determining capacities, the capacities for
choosing, acting, and living in accordance with one's interests,
projects, and goals. In this chapter, I shall trace the development
of the classical liberal principle of equal concern and respect by
examining the prior and prevalent Aristotelian conception of
equality as purely procedural. The strategy I shall use here is one
employed throughout: applying relational insights to reinterpret
concepts and conceptions central to equality analysis.

Applying the insights from the previous chapter about the relational features of language and of people helps to explain the appeal of procedural equality and at the same time shows why it
needs to be grounded by the classical liberal principle of equal
concern and respect. A discussion of classical liberal arguments for
equal concern and respect serves several purposes. It allows me to
emphasize the impact that liberal theory has had on our understanding of equality and to reconceive the classical liberal understanding of equal concern and respect in relational terms and then
register my commitment to it in the relational approach to equality that I shall advance. Most importantly, the discussion of classical liberalism begins the project of drawing attention to the
absence of an account of relationships in the liberal tradition. But
the project needs an idea introduced in the previous chapter: the
effects of standards of comparison on those who are in unequal
and oppressive relationships. This complex topic will require unpacking because it plays a vital role in the critique of liberal theory
in the chapters that follow. Carol Gilligan's *In a Different Voice* can
help us here.

The advantage of using Gilligan is that her work is well known.
The disadvantage is that in discussing aspects of her work for
which she is less well known, my understanding of her contribution is at odds with many of the interpretations that her research
has spawned. One of these important contributions is the uncovering of various unstated and taken-for-granted standards of comparison in traditional theory.[1] By challenging the tendency to
consider male norms the universal standards of comparison, Gilli-

gan's work can serve as a starting point for highlighting the effects of those standards with respect to the relationships and the beliefs that shape the lives of those people who are outside the norm. In the previous chapter, I emphasized that relationships are formed in and through social practices in ways that determine and circumscribe possibilities for those who are defined as different. A central insight in this chapter is that the perspectives of those in these relationships can provide information about inequalities that needs to be counted if we are to treat all people with equal concern and respect.

Procedural Equality: A Relational Critique and Reinterpretation

So far what has emerged from the examination of the language of equality by way of a conception is procedural equality, the Aristotelian conception based on the purely procedural test of treating like cases alike. The examination of Aristotle's own application of procedural equality in his political theory shows that his identification of relevant properties for sorting people allowed equality to be satisfied when unequals were treated unequally. As Rawls puts it, however, a defense of equality as a purely procedural principle "puts no restrictions upon what grounds may be offered to justify inequalities" (Rawls 1971, 507). He further notes that "[t]here is no guarantee of substantive equal treatment, since slave and caste systems . . . may satisfy this conception" (Rawls 1971, 507). Yet, some theorists who defend the rule of law, the activity of *consistently* applying the rules that are in place to cases identified as alike or equal, argue that something more substantive than the Aristotelian understanding of treating equals equally can be generated from a commitment to procedural equality alone. "To assume . . . that the rule of law cannot affect the substance of law is to sell short the notion of procedural justice. For in its very practice-based moral standards, it promises a minimum of justice which bears on the legal materials a judge can draw upon when he identifies law, not simply the manner in which he articulates his legal judgments. If the law must live up to a morality of procedure it will inhibit if not prevent the use of legal institutions to promote injustice" (Sypnowich 1990, 56).

The notion of procedural equality in the application of rules does indeed focus attention on the reasons for identifying certain differences as the basis for unequal treatment. However, the procedure of consistently and predictably applying rules for treatment in and of itself cannot ensure that Aristotelian grounds for unequal treatment of unequals are ruled out. As we discovered in the previous chapter, Aristotle certainly could and did provide reasons based on nature for treating some people unequally. By using insights from the previous chapter to show just how much a part of the everyday stream of life the activity of treating like cases alike is, we can discover both why procedural equality has intuitive appeal and why it is inadequate as a conception of equality.

The activity underlying procedural equality requires the same basic capacities of comparing and judging cases to be equal based on an agreed-upon standard of comparison, as was exhibited by the builders in their simplest language game of giving and receiving orders. Applying rules consistently and predictably is not unique to the activity of applying rules to people, but is the basic activity needed for being understood by others. As we learned with the builders, it is only against the backdrop of clarity, certainty, consistency, and predictability in the application of the rules that they can make sense of mistakes, questions, doubts, or inconsistencies in the identification of standards and in the application of rules. We appeal to this background of standards, rules, and justifications when there is doubt about the application of the rules, from the use of the simplest concepts to the most complicated versions of the rule of law that specify unequal treatment for unequals.

In the previous quotation, Christine Sypnowich is right to take clarity, certainty, consistency, and predictability as integral parts of such rule-governed activity as law, but these basic features of interactive and purposeful human activity and communication do not yet justify any conclusions that procedural equality has "intrinsic moral value" (Sypnowich 1990, 70). Consistent and predictable application of the laws cannot by itself get us beyond an Aristotelian account in which features can be used to group certain people as inferior and deserving of unequal treatment. The focus needs to move from valuing the consistent application of the actual rules that are in place in a community to studying the impact of the rules on people's lives and relationships. In other words, it is not the following of rules as such, but the rules that are followed in particular social and political contexts of purposive activity and interaction that brings in moral considerations. As we discovered in the previous chapter, this switch from the rules as such to their place in the context of language games is precisely what Wittgenstein argues for as a corrective to certain philosophical tendencies.

It is in thinking ourselves into the language games in which prescriptive statements are made that we understand how moral concepts function in people's lives. In following through what happens in the builders' game when they determine how women ought to be treated with respect to building, we learned how this sort of rule permeates people's lives in ways that affect their perception of themselves and others, their choices, their relationships, and even their beliefs about the structure of the world. In the course of describing these consequences, I argued for a broader understanding of morality as the actions and interactions of moral agents in all language games in a community of relationships. When we look beyond the mere procedure of consistently and predictably applying rules to the impact those rules have on lived lives, we discover what it really is about treating like cases alike that makes this procedure important and valuable.

Sypnowich realizes in part what we actually value in the consistent application of rules when she writes, "law must be framed in such a way that citizens can *plan their lives with some certainty* that the law's incursion into these plans will be consistent and intelligible" (Sypnowich 1990, 45, my emphasis).[2] An emphasis on enabling citizens to "plan their lives with some certainty" places the focus on the ways in which the whole background complex of standards, rules, and practices affects the lives of community members and the relationships they can enter into and form. It is now clear to us that it is the value we place on the freedom to plan a life and to engage in purposeful and creative activity as a member of a community that underlies any moral value we give to the procedure of applying rules consistently and predictably. This is the key insight of classical liberal theory.

The appeal of procedural equality has its explanation in the value we place on the human capacities for self-legislation and self-determination. People need consistency and predictability in the application of the rules that apply to them because this background enables them to pursue, develop, and actualize their interests, projects, and goals in interactive and purposeful contexts. We condemn inconsistency and unpredictability in rules as they apply to people because this places obstacles in the way of human flourishing and prevents people from freely pursuing their interests, projects, and goals. If I cannot know whether tomorrow brings a change in the rules so that my accumulated parking tickets bar me from applying for a job, for example, then it becomes impossible for me to plan my life with any certainty. However, certainty and predictability are not sufficient for ensuring that individual interests, projects, and goals will be treated with equal concern and respect and they are not sufficient for ensuring that damaging or oppressive relations do not result. These consequences are evident when we examine a now famous case of the strict application of procedural equality.

In the *Persons* case, the Supreme Court of Canada ruled in 1928 that because women were not persons they were not eligible to become senators. The decision, overturned by the Privy Council the following year, applied the rule of treating similar cases similarly. Women's difference justified exclusion from the Senate: they were not regarded as persons, and the British North America Act specified that only qualified *persons* were to be selected for the Senate.[3] The Supreme Court decision was viewed as a consistent and impartial interpretation of laws already in place that prohibited women from entering certain professions. Here, consistency and predictability in the application of the law were present, but resulted in placing barriers in the way of women's freedom to pursue interests, projects, and goals.

This brief discussion of the *Persons* case moves rather quickly over some complex issues. The case undermines the idea that procedural equality is an adequate test for equality in at least two respects, both of which are essential ingredients in the project of developing a relational account of equality. The first is an issue explored in the next two sections: the idea that consistency in the interpretation and application of the law will ensure that all people have the freedom to plan their lives needs to be supplemented by making equal concern and respect the foundation of theories of equality. If the process of treating like cases alike is to have any moral substance, it must rest on the fundamental requirement that each person be treated with equal concern and respect. This is precisely the central insight of classical liberalism, and it is this requirement that forms the foundation of all current theories of equality.

Second, the concept "dynamic realism," suggested in the previous chapter as a replacement for Hacking's "dynamic nominalism," is meant to capture the idea that categories are real in the sense that they describe real features of people, but also in the sense that they are created in factual moral and political contexts with concrete social practices that give significance to those features. Differences have their meaning in the context of human interaction and interpretation. When we apply these ideas to the *Persons* case, we undermine notions about law as an objective reflection of facts or about judges as objective and impartial interpreters of the facts. This point is related to one touched on in the previous chapter's discussion of the role of standards of comparison, and I shall expand on it in the last part of this chapter by making use of Gilligan's insights in *In a Different Voice*. The discussion in this chapter about the role of standards of comparison and the significance of perspectives will play a central role in the critique of Rawls's theory of justice in Chapter 5.

Classical Liberalism on Equality: The Theory

Most theorists credit liberal theory with rejecting Aristotelian-type determinations of who counts as equal and with expounding, if not always respecting, the thesis that all human beings are equal. Will Kymlicka explicitly describes accounts that discriminate among and group people on the basis of certain features to be a rejection of equality altogether. Kymlicka reasons that Nazi arguments, for example, do not merit consideration because they "deny that each person matters equally. . . . [T]hey reject equality . . . because they care more about some people's good than about others." He adds, "[c]onversely, when we affirm equality, it is . . . because we think each person's good matters equally" (Kymlicka 1989, 40). He uses the phrase "their claims are not informed by the *teachings* of equality" (Kymlicka 1989, 185, 240, my emphasis) to refer to those who deny that members of groups identifiable by features of race, gender, and class, for example, are equal or deserve equal concern and respect. Kymlicka takes liberal theory to be responsible for developing this "powerful ideal of equality": "the idea that every citizen has a right to full and equal participation in the political, economic, and cultural life of the country, without regard to race, sex, religion, physical handicap—without regard to any of the classifications which have traditionally kept people separate and behind" (Kymlicka 1989, 141).

What Kymlicka calls the "powerful ideal of equality" emerges from such classical liberal theorists as Hobbes, Locke, Kant, Rousseau, and Mill. Classical liberals provide the best-known arguments for why the intrinsic moral worth of each person makes equal treatment of all people foundational to equality. They describe various capacities unique and basic to human beings to argue for the equal moral worth of all persons: rationality, the capacity to make plans in the context of a life, and the capacity for pleasure and pain are some examples. Kant moves from an account of people possessing the capacity to reason to the moral principle that each person be treated as an end and never as a mere means. Utilitarians consider that respecting individual moral worth is satisfied when each person's interests count for one and only one in the calculation of utilities. In both cases, the argument moves from the specification of criteria for personhood, the possession of some relevant attribute (reason or interests, for example), to a discussion of the intrinsic worth of those attributes, to the prescription that a person deserves equal concern and respect by virtue of the fact that that person possesses the relevant attribute. The possession of the relevant capacity or capacities makes a person "a subject, an agent, a moral being to be valued, worthy of respect and concern" (Sypnowich 1990, 86).[4]

Some classical liberals explain the underlying argument for equal concern and respect in terms of the logical move from knowing and valuing our own capacities to conclusions about other human beings. We *value* our own freedom to plan and manage our life and that gives its protection moral force. Because it matters to us that we have this freedom, we are forced logically to value the freedom of others because we realize that they are like us in also having the requisite capacities and valuing their freedom to exercise these capacities. Further, we are forced logically to move from valuing each person's freedom to a commitment to procedural equality—all others like me ought to be treated equally.[5] Henry Sidgwick explains that the move from valuing my interests to valuing those of others is a logical and rational one that is based on the intuitive principle of rational benevolence: mere numerical difference does not justify a difference in treatment (Sidgwick 1966, 379–384).[6]

It is not difficult to grasp why the classical liberal ideal of equality has such force. In a historical context in which an Aristotelian conception of equality called for no more than classifying people according to certain similarities and then specifying that these "equals" be treated equally, the classical liberal argument that all people are similar in morally crucial respects is without question a radical and progressive move. By appealing to such basic human capacities as the ability to reason, to make plans, or to experience happiness, classical liberals reject the Aristotelian view that differences outside of these basic capacities could justify unequal treatment. This account of equality still operates with the rule that likes should be treated alike, but extends the criteria of "likeness" to cover all people who possess the relevant capacities. Until differences can be shown to be relevant to how people are treated, we presume equality: all people deserve equal concern and respect because they each possess the same morally relevant feature or features.

This understanding of equality has been variously referred to as "the postulate of equality" (Rosenfeld 1991, 21), "everyone's life matters equally" (Nielsen 1985, 8; 296; 301), and "the presumptive right of each person to be treated by society as a respected, responsible, participating member, regardless of the differences between persons" (Weinzweig 1987, 83). I prefer and shall continue to use Ronald Dworkin's phrase, "equal concern and respect" (Dworkin 1978, 180). Kai Nielsen states that he does not "know how to prove such a deep underlying moral principle" except to contrast it with a Nietzschean elitist meritocracy or an Aristotelian aristocracy, both of which hold that there are "quite different kinds of human beings . . . plainly not of equal moral worth" (Nielsen 1985, 8). As Nielsen puts it, equal concern and respect is taken to be the "point where justification comes to an end" (Nielsen 1985, 38; 268).

Nielsen's use of "justification comes to an end" is a well-aimed appropriation of Wittgenstein's use of the phrase in *On Certainty* (Wittgenstein 1969, §192). Wittgenstein uses the phrase to explain why some questions, doubts, and mistakes raised by philosophers, for example, make no sense outside of the language games in which they are used.[7] Justifications come to an end when we realize how the commitment to equal concern and respect for all people functions in our "stream of life" as a universal ideal, "a world-wide process and phenomenon" (Benhabib 1995, 252). The principle of equal concern and respect penetrates all language games and serves as an outlook or framework for moral and political theory. An Aristotelian conception of procedural equality that justifies grouping people based on sets of features and making the possession of these relevant to one's membership and participation in the moral community is a conception of equality that is no longer a live option in moral and political discourse. It is not as though descriptive differences no longer exist; rather they no longer form the basis for understanding some people to be inferior and deserving of unequal treatment. The commitment to moral equality is reflected in the constitutions of various nations and in such international documents as the United Nations' Declaration of Human Rights. These documents stipulate antidiscrimination rights as basic human and moral rights.

I have stressed the fundamental importance of equal concern and respect not only to demonstrate the historical importance of classical liberalism but also to indicate that the principle will be foundational to the relational approach to equality that I advance. However, it will look different as we will discover at the end of the chapter when I apply a relational critique to liberalism's understanding of what grounds equal concern and respect: the autonomous self-determining capacities of moral agents. But there are two topics to take up in connection with classical liberalism before we get there. First, before we give too much credit to classical liberalism for its revolutionary impact, we need to remind ourselves of how the "powerful ideal of equality" has worked and continues to work itself out in practice. In practice, the same differences that have had historical significance continue to be used to try and justify unequal treatment. In the next section, I discuss classical liberalism in practice as a way of introducing and discussing the second topic in the sections that follow: the two main lines of feminist criticism of classical liberal arguments.

Classical Liberalism on Equality: The Practice

Notoriously, even though classical liberals provide the foundational arguments for realizing that such differences as gender, race, and disability are irrelevant standards of comparison, irrelevant to the ways in which people ought to be treated, many still explicitly argue that people different in these very same ways do not have the requisite capacities to justify equal membership in the political community. Locke, for example, argues that all men "being furnished with like faculties, sharing all in one community of nature, there cannot be supposed any such subordination among us, that may authorize us to destroy another, as if we were made for one another's uses, as the inferior ranks of creatures are for ours" (Locke 1690, 457). Locke then sets about a few chapters later, in *Two Treatises of Government*, to explain that nature dictates women's subordination to the rule of the "abler and stronger" man and that women "consent" to this arrangement.

In a similar vein, Rousseau describes man in a state of nature as essentially free and equal. Yet he devotes sections of *Emile* to describing how women differ from men and need to be educated into their proper roles. Here are some of the steps Rousseau takes from similarity, to difference, to unequal treatment:

> But for her sex, a woman is a man; she has the same organs, the same needs, the same faculties. . . . Yet where sex is concerned man and woman are unlike; each is the complement of the other . . . where man and woman are alike, we have to do with the characteristics of the species; where they are unlike, we have to do with the characteristics of sex. . . . These resemblances and differences must have an influence on the moral nature; this influence is obvious, and is confirmed by experience; it shows the vanity of the disputes as to the superiority or the equality of the sexes; as if each sex, pursuing the path marked out for it by nature, were not more perfect in that very divergence than if it more closely resembled the other. . . . From this diversity springs the first difference which may be observed between man and woman in their moral relations. The man should be strong and active; the woman should be weak and passive; the one must have both the power and the will; it is enough that the other should offer little resistance (Rousseau 1760, 321–322).

The classical liberal precept of equal concern and respect did not guarantee that those who espoused the principle would extend equal consideration to all people. Some of the reasons for this return us to the discussion in the previous chapter about the close connections between identifying descriptive features and prescribing treatment. In a political context of inequalities already entrenched in social practices, descriptive differences have a prescriptive force that is difficult to eradicate. Think again of Chapter 2's descriptions of how builder A's perceptions and treatment of aspiring builder B emerge in a context in which his activities and interests are shaped by beliefs about what women are like, beliefs which in turn confirm the justifications for women's exclusion from building activities. Alison Jaggar makes the point when she writes, "women's social inequality often translates directly into scientific claims that women are 'naturally' different from or inferior to men. These claims, in turn, reinforce and so perpetuate women's subordination" (Jaggar 1987, 30).

Jaggar and many other feminists criticize classical liberal justifications for withholding equal treatment for some members. They use two main sorts of strategies. In the first strategy, critics draw attention to the inconsistencies in some of the classical liberal accounts of what makes people equal.[8] Here such basic principles as "mere numerical difference does not justify a difference in treatment" are put to the test in a strategy that questions the moral relevance of such differences as gender, race, and class. Demonstrating that one has the very same capacities specified by classical liberals as necessary and/or sufficient for membership is a powerful way of demanding inclusion in the community of equal members extolled by these political theorists. The historical success of this strategy illustrates the power of the classical liberal arguments. Its success also comes with pitfalls, as we will discover in Chapter 7.

At a second level of critique, one that will be central to my project and to which I now turn, critics have pointed out that the various criteria specified by liberals as necessary and/or sufficient for personhood and for equal treatment actually embody the particular norms of those in power and ignore or denigrate virtues and activities associated with those who are not.[9] It is difficult to expose these underlying assumptions. Gilligan's work is instructive in this respect.

The Role of Unstated Standards of Comparison

In the introduction to *In a Different Voice*, Gilligan provides a context for understanding her work by identifying the motivational factors that produced her interest in listening to women's voices as a way of undermining traditional theories about them. She recounts her dissatisfaction with traditional psychological theories of moral development: "the recurrent problems in interpreting women's development" and "the repeated exclusion of women from the critical theory-building studies of psychological research" (Gilligan 1982, 1). She notes that these "problems" had always been understood to "signify a problem in women's development" (Gilligan 1982, 2) and indicates that a shift in perspective enables one to adopt the following alternative explanation for observed differences in abilities: "[i]nstead, the failure of women to fit existing models of human growth may point to a problem in the representation, a limitation in the conception of human condition, an omission of certain truths about life" (Gilligan 1982, 2). Rather than take the accepted psychological theory of human growth as a given, *the* truth about moral development, Gilligan explores the possibility that the problem may be with the model used in the theory.

All of these comments about what prompted her research are repeated in "Letter to Readers, 1993," a new preface to *In a Different Voice*. Here, Gilligan takes the opportunity to reflect on her work of the last decade and on the reactions of her critics. She speculates about some of the underlying reasons for the resistance to taking account of what people say when they say something different and for the tendency to make value judgments about difference. She begins with basic points about relational features of speech acts in social contexts. "To have a voice is to be human. To have something to say is to be a person. But speaking depends on listening and being heard; it is an intensely relational act" (Gilligan 1993, xvi). In discussing interactions between psychologists and subjects, Gilligan notes her own tendency and the strong tendency on the part of researchers to fall into a "two-step process": "the process of listening to women and hearing something new, a different way of speaking, and then hearing how quickly this difference gets assimilated into old categories of thinking so that it loses its novelty and its message" (Gilligan 1993, xii).

Gilligan's discussion of the ease with which we fall into the "two-step process," encountering something new and then assimilating it by applying familiar categories, marks a feature of language discussed in the previous chapter. There, I emphasized that the whole background complex of standards, rules, and practices in a community serves as the base from which we learn a language and become members of a community. We make sense of what we encounter by relating it to that with which we are already familiar and understanding it in those terms. The builders find their place as members of their community by responding to the speech acts of others. They learn to communicate and interact with others by performing the actions and using the justifications for acting in the appropriate circumstances. The social practices ensure that one becomes familiar with the standards and rules that are accepted by community members. As we learned in Chapter 2, the consequences that follow from not placing what is encountered into the accepted categories go from incurring judgments of making mistakes to being viewed as deviant, incapable, or inferior.

When people become the objects of judgments, their very speech acts and actions are subjected to categorization and judgment. Gilligan explains that the effect of this tendency in traditional psychological research on and about women's experiences is double-edged. First, when researchers interview women and encounter something different, they quickly fall into judging what is said in terms of whether the source of the difference is nature or nurture and whether what is being said is better or worse than those speech acts that fit more easily into accepted and familiar categories. These questions are connected to issues raised in Chapter 2: metaphysical questions about whether differences are real or nominal, essential or socially constructed, and moral issues about the relevance of differences to questions of treatment. Second, the tendency to categorize and judge is repeated when theorists interpret research that falls outside familiar categories (including Gilligan's own research on psychological development) in terms of accepted and settled frameworks of thought: "[w]hen I hear my work being cast in terms of whether women and men are really (essentially) different or who is better than whom, I know that I have lost my voice, because these are not my questions. Instead, my questions are about our perceptions of reality and truth: how we know, how we hear, how we see, how we speak. My questions are about voice and relationship" (Gilligan 1993, xiii).[10]

Gilligan is not generally taken to be mainly concerned with "how we know, how we hear, how we see, how we speak," but her comments have obvious connections with the relational features of language and of people that I have been highlighting thus far.[11] Gilligan's thought can be further elucidated by building on her example of the interactions between the research subjects, Amy and Jake, and the Kohlberg psychologists who interpret and judge their responses to the Heinz dilemma. Amy and Jake, two eleven-year-olds, are told that Heinz cannot afford to buy a drug that can save his dying wife's life and the druggist who has the drug refuses to lower the price. They are then asked if Heinz should steal the drug to save his wife's life. Descriptions of Amy's and Jake's answers are generally used to illustrate the differences between a care and a justice approach to morality. I shall have more to say about justice and care and the connections between them beginning in Chapter 5. For now, I want to concentrate on the effects of unstated standards of comparison. Exploring the underlying relational dynamic between Amy and the Kohlberg interviewer is a vivid way of illustrating the impact of this kind of relationship on the way Amy perceives herself and her place in the world. Amy is the quintessential example of someone who fails to measure up on a scale of moral development understood to be the measure of psychological development for all people. In discussing this example, I shall move from outlining the effects of the dynamics of relationships to the perspectives of those detrimentally affected by them, and thereby make room for considering what it is about Amy's perspective that is valuable.

The Effects of Unstated Standards of Comparison

In the interview process, Amy is subjected to the "two-step" process. The Kohlberg interviewer comes already armed with a particular way of perceiving moral issues and judging moral development and interprets what research subjects say in terms of that framework. The framework represents in part the familiar categories and judgments in a social and political context that values the abilities to abstract from particular cases and formulate general principles as *the* way to solve moral problems. These are features of a justice approach that Jake articulates in his answer to the Heinz dilemma. Jake describes the dilemma as being like a mathematical problem (Gilligan 1982, 26). He assumes there are only two choices and calculates that Heinz needs to give priority to saving his wife's life and that stealing the drug is a minor offense for which the law will show leniency. Jake scores high on the Kohlberg scale.

When asked to respond to the question whether Heinz should steal a drug to save his wife's life, Amy's answers appear "evasive and unsure" to the Kohlberg interviewer. She says *both* that "there might be other ways besides stealing it, like if he could borrow the money, or make a loan or something" and that "his wife shouldn't die either" (Gilligan 1982, 28). Gilligan's point is that the question already constructs a particular framework that allows only two answers: stealing or letting die. When Amy starts to talk, the interviewer conveys feelings and attitudes of irritation and disappointment by repeating the questions and pressing Amy to explain her answers—giving her a chance to redeem herself and provide the answers that fit the construction of the dilemma as either stealing or letting die.

The interview process generates comparisons between the responses of Amy and those of Jake. Jake receives positive encouragement for his responses, encouragement that increases his confidence in his answers.[12] Amy, on the other hand, is judged to be someone who just has less ability than Jake to reason through moral dilemmas in a "correct" and "mature" way. Gilligan asks us to consider the full effects of these interactions by focusing on what happens when Amy picks up on these interactive cues of disappointment with her responses and realizes that her ability to think is being judged as inadequate: "[b]ut as the interviewer conveys through the repetition of questions that the answers she gave were not heard or not right, Amy's confidence begins to diminish, and her replies become more constrained and unsure. . . . [A]s she constructs the problem differently herself, Kohlberg's conception completely evades her" (Gilligan 1982, 29). The interactive relationship between Amy and the researcher creates self-doubt in Amy because the questions and concerns she takes to be genuine are viewed as irrelevant or indicative of inferior abilities.

If Amy is at all sensitive to the dynamics of the interactions and the comparisons it generates between herself and Jake, she realizes that the categorization and judgment of her responses ignore her perspective and "encourage her, in the name of development, to accept a construction of reality and morality that she identifies as problematic" (Gilligan 1986b, 329). Gilligan does not report any interactions that take place between Amy and Jake during or after the interview process, but we can easily imagine that outside of the interview process, Jake attributes his ability to come up with the "right" answers to the fact that he is male. If Amy is one of a number of girls in the research setting who make the same sorts of "mistakes" in their responses, then Jake's perceptions of what women are like will be reinforced. Gilligan's point is that when the results of this research are compiled and assimilated into theories of human moral development, conclusions are drawn about the inferior moral reasoning capacities of women in general in ways that affect how women are perceived and treated.

For Amy, several consequences (similar to those experienced by aspiring builder B) flow from the interactive relationship between her and the Kohlberg interviewer. Amy's ability to speak confidently and her opportunity to have herself understood and respected are restricted. In addition, when assumptions are made about Amy's capacities in terms of the Kohlberg standard of the ethic of justice, this limits the possibility of understanding Amy's different perspective as a legitimate way of exploring and doing things. What she says and how she behaves already have meaning ahead of anything she may see, feel, or say. Meaning is given to her difference in a way that affects both how others will understand her and how she will understand herself and her place in the community. The effects are evident in "personal doubts that invade women's sense of themselves, compromising their ability to act on their own perceptions and thus their willingness to take responsibility for what they do" (Gilligan 1982, 49).

This description of how judgments affect perceptions and perceptions affect judgments can be used to summarize several points made in the previous chapter and in this chapter so far. First, the description fills out the outline given in the previous chapter of how identifying and describing differences in people can affect those people. Second, it shows how identifying differences in people assumes particular standards of comparison, standards that are entrenched in social practices. The standards of comparison become so taken for granted that they are viewed as universal and true. They are assumed to be the points from which "knowing assertions of distinctions and differences" (Minow 1990a, 228) are made. Third, it sheds light on the complexity and difficulty of implementing the commitment to equal concern and respect in a context that continues to make properties that mattered in the past significant to current perceptions and treatment of people who have those properties.

Uncovering the biases underlying the assumption that one's perspective is an impartial and objective standard from which to judge others is a subtle and powerful kind of critique, one whose force is not always apparent. In an interesting discussion of a symposium in which several participants credited feminism with exposing androcentric bias in developmental psychology, Lynn Hankinson Nelson reports one psychologist as saying, " '*[a]nyone can see* that you can't build a theory about psychological development from studies limited to males. There is no need to assume there's a relationship between *feminism* and the ability to see that' " (Nelson 1994, 295, her emphasis). However, as Nelson points out and as Gilligan's studies show, selecting male-only research subjects was not so obviously wrongheaded to some psychologists. More importantly, the descriptions of how standards and rules are established and become entrenched in the very practices of community members engaged in interactive relationships shows how uncovering the assumptions and biases is no easy task.

Feminists have argued that male norms are so entrenched in social practices that they become invisible and are taken for granted. In a context where the predominantly male activities of competition and achievement in a public sphere serve as the norm against which all other activities are evaluated, women's activities, development, and reasoning capacities have been judged by theorists in many disciplines to be inferior. Martha Minow summarizes feminism's contribution to the uncovering of biases in traditional theory. "Many feminists find relational insights critical to any effort to recover women's experiences, because the exclusion, degradation, or devaluation of women by political theorists, historians, social scientists, and literary theorists implies and imposes a reference point based on male experience. Feminists have contributed incisive critiques of the unstated assumptions behind political theory, law, bureaucracy, natural science, and social science which presuppose the universality of a particular reference point" (Minow 1990a, 194). In illustrating the insidiousness of unstated standards of comparison, relational approaches present controversial challenges. As Minow points out in the context of law, "the switch in the focus of attention from the 'different person' to the social and legal construction of difference challenges long-established modes of reasoning about reality and about law" (Minow 1990a, 22–23).

In Chapter 2, I accepted an account of meaning that understands differences as real features of objects in the world, but added an account of how the selection and evaluation of difference is a product of social practices and political contexts. When those in power identify differences and group people accordingly, a whole set of rules is made applicable to all members of those groups in ways that shape the relationships they can enter into, limit their opportunities for participation and interaction with others, and determine the levels of freedom they have to develop their talents and capacities. Once we let go of the idea that current standards are the only objective and neutral ones and, as Gilligan advises, resist the tendency to fall into the two-step process of categorization and judgment, we are in a position to take different perspectives as valid points of reference, as perspectives that can provide valuable contributions to our understanding of social relations and of what is required to treat people with equal concern and respect.

Recall now that Hacking describes his model as a partial framework and admits that he "reflect[s] too little on the ordinary dynamics of human interaction" (Hacking 1986, 222). In the latter part of Chapter 2, I criticized Hacking's account of the two vectors of influence for not paying sufficient attention to the dynamics of human interaction or to the function of unstated standards of comparison. I argued that a key strategy in my relational approach is precisely to focus on the dynamics of human interaction and to do so in the context of concrete social practices and political contexts. Interactions between persons who have the power to label and those who are labeled tell us something about the social practices that shape relationships and the moral and political implications of being in those relationships. Relationships between those who have power and those who do not, between those who are taken to be the standard and those who are viewed as different from the standard, are interactive relationships and, as such, have the potential for changing political structures, but only if we take seriously the idea that those whose perspectives have been ignored or silenced have something to contribute.

The idea introduced in this chapter, that the perspectives of those viewed as different from the standard can enhance our understanding of equality, is central to the critique of liberal conceptions of equality in the next two chapters. For now, we can begin to examine the importance of this insight about the value of different perspectives, gleaned from our focus on the significance of relationships, by applying it in a preliminary way to a discussion of what Amy's approach can contribute to our understanding of what is needed to treat people with equal concern and respect.

The Value of Different Perspectives

Describing the interactions between Amy and the Kohlberg researcher draws out the consequences in one case of assuming particular standards of comparison as universal and true. Realizing that Kohlberg's scale is merely one possible standard of comparison for interpreting moral development allows us to shift our focus from understanding the Kohlberg standard as being the only measure of Amy's responses to understanding that her different approach is another equally viable way of understanding and structuring the world. In formulating his answer to the Heinz dilemma, Jake abstracts from the context of the particular people in and circumstances of the dilemma to articulate general moral rules against stealing other people's property and letting people die and then prioritizes the latter. He reasons that anyone in Heinz's position would and should steal the drug to save a person's life.

While Amy is also able to articulate the general moral rules that apply to this particular dilemma, her main concerns center on a breakdown of communication and relationship between Heinz and the druggist, Heinz and his wife, and his wife and the druggist. She worries about the possibility that not enough was done in the communication process before getting to the stage where nothing is left but the dilemma of either stealing or letting die. She wonders if enough has been done on the part of the druggist to listen, understand, and respond to what Heinz is saying and if enough has been done on the part of Heinz to communicate to the druggist his care for his wife and her health. In fact, Amy's concerns parallel those that Gilligan herself expresses about not enough being done on the part of researchers to take account of different perspectives. Amy is herself the object of a breakdown of communication similar to the one that she perceives as leading to the Heinz dilemma. Yet because the dilemma is constructed for her in a particular way, her concerns are taken to be irrelevant. She is assumed to be incapable of realizing the "real" problem and of making decisions in a sure and determined way. Her responses are "rendered incomprehensible by the Kohlberg frame" (Gilligan 1986b, 329). But what is it about Amy's approach that is different, insightful, and valuable? As we will discover in Chapters 6 and 7, the answer to that question is complex and multifaceted. But we can start by sketching an outline of that answer here.

Amy approaches the Heinz dilemma by locating it in the broader context of relationships. Her worries about the breakdown of communication and the severing of relationships permit an examination of an orientation that focuses on people in relationships. Once we make room for considering her approach as a valid way of thinking about moral problems, as a perspective different from Jake's in its concern for the effects of people's actions on relationships, we also make it possible to raise general questions about responsibility and interdependence not obviously open to the justice approach as Jake presents it. "Is the druggist charging an unreasonable price or a fair one? What are these people's social and financial resources? Is there no one they can call on? Are they racially or economically marginalized, and hence extraordinarily bereft of social resources? Can they not borrow the money, ask for credit? Are they an autonomous man-wife unit in solitary confrontation with the druggist?" (Code 1991, 161). When the "proper" answer to the Heinz dilemma is to steal the drug to save the life, questions about the background social practices that create the dilemma and put people like Heinz in the position of stealing to save a life are foreclosed.

The orientation that Amy presents is one that focuses on actual relationships and the impact of relationships on questions of identity, agency, and moral issues more generally. We are all in relationships, but what implications does an orientation that actually focuses on them as a way of thinking about moral agents and dilemmas have for moral and political theory? A quick answer would be that this orientation enables rather than hinders the possibility of raising the issues in the previously asked questions. A full and complex answer is to use the strategy adopted in this project and put to use in the next chapter: using an orientation that focuses on relationships to critically evaluate the application of the precept of equal concern and respect in liberal theories of equality and justice. But to finish this chapter, I want to return to a topic I raised earlier in the context of explaining the fundamental importance of the principle of equal concern and respect to all theories of equality. What is the equality that grounds equal concern and respect?

The discussion thus far of the relational features underlying the meaning of difference, the role of standards of comparison, the value of perspectives outside the norm, and an orientation centered on relationships can now be put to use in providing a different understanding of what grounds the foundational principle of equal concern and respect than that provided by classical liberals and incorporated in current liberal theory. So far, I have answered the question of what sort of equality grounds equal concern and respect in the very general terms of the basic human capacities for self-determination and self-legislation: agents who explore, pursue, and develop their interests, projects, and goals. Rawls's specific answer is "moral personality," to which I now turn as a way of differentiating and then sketching an alternative that I shall refer to as "moral personhood."

Moral Personhood: A Relational Interpretation of Equal Concern and Respect

Very late in *A Theory of Justice*, Rawls discusses the problem of identifying the kind of equality at the base of the view that all people are equal: "[t]here is no natural feature with respect to which all human beings are equal, that is, which everyone has (or which sufficiently many have) to the same degree" (Rawls 1971, 507). When he sets out to defend basing equality on natural capacities, he states, "[a]ll we have to do is select a range property . . . and to give equal justice to those meeting its conditions" (Rawls 1971, 508). Rawls then identifies the "range property" of moral personality: the capacity to formulate a conception of the good (a rational plan of life) and the capacity for a sense of justice, "a normally effective desire to apply and act upon the principles of justice" (Rawls 1971, 505). He further clarifies the idea of a range property by specifying that as a "condition for equal justice, the capacity for moral personality, is not at all stringent," that there "is no race or recognized group of human beings that lacks this attribute," and that "[o]nly scattered individuals are without this capacity, or its realization to a minimum degree, and the failure to realize it is the consequence of unjust and impoverished social circumstances" (Rawls 1971, 506).

I like the idea of identifying criteria for equality in terms of minimally sufficient conditions satisfied by a range of capacities, but I also think that we need to take care when identifying criteria that we do not presume existing structures that already exclude certain kinds of moral agents, activities, and values. In this respect, we can already raise questions about Rawls's account of moral personality. What constitutes a rational plan of life? Would everyone be equally or centrally concerned about satisfying preferences that shape their own particular conception of the good? Is the ability to formulate a "rational" plan of life crucial for determining who enters the original position and engages in critical thinking about equality and justice? How would an acknowledgment of the validity and value of the various perspectives of those in unequal and oppressive relationships affect our thinking about equality? Would inclusion of these perspectives change the reflections leading to agreement about the principles for structuring a just society? Do these perspectives shape a sense of justice different from that of those who constitute the norm? These are the kinds of questions that are raised when we apply relational insights to Rawls's account of moral personality, questions for which I shall explore answers in the detailed examination of Rawls in Chapter 5. For now, the questions allow me to provide a preliminary sketch of an account of moral equals that I refer to as moral personhood as distinct from Rawls's moral personality.

In Wittgensteinian terms, the concept of moral personhood can be said to form "a complicated network of similarities overlapping and criss-crossing: sometimes overall similarities, sometimes similarities of detail" (Wittgenstein 1953, §66). As was revealed in the context of discussing moral concepts in the previous chapter, moral agents are best understood as acting and interacting in all language games. They deliberate, formulate, and make decisions all in the context of planning a life in response to and in relationships with members of a community. Beliefs, judgments, moral behavior, and conceptions of the good are not incidental aspects of people's lives, but reflect who and what moral agents are in the particularity of all their relationships. The very capacities that Rawls identifies as criteria for equality, having a conception of the good and a sense of justice, need to be shown as emerging in and through particular relationships and social practices and to be evaluated in concrete social and political contexts. How we think about rationality or planning a life or justice is shaped by the relationships we are in.

The descriptions of Amy and of the builders acting and interacting in relationships in purposeful contexts shape a conception of moral personhood in terms of a self whose identity and self-concepts are structured in relation to others. The basis for moral equality is not any particular quality or qualities of a person's life, but takes shape in the whole network of activity and relationships within which people live. The description of the relational features of language and of people shows how individual capacities, activities, and choices take shape and have meaning in purposive and interactive contexts and in all sorts of relationships. Relationships are so fundamental and primary that we cannot conceive of individual interests, projects, and goals having meaning outside of them.

In connection with the "range property" that identifies criteria for what makes human beings equal, we need to bring into the foreground the most basic and fundamental features of personhood: we act, react, and interact as persons in a community of relationships. Like Rawls, Nielsen attempts to identify the kind of equality at the base of the view that all people are equal. Unlike Rawls, he focuses on features of people's sociality and interdependence: "in the ways that are most important, i.e., in our capacities for reciprocity, compassion, capacities to form life plans, to care for one another and the like, there are no, *a distinctive socialization apart*, significant differences between most people, so that we can say that we are equal here and that consequently each of us is of equal human worth" (Nielsen 1985, 185, his emphasis). I can now better explain why "moral personhood" captures what underlies equal concern and respect more adequately than "moral personality." Moral personhood is suggestive of moral agency as an ongoing process of engagement with others in a network of relationships shaped by social practices and political contexts. Autonomy is a capacity that emerges in and is exercised through relationships of all kinds and is best perceived as incomplete, tentative, and ongoing.

The concept of moral personhood sheds a different light on the classical liberal argument that moves from valuing my capacities to valuing other people's capacities. My ability to recognize that each person possesses the same valued capacities of self-legislation and self-determination depends on my living in relationships with others. Seyla Benhabib captures the primacy of social relations and the moral significance of this fact when she writes, "the self only becomes an 'I' in a community of other selves who are also 'I's. Every act of self-reference expresses simultaneously the uniqueness and differences of the self as well as the commonality among selves" (Benhabib 1987a, 170).[13] When we begin with the fact of our situatedness in relationships, a different light is also shed on liberal accounts of individuality and creativity with respect to self-determining capacities. In placing people's autonomous actions in a network of complex and ever-changing relationships, we highlight the concreteness of people's lives and the creativity and uniqueness with which people plan and manage their lives. Central to the notion of moral personhood is the feature of human diversity, diversity with respect to needs, capacities, and ways of being.

In an interesting twist on Rawls's idea of a range property, it is true to say that it is only in relations with others in a community of relations that we are able to identify the human capacities we share in common. Moral personhood, the kind of equality at the base of the view that all people are equal and deserve equal concern and respect, is intended to capture the idea that people are unique and creative social beings who act and interact in relationships of all kinds, of compassion, care, power, and oppression; relationships that can promote as well as hinder autonomy and opportunities. I can note for now and develop later the idea that liberal theory's cherished notions of autonomy, of moral agency, of justice, of rights, and of freedom are not relinquished in a relational approach; instead they are reconceptualized in terms of how these capacities and goals function and are given content in relationships.

By applying relational insights to the criteria Rawls comes up with, a richer and more complex account of moral equals emerges. Moral personhood is a concept designed to put aspects of sociality and relationality in the foreground in a theory of equality. The application of relational insights to the concepts of moral equality and of equal concern and respect already provides a contrast with some of the most basic ideas of liberal theory, one of which raises questions about how the self is conceived and why this matters to moral and political theory. I need to do much more to outline the self in liberal theory and to develop the rather sketchy ideas of a relational conception of the self presented here. That will be the task of Chapter 6.

Drawing Conclusions and Looking Ahead: The Builders and Equal Concern and Respect

In the account of moral personhood that I have sketched, people begin and remain in relationships and become persons by exercising self-determining capacities in and through relationships. They are engaged with others in interactive and purposeful activity and need to be in order to become members of a society. These features underlie the notion of moral equality and ground our commitment to equal concern and respect. Yet, the commitment to equal concern and respect is certainly much too general and needs to be given content. A commitment to equal concern and respect may be foundational to a theory of equality, but it is far from sufficient. On its own, it tells us little about what it is to treat people with equal concern and respect or about the structures that are needed to ensure that the precept is respected.

In the next two chapters, we will examine the two main theories developed by liberals to meet the demand for equal concern and respect. For now, we can take stock of some important aspects of the relational approach to equality developed in this chapter and begin to sketch the role of relational theory in enhancing an understanding of what is required for treating people with equal concern and respect. The three relational insights from this chapter are the importance of understanding the perspectives of those who are detrimentally affected by the relationships of inequality and powerlessness that they are in, the value of an orientation centered on relationships to an evaluation of moral and political issues, and the significance of the notion of moral personhood for revealing what people are like and what treating them with equal concern and respect will require. Let us return to the builders' community to apply these insights.

In learning the rule that excludes women from building, the builders not only treat women as nonbuilders, but because they learn the rule in the context of entrenched practices, they come to believe that their judgments reflect the only way the world can and should be structured. These judgments so fit into a stream of life that the established norms and social practices are presumed to be neutral and universal. From the perspective of those who fit the norm, various things about nonbuilders, for example, their activities, their relationships, and their values, tend not to be even noticed let alone understood. A case in point: from the perspective of the builders, a judgment that building is work but cleaning house is not would affect not only who is permitted to "work," but also attitudes about and aid for activities not perceived as work. Workers do things such as leave home, get paid, compete for building contracts, employ and manage builders, form unions, and formulate policies for structuring building communities. All of this constitutes work different from and more important than nonbuilding activities, activities that become part of the taken-for-granted background structure.

The first strategy outlined in the section "Classical Liberalism: The Practice" called for extending the criteria for moral equality to all those who have been excluded. In the case of the builders' community, this strategy would allow us to question women's exclusion from building activities. Women can build, and we ought to give them the same opportunity to compete for jobs and contracts as men have. The second strategy, developed from Gilligan's work on standards of comparison, would have us question the valuations and the structures, particularly when they result in diminished respect for the lives and activities of nonbuilders, and in the kind of treatment that places them in positions of marginality and powerlessness. Once we establish the case for examining different perspectives as equally viable and valuable ways of perceiving and structuring the world, we make room for considering the perspectives of those who are in relationships of powerlessness, oppression, and inequality as vantage points for understanding particular inequalities and for changing the structures that perpetuate unequal relations. We will discover that the first strategy constitutes the framework within which liberals tackle issues of equality. We need to keep the relational insights of the second strategy in mind as we turn to an examination of liberal theories of what is needed to satisfy the demands of the foundational commitment to equal concern and respect.

4

❦ ❦ ❦

Liberal Theory: From Formal to Substantive Equality of Opportunity

Introduction

Because people value their freedom to explore, pursue, and develop their life projects and goals, all liberal theorists agree that treating people with equal concern and respect means providing each person with an equal opportunity to pursue the goals he or she values. As Kymlicka and others explain,[1] however, a commitment to equal concern and respect is shared by such different theories as libertarianism, liberal substantive equality theory, radical egalitarianism, socialism, and Marxism:

> [E]very plausible political theory has the same ultimate value, which is equality. They are all "egalitarian" theories. . . . A theory is egalitarian in this sense if it accepts that the interests of each member of the community matter, and matter equally. Put another way, egalitarian theories require that the government treat its citizens with equal consideration; each citizen is entitled to equal concern and respect. This more basic notion of equality is found in Nozick's libertarianism as much as in Marx's communism. While leftists believe that equality of income or wealth is a precondition for treating people as equals, those on the right believe that equal rights over one's labour and property are a precondition for treating people as equals (Kymlicka 1990, 4).

69

While the commitment to the moral equality of all people is capable of generating very different theories of political structures needed to respect the precept, the factor that pulls all the theories together is respect for and protection of the basic capacities that make people deserving of equal concern and respect. We discovered in the previous chapter that we conceive the capacities differently when we begin with relationships rather than individuals. In this chapter and the next, I shall put that and other relational insights to use in an examination of the working out of the commitment to equal concern and respect within the liberal tradition.

Before we proceed to discuss liberal conceptions of equality, I need to note that there are inconsistencies in the terminology used to delineate theories of equality. In the previous quotation, for example, Kymlicka refers to the whole spectrum of equality theories as "egalitarian," in the sense that they all accept the foundational requirement that individuals be treated with equal concern and respect. However, most other theorists use "egalitarian" to refer to those theories that support measures for equalizing the distribution of goods. Nielsen takes libertarianism, for example, to be antiegalitarian, in the sense that it rejects state interference with the distribution of goods (Nielsen 1985, 132–135). How I use the terminology will become clear in the course of outlining and evaluating the two main liberal theories of formal and substantive equality. This project focuses on liberal theory's understanding of equal concern and respect, but, as Kymlicka notes, radical egalitarians, socialists, and Marxists all share a commitment to equal concern and respect. While I make use of critiques of liberalism by these theorists, it is in the context of borrowing relational insights from them rather than developing a full account of them.

Liberal Theory and Equality of Opportunity

Nielsen defines equality of opportunity as "the ideal of making opportunities for the various cherished positions in society completely open to free competition in which anyone can compete for those prized positions in society (positions which afford very different life-chances) and where they are awarded according to talent and achievement and not on the basis of social position, class, race, sex, friendship, or patronage" (Nielsen 1985, 133). But such a general description of equality of opportunity as an opportunity to compete in the race of life, does not yet explain how the ideal is satisfied or why it is so closely linked to liberal theory. Equality of opportunity is "a systematically ambiguous expression" (Macleod 1983, 370)[2] because it contains a number of variables, variables identified by Peter Westen in his analysis of the concept: "every opportunity is a chance of a specified agent or class of agents, X, to obtain a specified goal or set of goals, Y, without the hindrance of a specified obstacle or set of obstacles, Z" (Westen 1990, 169–170). This delineation of equality of opportunity into its constitutive variables provides a useful framework. Describing the complex of variables assumed in various conceptions of equality can explain why "equality of opportunity" is generally associated with liberal theory and "equality of well-being" or "results" or "wealth" with Marxist theories.

Liberal theory is generally distinguished from Marxist theory in its specification that the goal or set of goals (Y in Westen's formula) is the opportunity to compete in a free-market structure for relatively scarce educational, social, and economic goods. This still leaves unspecified the particular goals and the structures needed to obtain them: whether the opportunities are to compete for educational or employment positions or for social or economic goods. However, in liberal theory, opportunities exist in the context of competition in a free market. The qualifying phrase, "positions which afford very different life-chances," from Nielsen's definition of equality of opportunity, suggests that the structure within which the competition takes place can generate the kind of unequal outcomes that would be rejected in conceptions based on equality of well-being, or results, or wealth. So while equality of opportunity can be understood in a very general way as the opportunity to pursue interests, projects, and goals as a member of a community, maintaining the link between equality of opportunity and the basic liberal defense of a free-market structure is useful for keeping the distinction between liberal and Marxist conceptions clear.

Although the variable of goal (or set of goals) is fixed in liberal conceptions, specification of the two remaining variables generates different accounts of what is required to satisfy the ideal of equality of opportunity. Beginning in the next section, I shall discuss the diverse ways in which liberals fill in and describe the variables of agent or class (X in Westen's formula) and of obstacles (Z in Westen's formula) and come up with very different ideas about the competitors and of what the race should be like. But first, I want to mention the one specification of the variable of agent or class that is rejected by all liberals. Once again, this will illustrate liberal theory's departure from mere procedural equality.

In the Aristotelian understanding of equality, certain features are used to justify restricting opportunities for members identified on that basis. In terms of our framework of variables, Aristotelians deem that certain agents or classes of agents are justifiably excluded from competition altogether. Legally barring some people from pursuing their interests, projects, and goals because they are judged to belong to a class possessing features that make all its members unequal is an obvious infringement of the commitment to equal concern and respect. It is fairly easy to understand and eliminate the obstacles (Z) that result in this kind of unequal opportunity. The obstacles in this case are the rules and laws that prevent some people from having the same opportunity as others. Giving those who are excluded an equal opportunity requires the removal of the laws that forbid them from competing. The removal of these kinds of formal barriers results in an understanding of equal opportunity as purely formal: no one is barred from entering or competing in the race of life.[3] In liberal theory, formal equality is a necessary condition for satisfying the ideal of equality of opportunity, but it is not always sufficient. Disagreement then arises over whether something more is needed.

Amy Gutmann claims that in all liberal theory, equality is an idea "basic to the modern doctrine of individualism, equal respect for the human dignity of all people being essential to the realization of individual autonomy, the protection of privacy, and the opportunity for self-development" (Gutmann 1980, 18). Recognizable in this definition are the central elements of classical liberalism: the view of the self as a self-determining and self-legislating being, the value of these capacities, and the need to protect and promote them. Where liberals stand on the issue of whether formal equality is also sufficient for satisfying the ideal of equality of opportunity emerges from the different emphases on and interpretations of the other key elements of "individualism," "individual autonomy," "privacy," and "opportunity for self-development." In the next section, Robert Nozick's well-known libertarian defense of formal equality as both a necessary and sufficient condition for achieving equality will form the base for a critical analysis of two interconnected criticisms: that the conception of the self underlying libertarianism is impoverished and that the purely formal requirement is inadequate as a means to treat all people with equal concern and respect. While some of this is well-trod territory, it is worth pursuing because it will open the way to a relational account of equality, one that will serve to identify the positive and negative aspects of liberal substantive equality theory.

Formal Equality of Opportunity and Libertarianism

In the very first sentence of *Anarchy, State, and Utopia*, Nozick states that "individuals have rights, and there are things no person or group may do to them (without violating their rights)" (Nozick 1974, ix). His "strong formulation of individual rights" emerges from the classical liberal view of the individual as the ultimate unit of moral worth—from, as Nozick puts it, "the fact that there are distinct individuals, each with his own life *to lead*" (Nozick 1974, 34, his emphasis). Each individual has the capacity to pursue interests, projects, and goals and "to act in terms of some overall conception of the life one wishes to lead" (Nozick 1974, 50). Such capacities are intrinsically valuable because "[a] person's shaping his life in accordance with some overall plan is his way of giving meaning to his life; only a being with the capacity to so shape his life can have or strive for meaningful life" (Nozick 1974, 50). According to Nozick, a respect for individuality, separateness, and distinctiveness dictates that people be given the freedom to pursue their life plans unless those actions interfere with the freedom of others to pursue their life plans.

For Nozick and most libertarians, liberty is of primary value and flows from the equal moral worth of each individual: "as agents, we are creatures who can, and cannot but, make choices. We are also creatures who, as rational beings, can both have and give reasons for pursuing ends for ourselves. It is as members of this very special species that we may—and, I would say, should—demand the right to be left to our own devices; provided only that, and only in so far as, the devices chosen do not violate the equal rights of any others" (Flew 1989, 91). Libertarians thus place the emphasis on formal and negative conditions for protecting individual freedom as the way to treat individuals with equal concern and respect. In terms of questions of emphases, "individual autonomy" and "opportunity for self-development" are best achieved when people are left alone.

According to libertarians, individuals are free and equal under the law when there are no external barriers, including no state interference, in the individual lives of citizens. Libertarians defend "liberty-rights which impose on others only negative duties of non-interference" (Sumner 1987, 212). Individual rights to freedom of speech and property fit under the libertarian conception of rights as negative rights of noninterference. Nozick appeals to the Kantian imperative to treat people as ends and never as mere means and approves of what he takes to be Kant's universal and exceptionless support of the impermissibility of ever violating the liberty rights of individuals, even if the infringement would result in great benefits or good consequences for others. "To use a person in this way does not sufficiently respect and take account of the fact that he is a separate person, that his is the only life he has. He does not get some overbalancing good from his sacrifice, and no one is entitled to force this upon him—least of all a state or government that claims his allegiance (as other individuals do not) and that therefore scrupulously must be neutral between its citizens" (Nozick 1974, 33).[4]

Nozick defends property rights by arguing that provided goods were initially acquired under fair conditions, any redistribution of such justly acquired goods violates the strict inviolability of individual rights. In other words, Nozick rejects measures for equalizing the opportunities of competitors in the race of life as a violation of individual liberty. Nozick's defense of liberty and property rights is best illustrated by his famous Wilt Chamberlain example. Nozick asks us to suppose a society with an egalitarian distribution of goods and members committed to egalitarianism. We are to suppose that Wilt Chamberlain, a basketball star and idol, comes into this society and agrees to play games if 25 cents of every ticket goes directly to him. Nozick takes it to be obvious that if members of this society *voluntarily* elect to pay the 25 cents because they want to watch Chamberlain play, the resultant distributional inequality (Nozick supposes that Chamberlain ends up with $250,000 at the end of the season) is a perfectly fair and just outcome.

Nozick argues that anyone who values liberty and respects individual rights would think it unjust to prevent the members of this society from exercising their voluntary choice to pay Chamberlain the money to watch him play. "The general point illustrated by the Wilt Chamberlain example . . . is that no end-state principle or distributional patterned principle of justice can be continuously realized without continuous interference with people's lives. . . . To maintain a pattern one must either continually interfere to stop people from transferring resources as they wish to, or continually (or periodically) interfere to take from some persons resources that others for some reason chose to transfer to them" (Nozick 1974, 163). What should happen to individuals, and in particular, what should happen to the distribution of educational, social, and economic goods, simply emerges when we let competition among individuals for these goods in an unfettered free market have its way. Nozick's libertarianism is an example of formal equality theory, a theory that takes the removal of formal barriers to be both necessary and sufficient for achieving equality of opportunity.

To the libertarian, equal opportunity merely means equal treatment under the law. It does not mean that people are equal in their starting places in the competition or that the state is justified in trying to equalize starting positions. Formal equality theorists, in taking equality to be satisfied by purely formal means, discount the relevance of differences in initial starting positions. But an examination of the agents and their starting positions would appear to be highly relevant to an assessment of whether equal opportunity actually obtains. Recall the three variables in equality of opportunity statements. Those who argue for an assessment of obstacles (Z) hold that it is unjust that people who face differential obstacles in initial starting positions, such as lack of income for training or for proper nutrition, end up with unequal opportunities. While these sorts of barriers do not explicitly prohibit people from competing in the way that laws formally barring women and the poor from competing do, these barriers are also less visible and more intransigent than formal barriers and are thus more difficult to remove. In defending a situation that allows consequences to flow freely from Wilt Chamberlain exercising his superior talents, Nozick succeeds in perpetuating and magnifying these kinds of inequalities in initial starting places.

Fair Equality of Opportunity: The Basis for Substantive Equality Theory

No theorist has been as influential in conveying ideas of the importance of ensuring fair conditions as has Rawls in his account of "fair equality of opportunity." The basic question he poses in his analysis is whether it is fair that people who have the requisite talents and abilities face obstacles of social or biological disadvantages that prevent them from exercising their capacities to the fullest. Rawls discusses fair equality of opportunity in detail in a number of places in *A Theory of Justice* (Rawls 1971, 73, 83–89, 298–303). The definition and underlying justification for fair equality of opportunity is expressed in the following: "those who are at the same level of talent and ability, and have the same willingness to use them, should have the same prospects of success regardless of their initial place in the social system, that is, irrespective of the income class into which they are born" (Rawls 1971, 73). Rawls includes the condition of fair equality of opportunity in the second principle of justice: "positions are to be not only open in a formal sense, but . . . all should have a fair chance to attain them" (Rawls 1971, 73).

In Rawls's account of fair equality of opportunity, the possession of such features as natural and social endowments is the luck of the draw and taking them to be the basis for strong notions of individual desert and for entitlement to educational, social, and economic goods is unjust. Those who lose out in the lottery of life do not have the same opportunity to pursue their life projects and goals as those who are more fortunate. For Rawls, it is the luck of the draw that one is born into a wealthy family, and it is unjust if institutions are structured to give that person greater access to educational, social, and economic goods than is available to someone born into a poor family. It is the bad luck of the draw that a condition of poverty prevents one from pursuing interests, projects, and goals in the same way as wealthier others who have similar talents and abilities.

Rawls takes it to be "the most obvious injustice of the system of natural liberty" that it allows a distribution of assets to be "strongly influenced by natural and social contingencies . . . so arbitrary from a moral point of view" (Rawls 1971, 72). He explicitly rejects the Nozickean account that equal opportunity exists when no one is legally barred from competing in the race of life. For Rawls, formal equality's adherence to strict noninterference may be necessary, but it is not sufficient for securing conditions of fair equality of opportunity. Nozick's defense of an individual's freedom to acquire and hold the property he or she has "justly" acquired without interference results in the perpetuation of unequal opportunities. "[T]he existing distribution of income and wealth, say, is the cumulative effect of prior distributions of natural assets—that is, natural talents and abilities—as these have been developed or left unrealized, and their use favored or disfavored over time by social circumstances and such chance contingencies as accident and good fortune" (Rawls 1971, 72). While it is important to begin with the removal of formal and legal barriers that justified past discrimination and unequal opportunities for some, it is difficult to maintain, as Nozick does, that all people suddenly have equal opportunity when the barriers go down.

Nozick argues that allowing Wilt Chamberlain to accumulate capital is a fair outcome of voluntary choices on the part of members of this society. Rawls would want to address the inequalities that emerge when Chamberlain has the opportunity to play and the members of the society have the opportunity to watch him play under the conditions specified by Nozick. It is easy to imagine, for example, that the extra money that goes to Chamberlain could be used to provide better training facilities for his friends and relatives and that this would result in these people gaining an unfair advantage in the competition for places on the basketball team. We can imagine other long-range disadvantages that would accrue to the members of this society when Chamberlain is allowed to accumulate vast amounts of wealth. The differences considered by Rawls to be arbitrary from a moral point of view, natural abilities that one is born with and social advantages that one is born into, would be magnified in a society that justified and maintained the inviolability of individual rights of noninterference. While Chamberlain, his family, and his friends would have their negative rights protected, it would be at the expense of restricting the freedom and opportunities of those around them.

Rawls's assessment of informal barriers, the ways in which natural and social endowments affect one's chances in life and set up unfair advantages for some, forms the justification for a defense of positive measures for redistributing wealth and giving everyone a fair chance to compete in the race of life. Rawls's theory of justice, which specifies the conditions under which "fair equality of opportunity" can obtain, is a version of liberal substantive equality theory. In general, liberal substantive theorists argue that justice requires that special measures or programs be available to give all people substantively fair opportunity. Many people cannot realize their interests, projects, and goals under conditions that merely protect their right to noninterference from others. Positive social and welfare rights to health care, work, and education are examples of measures defended by substantive equality theorists as necessary for achieving equal opportunity and treating all people with equal concern and respect. Liberals who support positive rights have been variously referred to as "liberal egalitarians,"[5] "modern liberals,"[6] and "liberal substantive equality theorists."[7] I prefer the phrase "liberal substantive equality theory" and will use it to refer to liberals who support positive measures.

There is much more to be done to complete the outline and analysis of liberal substantive theory. The biggest task is to provide a detailed analysis of liberal theory's most well-known substantive equality theorist, Rawls. But this task will wait until the next chapter. In the next two sections, I want to reinforce some of the objections raised against libertarianism and thereby strengthen the arguments in favor of positive measures for achieving equality, but to do so by applying relational insights. To achieve this objective, I shall use two strategies: a new one, making use of important Marxist critiques of Nozick by G. A. Cohen and Kai Nielsen, and the familiar one of revisiting the builders' community and describing their activity and interactions in the light of our examination of liberal theory thus far. Together, these strategies will highlight the specific deficiencies of the purely formal requirement to treat individuals with equal concern and respect; the incoherence of the notion of a self abstracted from relationships in social practices and political contexts; the inadequacy of a defense of an unfettered free-market structure; and some of the particular inequalities revealed by a relational approach and missing in liberal theories.

The Significance of Social and Political Contexts: Reexamining Nozick's Chamberlain

Nielsen claims that Nozick "unrealistically assumes a genuinely free market society where people are busy, possessive individualists devoted to accumulating and bargaining and are concerned very centrally with protecting their private property" (Nielsen 1985, 65). Nielsen provides a multitude of sociological critiques in an attempt to "bring to light the fact that Nozick's empirical background assumptions are very uncritically and unreflectively held and that there is a kind of unworldly apoliticality to his account that is innocent of socio-political realities" (Nielsen 1985, 236). We could imagine that with different socialization and political structures, for example, people would be less concerned with the individual rights to private property than Nozick assumes. Cohen and Nielsen provide precisely this kind of argument in their convincing critique of Nozick's account of Wilt Chamberlain.

Cohen argues that Nozick concedes more than he realizes when he imagines that the fans are committed to egalitarianism. He convincingly shows that it is reasonable to think that because they are socialized in an egalitarian society the fans would not opt to give Chamberlain more money even if they need to in order to watch him play. As Nielsen puts it, it is reasonable to suppose that their commitment to egalitarianism would make them realize that "such Chamberlain-like contracts will introduce an inequality in *power* into the previously egalitarian society"—a consequence "which, by *their own standards and preferences*, they would not want to happen" (Nielsen 1985, 244, his emphasis). They would recognize that such seemingly individual voluntary acts of consent have public consequences that they would be unwilling to accept. In the face of realizing that undesirable consequences would flow from allowing disparities in wealth, it is likely that they would secure equality of resources over equality of opportunity to obtain resources. In fact, they would secure this precisely because they know that the latter freedom unfairly restricts the opportunity of some to pursue their interests, projects, and goals. Individual rights of noninterference would prevent some from obtaining, as Nielsen puts it, "an equality of life prospects" (Nielsen 1985, 7; 290).

Nozick assumes that people in any social and political context would choose in the way that he takes to be obvious. What he fails to realize is that the fans in his account choose as they do because they are socialized in a liberal society that accepts rights to property and values rights of noninterference. In such a society, the idea that unfettered competition among individuals should determine people's life chances is familiar and acceptable. Both Nielsen and Cohen question whether this idea would be so obviously acceptable in a different kind of society, one in which people do not place such high value on private property. The real force of their respective analyses, however, is the argument that even if Nozick is granted his point about the importance of voluntary choices, voluntary choices do not guarantee fair or just outcomes: not everything that "arises from a just situation as a result of fully voluntary transactions on the part of all legitimately concerned persons is itself just" (Cohen 1978, 151). Voluntary choices cannot by themselves bear the weight of moral assessments of whether equal opportunities obtain. As we will discover in the next chapter, this is an argument that Rawls puts to use in his call for reflective equilibrium, a methodology that creates fair conditions under which agreements about what is just can be reached.

Nielsen describes his theory as radical egalitarianism and Cohen describes his as socialist egalitarianism (Cohen 1995). Both are Marxists in that they reject the liberal defense of free-market structures because *unfettered* competition allows inequalities in wealth to determine inequalities in power. What their accounts have in common with liberal accounts such as Rawls's fair equality of opportunity is that they also defend a more egalitarian distribution of goods than can be obtained by the mere removal of formal barriers. They depart from Rawls in their analysis of the ways in which relations of power are integral to free-market structures and set up inequalities between capitalists and workers that cannot be rectified by a more equitable distribution of wealth. It is in this sense that Marxists in general can be said to defend conceptions that advocate equality of wealth or of life prospects, for example.

These Marxist insights about relations of power are important, but they do not capture the various kinds of relations of power that I underscored by describing how rules and practices create relationships among community members that restrict activities and opportunities for many. Power not only creates inequalities in relationships between capitalists and workers, but it is also a pervasive force in ordinary and personal relationships where differences other than class are present. These relationships affect perceptions of difference and self-concepts of those identified as different in ways that limit participation and restrict interactions with others. A relational approach takes these aspects of relationships to be relevant to an account of equal concern and respect. An examination of these relationships highlights what is missing in the libertarian account of agents and obstacles. Although questions will be raised later about equality of opportunity itself, for the sake of argument at this point in the analysis, let us suppose in the context of the builders' community that the opportunity is the one identified by liberals: an equal opportunity to build. We can now assess this opportunity in relational terms for purposes of highlighting the inadequacies of formal equality.

Revisiting the Builders' Community and Assessing Opportunities

In the society of builders, women are excluded from building activities. As a first step on the road to achieving equality of opportunity, formal and legal rules that support this exclusion would need to be removed. Nozick agrees that formal equality is necessary, but goes on to argue that it is also sufficient for obtaining equality. Without the formal rule that excluded her from building, aspiring builder B could have an equal opportunity to become a builder and obtain whatever rewards or goods go along with building. But does this account adequately capture the impact of the social practices in the builders' community on aspiring builder B? Will the removal of the laws barring her from being a builder now give her an equal opportunity to be a builder?

While removing formal barriers can begin to change the informal barriers (rules of conduct), relational insights about language and about people embedded in social practices and political contexts provide counterarguments to the idea that formal equality can by itself succeed in providing women with a fair opportunity to build. The removal of legal barriers can *begin* to change perceptions of what differences mean, but the category "woman" has a meaning that is embedded in the rules and practices of the community and determines the activities and interactions of members. Builder A must come to perceive women's differences as irrelevant for purposes of building, but he has constructed his perceptions of what women are like and of what it is to build around the rule that excludes women from building—and so has aspiring builder B.

In the idea that people become members of a community by interacting with others in purposeful contexts, we can begin to learn what is required for changing perceptions and self-concepts of aspiring builder B and those like her. Community members must learn to adjust all of the background assumptions. For example, they must revise the reasons given in the past for excluding women from building. The features of consistency and predictability in rule-following activity, outlined in the section in the previous chapter on procedural equality, are now obstacles to providing aspiring builder B with an equal opportunity to build. Builder A has constructed a whole system of beliefs in which he has learned to dispel doubts and explain mistakes by giving reasons for his actions. These reasons back up the interpretation and application of the rules that exclude aspiring builder B. Explanations and justifications are integral components of the feature of purposeful activity underlying the use of concepts. It is easy to realize how difficult it will be for the builders to change the standards of comparison and the rules for application and to respond to and interact differently with women.

Formal equality alone cannot erase the effects of a past, a historical context, in which treating like cases alike meant that features of some individuals were used to justify what is in fact unequal treatment. Members of groups discriminated against in the past have other barriers and obstacles to overcome besides those set out in the law. The meaning given to the actions and behavior of those classified as different lives on in the entrenched perceptions of members of groups as descriptively different and justifiably treated differently based on those differences. To believe that these factors no longer have an impact on the freedom of those who were identified, compared, and judged in this way is to assume that people can freely change the standards and rules that once formed their perceptions of and interactions with other people and that they can easily shed discriminatory beliefs and patterns of behavior. Social conditions of past overt discrimination against groups continue to have an impact on current perceptions and behavior. While Nozick could hardly deny that these factors have an impact on people, he would, however, claim that they are irrelevant to an analysis of opportunities. But even under Nozick's own terms this will not work, precisely because these factors limit the freedom so central to his account.

The description of what happens when rules that exclude aspiring builder B from building are removed should convince us of the inadequacy of viewing aspiring builder B as suddenly having an equal opportunity to build when the rules for exclusion are removed. Libertarians fail to grasp the difficulty involved in changing perceptions and behavior and ignore the ways in which these perceptions continue to be obstacles to the freedom of some people even in a society now committed to treating all people with equal concern and respect. These factors result in inequalities that limit the opportunities of some people, namely, members of groups who have suffered a history of disadvantage, marginalization, and discrimination. An account of individual freedom and equal opportunity needs a corresponding account of the ways in which beliefs about an individual's proper role and function continue to have discriminatory effects all the way from educational to career opportunities. Perceptions and beliefs about people are shaped in everyday practices in ways that limit some people's opportunities to interact with others and to participate in certain activities.

Recall the complex of relational features of language and of people identified in Chapter 2: relationships of similarity and difference are shaped in social practices by community members; standards and rules are established in relationships with others and for particular purposes; and learning the standards and following the rules are conditions for being understood by others and accepted in relationships in communities. These relational features show that obstacles and opportunities need to be understood and assessed in the whole background complex of the standards, rules, and practices in a community. When we take the perceptions and beliefs that are entrenched in rules and practices to be relevant to an assessment of the fairness of the competition, it becomes evident that the relationships in the builders' community generate such obstacles as diminished confidence, self-respect, and power, obstacles that continue to result in unequal opportunities.

Now recall two of the relational insights developed in the previous chapter: the importance of understanding the perspectives of those who are detrimentally affected by the relationships of inequality and powerlessness that they are in and the significance of the notion of moral personhood for revealing what people are like and what treating them with equal concern and respect will require. Applying these insights shows that at minimum Nozick is guilty of theorizing about the self in abstraction from the social practices and political contexts within which people interact. In assuming that anyone would value freedom to such an extent that they would be oblivious to the effects on others of Chamberlain's increased wealth, Nozick also assumes the perspective of someone who is not disadvantaged by a decision to pay Chamberlain to watch him play. The insights about perspectives from the previous chapter would support an argument that there is a much greater chance that those who are affected by the resultant inequalities in wealth in terms of opportunities and of levels of power and freedom would reason as Cohen and Nielsen suggest in their analyses of the significance of social factors in the shaping of people's beliefs and values.

While it may be true that a "person's shaping his life in accordance with some overall plan is his way of giving meaning to his life" (Nozick 1974, 50), persons give meaning to and shape their lives only in relationships with others in social contexts. Rather than begin with "the fact that there are distinct individuals, each with his own life *to lead*" (Nozick 1974, 34, his emphasis), we could just as easily use people's sense of community and cooperativeness as a starting point for theorizing about conditions for treating persons with equal concern and respect. This is what the Nielsen and Cohen analyses of the Wilt Chamberlain example teach us and it is what my account of moral personhood is meant to capture. The respective analyses emphasize the embeddedness of people in social practices and political contexts, an embeddedness that has us question freedom as an absolute value in and of itself. We can now add to this analysis the idea that the perspectives of those in the sorts of relationships that create and perpetuate disadvantages provide insights about the structures needed to satisfy the requirement to treat all people with equal concern and respect. But our critical evaluation of libertarianism raises additional questions that need to be answered in a project targeting liberal theory more generally. Liberal substantive theorists' particular assessment of agents and obstacles provides them with a defense of positive measures for equalizing the initial starting places in life. How does this kind of assessment fare with respect to satisfying the demand for equal concern and respect?

Drawing Conclusions and Looking Ahead: A Relational Approach to Equality

So far, in my account of equal concern and respect, equality of opportunity in the general sense of an equal opportunity to pursue interests, projects, and goals remains important, an element necessary to treating people with equal concern and respect. But it is as yet an open question whether equality of opportunity in the specifically liberal sense of competition in a free-market structure will be sufficient for achieving conditions that allow all people to be treated with equal concern and respect. My primary argument is that equality analysis needs to take account of relational factors. Although the target in this project is equality of opportunity theorists, the discussion of resources and of well-being is always but a short distance away. While the examination of what description of equality best fits my relational account will be left to the end, we already know that the emphasis on relationships in social contexts moves the focus from what individuals in and by themselves need to flourish to what individuals in relationships and affected by various social practices need to flourish. As a first attempt to articulate what sort of theory of equality a relational approach supports, we can observe that we need considerable equality of resources in order to achieve genuine equality of opportunity broadly conceived. Yet, while evidence for this observation will be particularly strong in Chapter 8's discussion of affirmative action, that discussion will also reveal that equal resources are far from sufficient for meeting the demands of equal concern and respect.

Whether we identify the equality aimed for as opportunity, wealth, welfare, life prospects, resources, capabilities, results, or well-being, the measure for determining the achievement of equality is whether we have conditions that treat all people with equal concern and respect. Liberal theory has been instructive here. In their critical analyses of particular strands within the liberal tradition, liberals themselves have provided more enriched accounts of personhood and more substantive understandings of equality than is true of classical liberals and libertarians. In their defense of positive measures for equalizing opportunities, liberal substantive theorists have taken us in the direction of a concept of equality of resources: achieving fair equality of opportunity means providing all people with the resources to pursue their interests, projects, and goals.

Both Marxists and liberal substantive theorists defend a more egalitarian distribution of goods than can be obtained by the mere removal of formal barriers. Both kinds of theories take us beyond libertarianism in revealing the inadequacies of purely formal and negative conditions for treating people with equal concern and respect. Simply letting competition among individuals for scarce educational, social, and economic goods in an unfettered free market have its way perpetuates and creates inequalities in life prospects and in opportunities. Rawls recognizes this in his defense of a redistribution of wealth as one positive measure for removing morally irrelevant obstacles and making the competition fair. We have noted in a preliminary way that Marxists argue that any defense of disparities in wealth allows inequalities in power and life prospects to persist. We have also noted that in focusing their critique of liberalism on the inequalities generated by a free-market structure, Marxists have tended to ignore other kinds of relations of power and the inequalities these relationships generate. As we work through a detailed examination of Rawls's theory of justice, it will become evident that a failure to recognize the inequalities generated by certain relationships is also one of the shortcomings of liberal substantive equality theory. Attending to these inequalities raises doubts that aspiring builder B is treated equally when she is given *either* a formal or fair opportunity to build.

5

❦ ❦ ❦

Rawls and the Original Position: Moving from Monologue to Dialogue

Introduction

William Griffith describes Rawls's theory of justice in these terms: "Rawls' *A Theory of Justice* is the central work which has most shaped recent theoretical debate about equality as an ideal, both in terms of how it should be conceived and how it may be justified. Perhaps because its remarkable influence reached beyond Anglo-American academic philosophers . . . leading most theoreticians of equality to compare or contrast their positions with Rawls', it serves well as an organizing position around which to array other views" (Griffith 1994, 13). This quotation leads the chapter because it allows me to explain that my discussion of Rawls is framed in two respects. First, I will follow the theorists Griffith describes and use Rawls as a focal point around which to evaluate liberal substantive equality theory generally and Rawls's formulation of the original position as a vantage point for critical thinking about equality and justice more specifically. Second, it will become clear that my own contribution to the vast literature is shaped by and emerges from the wide range of critiques already available on Rawls.

Recall now the questions posed in Chapter 2 in connection

with Rawls's account of moral equals as having the capacities for forming a rational plan of life and for a sense of justice. What constitutes a rational plan of life? Would everyone be equally or centrally concerned about satisfying preferences that shape their own particular conception of the good? Is the ability to formulate a "rational" plan of life crucial for determining who enters the original position and engages in critical thinking about equality and justice? How would an acknowledgment of the validity and value of the various perspectives of those in unequal and oppressive relationships affect our thinking about equality? Would inclusion of these perspectives change the reflections leading to agreement about the principles for structuring a just society? Do these perspectives shape a sense of justice different from that of those who constitute the norm?

In this chapter, I shall explore answers to these sorts of questions by first outlining Rawls and then revising what needs to happen in the original position for principles of justice to emerge. Rawls takes it to be a positive feature of his method for arriving at principles of justice that any moral person can enter the thought experiment of the original position, stand apart from his or her own particular ends and other people, and by him- or herself obtain a point of view that is impartial about the prospects and perspectives of anyone in a potential society. I shall argue that we need people with all their encumbrances and in all their embeddedness in social and political contexts engaged in critical thinking about different perspectives to know what equality is and requires. In other words, we need to place relationships in the foreground in an analysis of equality.

The Framework: The Original Position in *A Theory of Justice*

We learned in the previous chapter that Nozick considers that the talents and abilities an individual has and the property an individual acquires under "just" conditions generate a strong entitlement to the benefits that flow from this possession of talents and goods. Rawls rejects this account and views such descriptive features as "aspects of the social world that seem arbitrary from a moral point of view" (Rawls 1971, 15). Rawls's theory is the outcome of a search for "a conception of justice that nullifies the accidents of natural endowment and the contingencies of social circumstance as counters in quest for political and economic advantage" (Rawls 1971, 15). Giving substance to treating each person with equal concern and respect means minimizing the disadvantages that accrue to those whose differences have justified unequal treatment in the past and continue to result in unequal opportunities now. Rawls undermines formal equality as a *sufficient* condition for satisfying the requirement to treat individuals with equal concern and respect by appealing to considered judgments about the fairness of allowing morally arbitrary features to result in disadvantages and unequal opportunities. Fair equality of opportunity theory holds that people with similar talents and abilities should not be disadvantaged by features such as race, gender, and disability or by factors such as class, geographical location, and wealth. The original position is Rawls's method for theorizing about the conditions needed for achieving such fair equality of opportunity.

The original position is a thought experiment in which we imagine ourselves behind a veil of ignorance where knowledge of our particular features, ones that Rawls takes to be morally arbitrary, is suppressed. Behind a veil of ignorance, Rawls specifies that the parties to the original position have no knowledge of their individual "class position or social status," their "fortune in the distribution of natural assets and abilities," or their life plans, their particular conceptions of the good. Rawls further stipulates that they have no knowledge of particular circumstances such as the "political or economic situation" or the generation to which they belong (Rawls 1971, 137). These restrictions on the knowledge that parties to the original position can have are intended to establish fair bargaining procedures, ones that will allow the parties to reach agreement about principles of justice for structuring their society.

The parties to the original position have enough knowledge of general facts to get the bargaining going. They know that they will have interests and projects that they will want to be able to explore, pursue, and revise, what Rawls refers to as the capacity to form a rational plan of life, a conception of the good. They know that there will be differences in natural and social endowments and that political structures can and do allow these endowments to affect the distribution of goods: "[t]hey understand political affairs and the principles of economic theory; they know the basis of social organization and the laws of human psychology" (Rawls 1971, 137). For Rawls, this general knowledge includes the capacity for a sense of justice, "a skill in judging things to be just and unjust, and in supporting these judgments by reasons . . . [as well as] some desire to act in accord with these pronouncements" (Rawls 1971, 46). Rawls takes these two capacities, the capacity to form a rational plan of life and the capacity for a sense of justice, to be the criteria for possession of "moral personality" (Rawls 1971, 12; 19; 505) and takes moral personality to be the basis of equality (Rawls 1971, 504–510).

The "parties in the original position are equal. That is, all have the same rights in the procedure for choosing principles; each can make proposals, submit reasons for their acceptance, and so on. Obviously the purpose of these conditions is to represent equality between human beings as moral persons, as creatures having a conception of their good and capable of a sense of justice" (Rawls 1971, 19). Having only that knowledge of those "traits that characterize us as equal rational and moral beings—capable of giving our lives meaning and of recognizing political and moral duties and obligations" (Gutmann 1980, 165), the parties in the original position are viewed as beginning on an equal footing from which to bargain for conditions that will ensure equal concern and respect for their individual life projects and goals no matter what these turn out to be. The bargaining gets under way with bargainers who are equally rational and moral beings. These constraints are intended to clarify our thinking about equality and justice. Rawls uses the original position as a way of structuring institutions so morally irrelevant differences do not unfairly determine the distribution of social goods or the valuation of individual life plans.

The original position is an ingenious device. It asks us to reason about the principles we would agree to be governed by if we did not know where and who we would be. According to Rawls, the restrictions placed on knowledge and the constraints on the bargaining that ensues create a point of view from which anyone can reason in an impartial way about differences in natural and social endowments and about different conceptions of the good. Because I could turn out to be anyone in any place, I would not choose an institutional framework that would place me in a disadvantaged position if I turned out to be black, or poor, or disabled. Self-interest alone would motivate me to bargain for principles of justice that ensure that morally arbitrary natural and social endowments do not determine in advance the distribution of social goods or the opportunities open to me. Rawls argues that mutual disinterest with respect to possible positions and places in society characterizes the parties. In the original position where the parties begin from a state of equal moral worth, the specific formulation of moral personality, Rawls argues that the principles of justice that they would agree to adopt would be, first, that "all social primary goods—liberty and opportunity, income and wealth, and the bases of self-respect—are to be distributed equally" and, second, that "social and economic inequalities are to be arranged so that they are both: (a) to the greatest benefit of the least advantaged . . . and (b) attached to offices and positions open to all under conditions of fair equality of opportunity" (Rawls 1971, 302).

At least in his early work, Rawls views the principles of justice as universal and absolute. His conviction that knowledge of the particularities of one's position in life would result in unfair bargaining advantages leads him to formulate the original position as "an Archimedean point from which the basic structure itself can be appraised" (Rawls 1971, 260). He conceives this point of view as fitting into a philosophical tradition that "has assumed that there exists some appropriate perspective from which unanimity on moral questions may be hoped for, at least among rational persons with relevantly similar and sufficient information. . . . Different moral theories arise from different interpretations of this point of view, of what I have called the initial situation" (Rawls 1971, 263–264). Rawls's interpretation of this point of view emerges from a process that he calls "reflective equilibrium."

Reflective equilibrium is the process of considering our firmest convictions and adjusting our principles in the light of an examination of conditions and particular cases: "[b]y going back and forth, sometimes altering the conditions of the contractual circumstances, at others withdrawing our judgments and conforming them to principle, I assume that eventually we shall find a description of the initial situation that both expresses reasonable conditions and yields principles which match our considered judgments duly pruned and adjusted" (Rawls 1971, 20). If it seems as though the conditions placed on the original position are too determinate, then the test of reflective equilibrium allows us to move back and forth from the principles to the original position and from the original position to the principles for fit with our considered judgments about what is reasonable and fair.

Reflective equilibrium plays an important role for another reason. Sandel says of Rawls's theory: "[n]ot only did his contract never really happen; it is imagined to take place among the sorts of beings who never really existed, that is, beings struck with the kind of complicated amnesia necessary to the veil of ignorance. In this sense, Rawls' theory is doubly hypothetical. It imagines an event that never really happened, involving the sorts of beings who never really existed" (Sandel 1982, 105). Sandel's work is well-known for dealing with that aspect of the original position that generates metaphysical or ontological questions about the "beings who never really existed," an objection I shall examine in the next chapter. But we can address at least one aspect of Sandel's objection that Rawls imagines "an event that never really happened" rather quickly. Though, as we will discover in the rest of this chapter, from another point of view it merely raises other questions about what happens and should happen in the original position.

Rawls states early in the first chapter of *A Theory of Justice*, "I have emphasized that this original position is purely hypothetical" (Rawls 1971, 21). Sandel's objection, then, seems to miss the mark. The original position is an imagined initial situation designed to clarify our thoughts about the institutional structures that are needed to treat each person with equal concern and respect. It is not an event that happened or could happen, but there is another underlying issue. Rawls tells us that any binding force the principles may have does not come from their emergence in an agreement reached in "an actual historical state of affairs, much less as a primitive condition of culture" (Rawls 1971, 12). This does immediately raise the question, as Rawls himself is aware, about the moral status and force of principles generated by a mere thought experiment: "why, if this agreement is never actually entered into, we should take any interest in these principles, moral or otherwise" (Rawls 1971, 21).

As a brief response to the question, we can say that Rawls, unlike Nozick, does not assume that principles are morally binding merely because an agreement is reached voluntarily. To repeat an argument from the previous chapter, not everything that arises out of "fully voluntary transactions on the part of all legitimately concerned persons is itself just" (Cohen 1978, 151).[1] Rawls defends fair equality of opportunity by giving weight to our considered judgments about what is fair and just. Moreover, Rawls stipulates that the parties reach an agreement about principles of justice by using the test of reflective equilibrium, a process in which the parties move back and forth between specifying the conditions and formulating the principles by testing them against our considered judgments about what is fair. Reflective equilibrium is a process in which deeply held convictions, principles, and moral justifications all play a role in reaching an agreement about principles. These descriptions of what happens in the original position would appear to set moral constraints that would make the principles binding on morally rational beings.

In a nice summary of the point and purpose of the original position, Rawls writes, "[t]he original position is defined in such a way that it is a status quo in which any agreements reached are fair. It is a state of affairs in which the parties are equally represented as moral persons and the outcome is not conditioned by arbitrary contingencies or the relative balance of social forces" (Rawls 1971, 120). But the delineation of constraints on what the parties to the original position know has become precisely the target for the most well-known objections to Rawls, ones about the Rawlsian self. These objections range from claims that this self is too "thin" to generate principles at all to claims that this self is too "thick" and merely represents the biases of the liberal individualist, competitive, and possessive self. The charge of excessive individualism is well known; some take it as a justification for rejecting all liberal theory. I shall examine questions about the liberal self in the context of developing a contrasting relational conception of the self in the next chapter. But first, I need to put the familiar strategy of applying relational insights to work in an evaluation of Rawls's formulation of the original position as a device for critical thinking about equality and justice. We will discover that this critique of Rawls already reveals quite a bit about what people are like and what they need to flourish, a critique that will be the backdrop against which to construct an account of a relational theory of equality.

Recipe for Bias: Take Original Position, Add Women, and Stir

Rawls uses the veil of ignorance to find a point of view removed from arbitrary contingencies and morally irrelevant discriminations, a point of view removed from the biases of individual perspectives and interests. This point of view is an impartial perspective from which to think about equality and justice and from which to make reasonable assessments of what is needed to achieve equality. Once the impartial point of view is obtained, Rawls believes that a fair amount in the way of uniformity in reasoning about equality and justice will obtain. Note that the thought experiment can be conducted alone and the parties are interchangeable. At one point, Rawls imagines that the parties communicate through a referee, but takes the referee to be superfluous and communication in the original position to be nothing like "bargaining in the usual sense" because the parties are so similarly situated that "the deliberations of any one person are typical of all" (Rawls 1971, 263). Bargaining implies that the parties are differentially situated and can negotiate terms advantageous to them. Such a procedure will not generate fair principles. I want to question three aspects of this method of thinking about equality and justice: the idea that there is an impartial perspective that can generate unbiased judgments about others, the characterization of the parties as mutually disinterested, and the coherence of the notion that a moral reasoner could do it alone. Susan Moller Okin's careful analysis of Rawls's theory of justice in *Justice, Gender, and the Family* is a good place to start.

Okin examines Rawls's seemingly innocent presumption that those in the original position are heads of households speaking for and representing the interests of the next generation. There is little question for Rawls or for the reader that "heads of households" means males representing and speaking for women and children. Okin demonstrates that Rawls is guilty of assuming that "life within the family and the relations between the sexes are not properly regarded as part of the subject matter of a theory of social justice" (Okin 1989, 92). The assumption is that matters of justice are not applicable to the private sphere of the family, which is characterized instead by sentiments of benevolence, care, mutual dependence, and an identity of interests. Okin claims that it is precisely in the hierarchical structure of the family that sex roles are still rigidly defined in ways that restrict freedom and limit opportunities. She views the erasure of women's experiences from traditional theories of justice as a persistent barrier to achieving equality: "[u]ntil there is justice within the family, women will not be able to gain equality in politics, at work, or in any other sphere" (Okin 1989, 4).

Okin attempts to salvage Rawls, and liberal theory in general, by incorporating feminist concerns about disadvantage and discrimination perpetuated by the institution of the family into Rawls's theory of justice. Okin argues that the people in the original position need to know that the difference of gender is an important factor structuring institutions in ways that perpetuate inequalities. By making use of Rawls's endorsement of self-respect as "the most important primary good" (Rawls 1971, 440), she argues that we need conditions that allow group members to develop "an equal sense of respect for themselves and equal expectations of self-definition and development" (Okin 1989, 104–105). The discussions of the builders and of Amy show how the devaluation of women's traditional caring roles have damaging effects on self-concepts and identity. If we take seriously that the original position is the point of view from which to reason about conditions for treating all people with equal concern and respect, then, as Kymlicka points out: "[f]rom a position of equality, women wouldn't have agreed to a system of social roles that defines 'male' jobs as superior to, and dominating over, 'female' jobs. We have every reason to believe this, since those gender roles were created not only without the consent of women, but in fact required the legal and political suppression of women" (Kymlicka 1989, 93; 1990, 87).

While Rawls adds gender to the list of features the parties in the original position have no knowledge of in his later work (Rawls 1993, 25), he never mentions gender as a factor that can result in disadvantages and unequal opportunities in *A Theory of Justice*. Okin's main contribution is to argue that the mere addition of gender is not sufficient. When we are forced to think about the effects of considering gender in the original position, the result is a more radical restructuring of society than Rawls imagines. To grasp how this argument works, we need to abandon Rawls's description of the mutual disinterestedness and interchangeability of the parties to the original position and his consequent presumption that they would all reason in the same way. Instead, a correctly structured original position requires that difference be acknowledged in a much more fundamental way than Rawls realizes. When we incorporate gender, for example, as a difference that results in particular unequal opportunities and specific disadvantages in many social and political contexts, we can no longer blithely assume that the family is beyond justice. But in order to realize this, we need to reformulate what should take place in the original position.

Okin considers empathy to be the condition that best describes what goes on in and is required of the parties to the original position (Okin 1989, 101–109). In the bargaining procedure, I do not perceive myself as potentially anyone, but I perceive myself as someone who may be disadvantaged because of particular kinds of differences. Okin argues that the original position may require impartiality and neutrality about the value of difference and of different conceptions of the good, but it also requires an ability to empathize with different points of view, and this requires understanding the disadvantages that result from particular differences.

Empathy is best described as a cognitive capacity in which one grasps the configuration of both another's reasons for a particular position and the feelings or experiences that accompany those reasons. As a person in the original position, I would not imagine myself as no different from anyone else, but instead I would be forced to place myself in each person's position and imagine what each possible life might be like.[2] Okin concentrates on the difference of gender, but an incorporation of empathy as I just described it shows why imagining myself in the position of any disadvantaged person requires that I know quite a bit more about the consequences of difference than simply "I do not want that to be me."

Can Okin's incorporation of empathy save Rawls's theory from the feminist criticisms of bias and salvage the original position as a useful device for generating principles by which we would agree to be governed? Sypnowich argues that Okin's incorporation of empathy is neither a valid interpretation of Rawls nor a positive addition to the formulation of the conditions placed on the original position. "The veil of ignorance denies us the information about ourselves or others that would enable us to step in other people's shoes in the empathetic way that Okin commends. Moreover, the point of the veil of ignorance is precisely to avoid appeal to such motives as empathy or altruism. . . . It is part of the attraction of Rawls's theory that he drives us to take account of the needs of some hypothetical worst-off person without demanding any skills of empathy on our part" (Sypnowich 1993b, 495).

Rawls does indeed say that the parties in the original position "are mutually disinterested rather than sympathetic" (Rawls 1971, 187). However, Sypnowich mistakes empathy for sympathy, as is evident when she explains the unreasonableness of Okin's incorporation of empathy by giving examples of the difficulty of "empathizing" with the sexist or requiring that the sexist "empathize" with the nonsexist (Sypnowich 1993b, 495). But it is perfectly possible for me to empathize in the sense of understanding the position of the sexist, the reasons he gives, for example, for his belief that women lack certain capacities as grounds for his differential treatment of them, without sympathizing with him. Whereas empathy requires understanding the reasons for a position and knowing the feelings that accompany those reasons, sympathy suggests that one be able to feel concern for what another feels, as in the case of sympathizing with someone who grieves over the death of a loved one. Although Rawls clearly took mutual disinterest to characterize the bargainers, what he himself describes as the capacity for a sense of justice, the ability to provide reasons for judgments and to consistently match reasons and judgments, is more compatible with empathy as I describe it and Okin endorses it.

Okin's interpretation of the original position as requiring empathy gives content to the bargaining in a way that is absent when the thought experiment requires that we merely imagine a world where differences no longer matter to life prospects. If we add relational insights about how difference is created and maintained in social practices and political contexts, we will be able to discover a deficiency in Okin's critique too. We have already noted that Okin focuses on gender, and we used a general account of empathy to extend the analysis to other differences. The assignment of difference can result in exclusion, powerlessness, and disadvantage, and the empathy that Okin introduces is the least that would be required for understanding what it is like to be anyone who does not fit the norm and who is outside the center of influence and power. For Okin, however, the original position remains a heuristic device, a thought experiment, into which you or I or any individual can think ourselves by ourselves in order to come up with principles of justice. In other words, the original position still reflects the deliberations of a solitary moral reasoner.

So far, I perform the thought experiment by thinking about other possible positions, imagining and finding out about the consequences of being in those positions, empathizing with those imaginary others, and then coming up with principles of justice. As a thought experiment, the original position is or at least can be a solitary endeavor and there need be no communication among people with different points of view. We learned that Rawls explicitly supports this interpretation when he says that any one person can engage in the thought experiment of the original position and obtain a point of view removed from the particularity of different perspectives. Even after extending Okin's account of empathy, we are left with the notion that a solitary moral reasoner, though ignorant of his or her life prospects and in this sense neutral, could otherwise understand all points of view by empathizing with different others. But if we suppose real empathic understanding can only emerge from and become possible through relationships with others, then two things become apparent. First, the capacity to empathize assumes a background of our embeddedness in a network of relationships with others. Second, if empathy is to succeed in revealing what justice requires, then we need to engage in actual communication with others and not just in empathic imaginings about different others from our own perspective and point of view. Such dialogue will allow us to question something else that Okin retains in her revised original position, the idea that something very much like Rawls's principles of justice would be selected.

Bias and Points of View

One example Rawls gives of the laws of moral psychology known to the parties in the original position is that they have general knowledge of the need for "securing the stability of social cooperation" (Rawls 1971, 138). They go into the original position aware of difference and conflict and of the need to arbitrate and settle conflicts in order to achieve stable social relations. Once we allow this much knowledge about society and people, however, we begin to undermine the notion of a solitary moral reasoner who can think critically about equality and justice outside of a presumed background complex of relationships in social practices and political contexts. In her critique of the idea of a solitary moral reasoner, Marilyn Friedman argues that "no individual begins such an exercise ex nihilo; a background of interpersonal experience, including dialogue with others about moral matters, is a practical necessity in order for someone to have the ability to engage in isolated moral thinking. And professional philosophers employing 'monological' methods for seeking impartiality are nonetheless certainly talking to each other" (Friedman 1993, 15). The very ability to engage in Rawls's thought experiment relies on our embeddedness in communal rules and practices where reasons and justifications are given for reflection on and critical thinking about justice.[3]

We can think critically about equality and justice only when we are already embedded in social relations of particular sorts. We can specify what it is to empathize with another only because we are already situated in relationships and can thus imagine what it would be like to occupy another's position. In other words, it is only in assuming our inherent sociality and embeddedness in relationships that we can empathize with the positions of anyone and everyone. When we learn what is required of empathy in this way, we are brought back to my account of moral personhood, an account of moral equals as concrete persons situated in an ongoing process of engagement with others in a network of relationships shaped by social practices and political contexts. This account of moral personhood explains how and why empathy and not mutual disinterest should characterize the parties in the original position. To imagine ourselves without such a basic human capacity is not to add anything positive to a process of reasoning about just principles for structuring a society. Empathy also better explains why one would agree to be governed by the principles generated through the bargaining procedure.

When the focus returns to relationships, this generates a new understanding of empathy, one that undermines the notion that a solitary moral reasoner could gain a full understanding of the situation by empathizing with different points of view. Empathy, as I have described it, challenges the idea that solitary reasoners ultimately interested in satisfying preferences that shape their own conception of the good characterizes the parties, as well as the idea that such reasoners can come up with principles of justice. We need to know about the actual lived lives, the social and political structures, and the emotions that motivate and hinder people in particular lives because these facts and knowledge about them reveal inequalities and injustices that tend to go unnoticed. Notice that we have returned to the insight provided in Chapter 3 about the importance of understanding the lives and perspectives of those who are detrimentally affected by the relationships of inequality and powerlessness that they are in.

In an objection that at first glance appears to miss the point of the original position, Minow puts forward the idea that perspectives are relevant to an analysis of equality. She says of Rawls's formulation of the original position: "the very form of his questions presumes that the person behind the veil of ignorance is not the worst-off person. It assumes some essence of a self preexisting one's situation, and anyone would approach the possibility of being worst off the same way. . . . Rawls' question is put only to the particular person who is not the worst-off, a particular person who is not likely to understand fully the situation of the worst-off" (Minow 1990a, 151). Minow appears to miss the point because it seems obvious that everyone would think in terms of avoiding the worst-off position; even the worst-off would. Yet, the underlying argument is that the point of view Rawls describes in the original position and assumes as neutral and universal is actually a particular point of view, that of the advantaged. From this point of view, assumptions are made about what it would be like to be disadvantaged that do not necessarily correspond to the facts. The effects of assuming that this point of view is neutral and unbiased can be filled out by discussing the Poverty Game, an example used by Lorraine Code in *What Can She Know?*

The Poverty Game is a game created by six women on welfare, a game designed by them in such a way as to enable anyone to imagine what it is like to be on welfare. To play the game, each player thinks herself into and assumes the identity of a woman who lives below the subsistence level. Code describes the details of the game: "[r]ecordings of autobiographical stories, played as the game progresses, contribute to this imaginative exercise. Facilitators act as welfare workers and other public officials to simulate the pressures and obstacles the women encounter. Months of living with not enough to live on and no prospects of improvement are condensed into the day it takes to play the game" (Code 1991, 265). The game is similar to the original position in that it requires imagining oneself in another's place. It is dissimilar in that it takes the details and experiences of a life lived by someone in this sort of worst-off position to be essential to understanding what it is like to be that person. What the players find out is that women on welfare are isolated. Because they have limited and controlled access to their welfare workers, "it is hard for them to *know* about how to better their situation, cope with unexpected crises, or claim their rights and privileges" (Code 1991, 265, her emphasis). In the game, players are presented with problems of sick children and late checks. To recreate the facts of isolation, the rules forbid the players to communicate or consult with other players about the problems with which they are confronted.

Playing the game, spending a day imitating living the life of someone on welfare, only touches the surface of understanding the effects of the fear and isolation of trying to survive day by day when one is actually on welfare. When the game ends, most players go back to less disadvantaged lives. Those not on welfare and just reading about how the game is played are even further removed from knowing what it might be like to live on welfare. Laurence Thomas casts doubt on our ability to understand very much at all about someone's lived experiences without being in contact with them. "[I]t is possible that a person can have the intellectual belief that as a group Xs have the intellectual wherewithal or moral stamina of any other group, but not have the corresponding emotional configuration, since the person has never experienced any X as an equal. And the truth of the matter is that one does not know what it is like to experience X as an equal by reading books about Xs or watching moving documentaries or whatever" (Thomas 1994, 134). We find in Thomas's description of what is required to really know the position of another the two elements of empathy I outlined: knowing the factual details of inequalities experienced by particular others and knowing the experiential effects of those inequalities on particular lives. It is in knowing the details and experiences of particular disadvantaged lives that we come to feel the injustice of those inequalities. The argument here, as in Chapter 3, is that we can obtain this knowledge of particular inequalities and injustices when we pay attention to the perspectives of those who are disadvantaged.

Playing or reading about the welfare game provides at least a bit of contact and context for understanding the inequalities experienced by those on welfare. The bit of information we are given about the lives and experiences of the women on welfare begins to undermine stereotypes prevalent in our own society of welfare recipients as lazy, taking easy handouts, and able but unwilling to work. If we have never experienced what it is like to live on welfare, then knowing about the facts of isolation and lack of information forces us to acknowledge some taken-for-granted assumptions; for example, that aid or information about resources is easily obtainable for everyone. Unless we know the details of these lives lived in isolation and subjected to stereotypes, it is easy to take for granted the notion that people can just help themselves and to believe that their misfortune is a result of their own lack of desire or effort to change their lives. From a position of advantage, it is too easy to think in terms of "I made it on *my* own; you can and should make it on *your* own."

Code uses the welfare game to make a point about theories of knowledge that have "no place for analyses of the availability of knowledge, of knowledge-acquisition processes" (Code 1991, 266). The assumption is that "cognitive agents are virtually interchangeable, their specific and concrete situations within material, political, and ideological contexts, without epistemological significance" (Nelson 1994, 306). These insights about the significance of the identity of the knower, of different points of view, can be applied to an account of what is needed for critical thinking about equality and justice. The specific and concrete lives lived by persons in particular social and political contexts are not mere biased points of view that create unfair bargaining advantages. Knowledge of the details and experiences of actual lived lives (and the facts will vary from one sort of position to another and result in different kinds and levels of disadvantage) reduces the potential for biased judgments about the lives of others.

We may begin with the foundational requirement that persons be treated with equal concern and respect, a requirement I take

Okin to defend when she incorporates empathy as a condition of the original position, but the commitment to equal concern and respect is violated when we believe that there is a single point of view from which to understand and speak for distinct and different others. Just the knowledge alone that we have emerged from a history of discrimination in which differences justified unequal treatment and that these differences continue to be highly relevant to how people are treated should undermine confidence about being able to engage in monological reasoning from some isolated point of view. The elimination or reduction of bias in judgment requires not that we imagine our differences away, but that we attend to the detail of the particularities of people's lives as they perceive them. Impartiality, in the sense of the ability to treat each person with equal concern and respect, is achieved not through the monological thinking of a solitary and isolated moral reasoner, but through a communicative process of an ongoing dialogue among different points of view. While Rawls obviously recognizes the fundamental importance of the human capacity to plan a life, he is inattentive to the significance of a plurality of different life plans, as his confidence that any one can, all by themselves, engage in impartial thinking about the lives of different and concrete others displays. Treating all people with equal concern and respect requires empathy of a kind gained from dialogue, a communicative approach that can give us knowledge of the particularities of how people understand and live their lives.

Dialogue: Eliminating Bias and Achieving Impartiality

In *What Are Friends For?* Marilyn Friedman endorses Rawls's underlying goal of eliminating bias, but argues that this is achieved precisely by acknowledging and understanding different points of view, not by assuming a neutral and universal perspective. What needs to take place in the original position is not the monologue of a solitary reasoner, but a dialogue among different points of view. Friedman argues that "biases are best discerned in intersubjective dialogue among persons of different standpoints, including those who are the victims of bias and are therefore likely to be best situated to discern the biases against them in the thinking and practices of others" (Friedman 1993, 3). Empathizing requires real concrete relationships with the empathized in which they tell us about the inequalities they experience and how they are affected by them and not just having general knowledge of how some differences result in unequal opportunities and lower income levels. Empathy, as I have described it, also involves humility with respect to claims to know other points of view. As the welfare game shows, what we claim to know about lives very different from our own "*underdescribes* those standpoints" (Friedman 1993, 21, her emphasis).

Friedman rejects the model of the solitary reasoner in some neutral position and opts for a model of people embedded in relationships and dialogue with others. "Dialogue allows us each the opportunity to strive to correct the biases of others by expressing our own points of view. However arduous and plodding this alternative method may be in practice, it does not possess the disturbing feature of requiring someone who was gravely harmed by another to adopt the perspective of the wrongdoer as a condition for engaging in critical moral thinking" (Friedman 1993, 23–24). What Friedman describes is an impartiality tempered not by sympathy, but by an empathic and intellectual understanding of points of view of the sort that emerges from interactive relationships and communication with others.

The constraints on knowledge and motivation that Rawls places on the original position will not generate just principles. The original position needs to incorporate both aspects of empathy, understanding the reasons for particular inequalities and being aware of the emotional configurations that accompany those inequalities. We need adequate knowledge of the particularities of different perspectives to be able to think critically about the conditions needed for treating people with equal concern and respect, the point and purpose of the original position. Seyla Benhabib calls these perspectives the "standpoint of the concrete other" and says that acknowledgment of perspectives "requires us to view each and every rational being as an individual with a concrete history, identity, and affective-emotional constitution" and "to comprehend the needs of the other, his or her motivations, what she searches for, and what s/he desires" (Benhabib 1992, 159). We acquire this knowledge through dialogue, and this insight is central to work in the area of communicative ethics by theorists such as Habermas and Benhabib.

Benhabib begins with Habermas's model of communicative ethics, which she describes as "the processual generation of reasonable agreement about moral principles via an open-ended moral conversation" (Benhabib 1992, 37), and develops an account that she calls "interactive universalism" (Benhabib 1992, 6; 153; 165).[4] In Benhabib's version of communicative ethics, critical thinking begins with the acceptance of two foundational principles: we ought to treat everyone with equal concern and respect (the generalized other) and we ought to treat each other as concrete human beings whose capacity for self-definition ought to be enhanced (the concrete other) (Benhabib 1992, 164). Together, these substantive moral norms recognize "the plurality of modes of being human" (Benhabib 1992, 153) and give value to "what differentiates us from each other" (Benhabib 1992, 159), the ways in which individual lives are planned and managed with creativity and uniqueness. While Rawls also underlines the fundamental importance of the human capacity to plan a life, his confidence that we can render impartial and neutral judgments about the lives of different concrete others fails to take seriously the distinctiveness and uniqueness of persons. Without knowledge of the details and experiences of concrete others, we end up where Rawls does: arriving at principles that are "defined surreptitiously by identifying the experiences of a specific group of subjects as the paradigmatic case of the human as such. These subjects are invariably white, male adults who are propertied or at least professional" (Benhabib 1992, 152–153).

Benhabib takes difference, the uniqueness of each life, to be morally relevant to critical thinking about moral principles and the reason for promoting dialogue among concrete selves. In Benhabib's account of communicative ethics, each person deserves equal concern and respect, and respect for others is enhanced when we think from the perspective of concrete others.[5] In other words, the universal and foundational moral principle of equal concern and respect is given content when it is placed in the context of the concrete lives of persons. Two things will be important in my critical analysis of Benhabib's account. First, she too suggests that the interactive dialogue can be accomplished alone: "to think from the perspective of everyone else is to know how to listen to what the other is saying, or when the voices are absent, to imagine to oneself a conversation with the other as my dialogic partner" (Benhabib 1992, 137). Second, I shall also defend a version of the universal principles she provides, but argue that the relational approach I have been advancing calls for a shift in emphasis for the second principle she specifies.

We learned in Chapter 2 that how difference is perceived and understood in social practices and political contexts affects one's ability to plan and manage a life. Like Benhabib, we do not jettison the classical liberal focus on the human capacity for self-definition as the basis for the principle of equal concern and respect. Benhabib argues that enhancing the general capacity for self-definition calls for an examination of the standpoint of concrete others as a way of promoting equal concern and respect for each and every person. I want to contextualize and concretize equal concern and respect even further by calling for an assessment of how the capacity for self-definition is enhanced or restricted for concrete others by particular social practices and in certain political contexts. I think a full account of and respect for the unique self-defining capacities of particular concrete others calls for an analysis of the specific network of relationships in which they are embedded. Perhaps Benhabib would not disagree, but such an analysis, I suggest, undermines the adequacy of the possibility she allows: that one can "know how to listen to what the other is saying" by imagining "to oneself a conversation with the other" (Benhabib 1992, 137). Imagining to ourselves a conversation with a concrete other will not allow us to learn fully the complexities and subtleties of the effects that the particularized network of relationships has on a concrete person's self-defining capacities. Most importantly, an examination of the network of relationships reveals patterns and shared experiences that can tell us about inequalities generated by social practices and in political contexts for those who are members of disadvantaged groups.

The starting point is the idea that we need to theorize about equality and justice in the context of considering moral agents as engaged with others in a network of relationships shaped by social practices and political contexts. When we begin here, a slightly different light is cast on Benhabib's second principle of the "concrete other": we ought to treat each other as concrete human beings whose capacity for self-definition ought to be enhanced. Recast, the second principle would look something like the following: we ought to treat each other as concrete human beings whose capacity for self-definition is shaped by relationships and expresses ways of being and modes of human interaction that ought to be respected. I shall shorten the formulation and refer to the principle as "respect for human diversity and ways of being."

Together, the two principles bring the significance of concrete perspectives into the foreground but allow us to assess those perspectives in the context of the relationships shaped by particular social practices and political structures. When we focus on the network of relationships, we begin to notice patterns both in the stories told by individuals with concrete histories and identities and in the social and legal structures that make the stories possible, patterns that make us attend to the inequalities experienced by concrete others in specific contexts. The principles of treating everyone with equal concern and respect and respecting human diversity and ways of being are general and universal and form the base for the relational theory I defend. Now we turn to the structure of the dialogue and begin to draw out how the two principles can be given content.

Nielsen captures to some extent what I want to advocate as part of a dialogic approach in his account of what he calls "wide reflective equilibrium." Nielsen expands on Rawls's version of reflective equilibrium by considering the social and political contexts within which reasoning about justice takes place to be relevant to the deliberations and negotiations. Nielsen defends a process whereby we bring under reflection and into equilibrium not only the considered convictions and general moral principles that Rawls describes but also the particular social practices and political contexts within which the convictions and principles are or will be situated. For Nielsen, wide reflective equilibrium under these conditions shapes "a consistent and coherent cluster of beliefs" that reasonable persons would be willing to accept and support. "The consistent set we seek is not only of specific moral convictions and more general principles but of whole theories of morality, conceptions of the function of morality in society, factual beliefs about the structure of society and about human nature, beliefs about social change (including beliefs about how societies will develop or can be made to develop) as well as specific historical and sociological beliefs about what our situation is. The equilibrium we seek is one in which all these elements are put into a coherent whole where the aim remains to maximize coherence"

(Nielsen 1994b, 523–524).[6] My model of a dialogic enterprise would depart from Nielsen's account in several ways, however. First, I would reject the suggestion implied in Nielsen's account (and Benhabib's), that wide reflective equilibrium can be achieved by a solitary moral reasoner. Second, I want to particularize even further the people we are reflecting about and the social practices and political contexts within which they interact. Lastly, I want to insist that adequate reflection on different perspectives needs information about the details and experiences of the lives of those who exist in oppressive and unequal relationships; information that contact, dialogue, interaction, imagination, and empathy can uncover and reveal.

Dialogue particularizes inequalities and disadvantages shaped by social practices and in political contexts. The interaction and dialogue of different people differentially affected by the dominant discourse makes them evident and concrete. Charles Mills puts it well when he writes, "[t]he fact that noumenal individuals confront one another phenomenally in the factory as capitalists and workers, in the family and bedroom as men and women, in the streets as whites and blacks, is crucial to a comprehension of the specific obstacles people face in the realization of justice. Similarly, the beliefs, norms, values, theories, conceptions of the good that concrete individuals have—much of which is stripped away by the Rawlsian veil—may often be a necessary epistemic contribution towards articulating a morally superior ideal" (Mills 1994, 11). We caught a glimpse of what dialogue can teach us in the example of the women on welfare. In learning about the details of their lives, we learn that their isolation and lack of information contribute to their hardship and lack of opportunity, and we confront stereotypes of them as lazy or incompetent, stereotypes reflected in policies that require they explain and justify their day-to-day activities and choices. But what will dialogue achieve by way of critical thinking about the structures that are needed to treat people with equal concern and respect? Will this dialogue generate universal principles of justice for structuring social and political institutions? The approach I shall adopt for answering these questions is to examine whether Rawls's principles of justice will do. In revealing some of the shortcomings of Rawls's difference principle in particular, a sketch of a different theory will emerge.

Human Diversity: The Difference That Difference Makes

Rawls's task for the parties to the original position is to formulate principles of justice that will best give them the means to pursue the life projects and goals they know they will have and value, no matter what their starting positions are like. Because the original position is assumed to be a point of view abstracted from difference, the means are presumed to be resources that will provide everyone with fair equality of opportunity. For Rawls, the resources are primary goods, "things that every rational man is presumed to want" (Rawls 1971, 62), and include "rights and liberties, opportunities and powers, income and wealth" (Rawls 1971, 92). We discovered that problems emerge when a commitment to the moral equality of all people pushes theorists like Rawls in the direction of ignoring "interpersonal diversities," "by taking 'no note of them,' or by 'assuming them to be absent' " (Sen 1992, 30). We need to take account of difference at the start of our inquiry into what is needed to treat people with equal concern and respect. Amartya Sen argues that the significance of the plurality of difference forces us to reassess Rawls's second principle of justice, the difference principle that justifies inequalities in the distribution of social and economic goods if it is to the benefit of the least well off. By questioning the difference principle, Sen also casts doubt on Rawls's account of equal liberties.

Sen commends Rawls for formulating a substantive theory that goes beyond libertarianism in acknowledging that large disparities in resources and wealth lead to inequalities in freedom and opportunity (Sen 1992, 38). However, he argues that in focusing on the distribution of material goods as the means for achieving equality of opportunity, Rawls does not give adequate attention to the ways in which equal means can still result in "serious inequalities in actual freedoms enjoyed by different persons" (Sen 1992, 81). A proper assessment of equality requires an account of how diverse needs and capabilities result in inequalities in freedom and opportunity that cannot be entirely rectified by a difference principle that merely increases income: "[e]quality of freedom to pursue our ends cannot be generated by equality in the distribution of primary goods" (Sen 1992, 87).

Concentrating attention on the capabilities and needs of different others raises questions about the difference principle as formulated by Rawls. We will raise other questions about the inequalities in wealth justified by the difference principle in the next section, but for now we need to examine Sen's important account of how differences are relevant to an assessment of the freedom people have to meet their needs or develop their capabilities. As he puts it, many people "have characteristics—age, disability, disease-proneness, etc.—that make it more difficult for them to convert primary goods into basic capabilities, e.g. being able to move about, to lead a healthy life, to take part in the life of the community" (Sen 1992, 82). Sen's vital contribution to a growing literature on needs and capabilities becomes apparent when we contrast his criticism that Rawls ignores certain relevant differences with what seems to be a similar criticism by Brian Barry.[7]

Like Sen, Barry also examines deficiencies in Rawls's account of differences. Unlike Sen, Barry argues that the problem is that Rawls's principles do not allow *more* material goods to be given to those with particular differences. "For Rawls a pound is a pound is a pound. Whether some people need more pounds to get to the same place as others is irrelevant. The result of this dogma is to prevent anyone from being able to claim that because of special handicaps or disadvantages he needs more income than other people to achieve the same (or less) satisfaction. Thus we rule out special allowances for the blind or otherwise handicapped, or to the sick and infirm, or to pregnant women, designed to offset the special expenses associated with those conditions" (Barry 1973, 56). Sen, I think correctly, perceives that Rawls's difference principle *does* allow those with particular disadvantages to receive more income. Sen's contribution is to argue that while giving more primary goods such as income to the least well off obviously goes in the direction of increasing well-being, it still fails to address inequalities that remain in particular cases.

Because Rawls concentrates on primary goods as material goods and on a distribution and redistribution of these goods, some people will remain just as disadvantaged even when they obtain more of them. Giving more material goods to those whose inequality is a result of different capabilities or needs will not always help them to transform those goods into genuine opportunities to pursue life projects and goals. Inequalities experienced by disabled persons or by pregnant women in the workplace, for example, occur at the level of reduced capabilities and increased needs. In the case of persons with disabilities, perhaps more income can provide costly equipment and home care, but it will not change a workplace structure designed for able-bodied people or stereotypes of physically disabled persons as mentally incompetent, for example. In the case of pregnant women in the workplace, perhaps more money will bridge the early care period with maternity leave, but it will not change workplace structures that do not accommodate child-care responsibilities or stereotypes of mothers as less career oriented and more suited to child rearing activities.

Like Okin, Sen attempts to salvage Rawls by incorporating his account of inequalities in needs and capabilities into Rawls's theory of justice. Rawls's endorsement of improving the condition of the least well off is Sen's opening for advocating the need to assess inequalities by attending to the diversity of people who are in the least advantaged places in society. "Rawls's general argument for focusing on the least advantaged does apply here (for reasons of 'fairness' that he has analysed so powerfully). That certainly provides reason enough to take seriously the claims of attainment equality even when the maximal achievements are quite diverse" (Sen 1990, 92). Unlike Okin, however, Sen is less confident that his critique of Rawls and call for revisions will generate a complete or universal theory of justice. In some of his most recent work, Sen states that in his analysis of capabilities and needs, he has "not gone beyond outlining a space and some general features of a combining formula, and this obviously falls far short of being a complete theory of justice" (Sen 1995b, 268).

Sen's account is important because it retains the classical liberal focus on an individual's capacity for self-determination and shows that valuing and enhancing this capacity requires an assessment of inequalities in terms of the diverse needs and capabilities of different people. His analysis shows how one's freedom to pursue interests, projects, and goals is affected by situations of increased needs and reduced capabilities. Sen highlights human diversity. Attending to the particularities of difference undermines complacency in the belief that equality is achieved when people's basic needs for food and shelter are met. A theory of equality must pay attention not only to distributing material goods as the means to freedom but also to the ways in which different needs and capabilities limit one's freedom to pursue interests, projects, and goals. Differences are not irrelevant to critical thinking about what is needed to treat all people with equal concern and respect.

Sen's assessment of the needs and capabilities of different others rests on descriptions of particular people who are least well off. I want to emphasize that the needs and capabilities of the least well off are shaped in and through relationships and, in particular, relationships between the powerful and powerless. The disabled person and the pregnant woman in the workplace are defined and judged in relation to the norms of the able-bodied person and male worker. Sen rightly argues that giving people with these sorts of needs and capabilities more income will not address their inequalities. He elects to revise Rawls's account of what is needed to achieve equality by examining more carefully the position of the least well off. Another way to revise Rawls is to examine more carefully what should fall under the concept of "primary goods" and to start with Rawls's own account of self-respect as an important primary good. A formulation in terms of self-respect puts relationships back into the analysis of whether equality obtains in a way missing in Sen's account.

Rawls adds self-respect to the list of primary goods early on in *A Theory of Justice* (Rawls 1971, 62, 92), but he postpones discussion of it until Part Three, where he deals with an examination of conceptions of the good. After listing the broad categories of the primary goods, Rawls adds as an afterthought, "[a] very important primary good is a sense of one's own worth; but for simplicity I leave this aside until much later" (Rawls 1971, 92). Rawls defines self-respect as including "a person's sense of his own value, his secure conviction that his conception of his good, his plan of life is worth carrying out" and as implying "a confidence in one's ability, so far as it is within one's power, to fulfill one's intentions" (Rawls 1971, 440). If we combine this definition with Rawls's statements about self-respect as "perhaps the most important primary good," then it seems fairly obvious that those with different needs and capabilities do not necessarily gain self-respect when they are merely given more of the other primary goods.

We need to examine the inequalities that result from diminished levels of self-respect or distorted perceptions of the capabilities and needs of different and concrete others. We have in front of us a way for doing this: a restructured original position in which dialogue among multiple kinds of people about the effects of social practices and political conditions on freedom and opportunity takes place. An account of how particular needs and capabilities are understood and shaped in social practices and have an impact on levels of freedom and self-respect is obtained through dialogue and interaction where the perspectives of those identified as different are taken seriously. Obtaining a primary good like self-respect requires attending to the lives and experiences of those whose perspectives have been absent or ignored in theories of justice.

The idea that impartiality can be obtained by assuming a point of view removed from difference needs to be abandoned. There is no impartial and neutral point of view removed from the perspectives of concrete persons embedded in social practices and political contexts. If anything, assuming the point of view of the solitary moral reasoner described in traditional moral and political philosophy makes it more difficult to acknowledge and assess some kinds of inequality because it masks the biases contained in it. In our analysis thus far, the moral point of view Rawls assumes in his own critical thinking about justice seems to be that of a well-off, able-bodied male who speaks for and makes assumptions about the lives and experiences of different others. From a vantage point that he takes to be neutral and impartial, what Rawls actually knows about different perspectives is partial, inadequate, and distorted.

Through the synthesis and development of arguments and ideas provided by numerous critiques of Rawls, we now have a very different picture of what needs to happen in the original position to generate principles of justice all would agree to be governed by. So little remains of the conditions Rawls designed as necessary for fair bargaining procedures that we may wonder if we should retain the methodological device of the original position at all. I suggest we should. The ingenuity of the original position lies in the simple but powerful idea that moral principles derive their force not from some a priori reasoning removed from experience and the contingencies of the world, but from critical moral reasoning about and in the world we live in. Rawls simply asks us to think about what principles we would agree to abide by if we did not know how things would turn out for us, and this ensures that everyone is treated with equal concern and respect. I have retained the idea of the original position as a device for clarifying what equality means and requires and arrived at the foundational moral principles of treating everyone with equal concern and respect and respecting human diversity and ways of being.

Sen draws our attention to the significance of human diversity for an assessment of equality. I highlighted the relevance of social practices and political contexts for an understanding of human diversity and this, I want to argue, draws our attention to the ways of being of those whose differences have been made significant to their life prospects and levels of freedom and self-respect. In order to retain the device of the original position as a tool for achieving impartiality about different others, we need to focus on the method of reflective equilibrium in the context of dialogue among different people differentially affected by social practices in various political contexts. I have been defending a very broad application of wide reflective equilibrium, but I need to give the methodology that structures the dialogue more content to uncover just what would emerge from this revised original position.

Constraints on Dialogue: Justifications, Assessments, and Communities

Critical thinking about equality and justice begins with the foundational principle of equal concern and respect, a principle reflected by the incorporation of empathy into the original position. Empathy requires more in the way of knowledge about the details and experiences of lived lives than can possibly be handled by a solitary moral reasoner. What needs to take place in the original position is communication among multiple kinds of people about the inequalities generated by particular social practices and in specific political contexts. The original position needs to contain experiences of the widest possible variety of people in interaction and communication with others in social and political contexts. This requirement generates the principle of respect for human diversity and ways of being. The principles then structure the dialogue so that inequalities and injustices of all kinds are confronted and addressed.

In a critique that specifically targets Okin's revisions to the original position, Ruth Anna Putnam defends the importance of "enhancing one's ability to recognize a multiplicity of 'least advantaged' positions and an ability to hear and heed the complaints raised from these perspectives" (Putnam 1995, 323). However, she does not think that these perspectives will or should change the substance or content of universal principles of justice. In her view, we need to retain something very close to Rawls's original position and its emergent two principles of justice that structure the basic institutions. Only *after* the general and universal principles structure the basic institutions do we need to tinker with the second level policies and legislation that an incorporation of different perspectives will demand.

Like me, Putnam thinks that Okin's incorporation of women into the original position leads to a demand for inclusion of other perspectives.[8] Unlike me, however, Putnam thinks that this inclusion cannot be sustained or managed in a device like the original position: "a small tear in the veil of ignorance would lead . . . to it being rent altogether" (Putnam 1995, 310) and "attempts to widen the scope of justice have opened a line of reasoning which threatens to *fragment* justice by emphasizing the diverse particularities of those to whom justice applies" (Putnam 1995, 302, her emphasis). Putnam gives three reasons for rejecting the idea of opening up the original position to diverse perspectives and knowledge about the details of them. First, the task of incorporating diverse perspectives is not only endless but runs the risk of misrepresenting those who are members of more than one disadvantaged group. The answer to these difficulties, according to Putnam, would seem to force us to include the perspective of each and every concrete individual, and this would tell us very little about what justice requires. The next chapter will be devoted to answering this sort of objection to the notion of perspectives. The second objection, that it will not be possible to "come to an agreement on any conception of justice," and the third objection, that "it is impossible to perform the suggested thought experiment" (Putnam 1995, 317), constitute direct attacks on the revisions to the original position that I have advanced in this chapter.

In the remainder of this chapter, I want to question two assumptions underlying Putnam's objections to including the perspectives of the disadvantaged in the original position: the assumption that their inclusion will not affect the principles of justice that would emerge from the deliberations and the assumption that their inclusion would be so unwieldy and conflictual as to block agreement about principles of justice. I think that G. A. Cohen's insightful critique of Rawls in "Incentives, Inequality, and Community" is instructive on both fronts. While Cohen's concern is not with providing an appropriate description of the original position, he gives the kind of analysis of people in communities that puts the focus where it needs to be. Not only does Cohen raise doubts about the "justice" of the difference principle, doubts different from and in addition to the ones raised by Sen, but his account will allow me to suggest mechanisms for engaging in dialogue that answer Putnam's worries about too many perspectives generating too many conflicts among individual parties.

Cohen's specific target is the incentive argument that he takes to be pervasive in and assumed by liberal theory as a justification for inequalities in wealth. The gist of the argument is that inequalities in wealth serve as an incentive for the talented to work harder and produce more than they would if everyone had the same amount of material goods. Moreover, because the rich and talented are motivated to work harder when they have more material goods, they generate the kind of wealth and opportunities that allow everyone to benefit, particularly the least well off. We have already noted that Rawls rejects Nozickean justifications in terms of desert and entitlement for inequalities in wealth. We also know that the difference principle justifies inequalities in the distribution of social and economic goods if it is to the benefit of the least well off. In one place, Rawls narrows the range of possible justifications for these inequalities and appears to leave us with what Cohen identifies as the incentive argument: "the greater advantages of some are in return for compensating benefits for the less favored; and no one supposes that those who have a larger share are more deserving from a moral point of view. Happiness according to virtue is rejected as a principle of distribution (§48). And so likewise is the principle of perfection: regardless of the excellences that persons or associations display, their claims to social resources are always adjudicated by principles of mutual justice" (Rawls 1971, 536).

Cohen does not refer to them, but Rawls's interesting comments about envy in the less frequently discussed third part of *A Theory of Justice* support the idea that Rawls assumes an incentive argument.[9] In outlining what rationality entails, Rawls specifies the following: "[t]he special assumption I make is that a rational individual does not suffer from envy. He is not ready to accept a loss for himself if only others have less as well. He is not downcast by the knowledge or perception that others have a large index of primary social goods" (Rawls 1971, 143). Presumably, it is irrational for the less-advantaged to envy the rich because their envy would result in principles that remove inequalities in wealth, a removal that would reduce the incentive for the well-off to develop their talents and generate benefits such as creating employment opportunities for the poor. Rational and mutually disinterested parties would acknowledge that envy for the rich and talented makes everyone worse off.

Let us examine this presupposition in the light of the argument that the point of view in Rawls's version of the original position represents the perspective of the advantaged. From the perspective of the advantaged, it would seem irrational for the poor to envy the rich because the greater wealth of the rich can only benefit the poor, an assumption already present in Rawls's difference principle that allows these inequalities only when they are to the benefit of the least well off. But this seems to beg the question of why the inequalities in wealth are necessary. Is it because the rich will have no incentive for working hard and thereby generating benefits for all unless they are given more income? Is it that an equal distribution of wealth *actually* makes everyone worse off? Rawls suggests an affirmative answer to both questions when he writes, "there may be forms of equality that do spring from envy. Strict egalitarianism, the doctrine which insists upon an equal distribution of all primary goods, conceivably derives from this propensity. What this means is that this conception of equality would be adopted in the original position only if the parties are assumed to be sufficiently envious" (Rawls 1971, 538–539). Envy does not characterize the parties in the original position because envy would generate policies that removed inequalities in wealth. Rawls assumes that these inequalities are the kind of incentives that people need to develop their talents and skills in ways that benefit everyone *and that the disadvantaged would recognize this*. The latter is precisely what Cohen calls into question.

Cohen argues that, on at least one reading, Rawls assumes that inequalities in wealth are necessary because "talented people lack a certain sort of commitment to equality" (Cohen 1995, 379) and that this reading contradicts the raison d'être of the original position. Cohen mounts a case against the incentive argument on the grounds that it violates a condition of community. To be part of a community, citizens need to be able to provide what Cohen refers to as "comprehensive justifications" (Cohen 1995, 347), justifications for principles and policies that stand as reasonable and acceptable to all its members. Cohen argues that the incentive argument seems reasonable when it is uttered in third-person impersonal statements that take the following form: because the talented rich will not work as hard if they do not have incentives such as greater wealth, everyone will be made worse off. Cohen argues that the incentive argument cannot serve as a comprehensive justification for inequality when it is uttered by the talented rich in first-person interpersonal statements that take the following form: because I, a talented rich person, will not work as hard unless I have incentives such as greater wealth, you, the poor, will be worse off.

Cohen argues that when the incentive argument is put in the first-person interpersonal form, it becomes clear that the rich make it the case that the poor are worse off. On the lips of the rich, the incentive argument displays relations between rich and poor that lack a communal character. In Cohen's words, the incentive "argument is generally presented in thoroughly third-personal terms and, relatedly, as though no question arises about the attitudes and choices of the rich people it mentions. When, by contrast, we imagine a talented rich person himself affirming the argument, the background issues of equality and obligation come clearly into view, and, if I am right, the rich are revealed to be out of community with the poor in respect of the economic dimension of their lives" (Cohen 1995, 354).

To understand the full force of Cohen's case against the incentive argument, it will be useful to pick up on an aspect of his case against Nozick's account of Wilt Chamberlain discussed in Chapter 4. There, it became clear that Nozick was wrong to assume that anyone would reason in the same way, which is to allow disparities in wealth in order to satisfy the immediate preferences to watch Chamberlain play. People socialized in an egalitarian society would be more likely to understand that allowing individuals to satisfy their preferences without regard to the effects of those preferences on the lives and freedom of others would generate the kind of inequalities they would not want. These sentiments are not indicative of irrationality or envy. At the bottom of the incentive argument is the threat that the well off will not produce if the unequalizing incentives are withdrawn. This is precisely a constraint created by an inegalitarian attitude that runs counter to the spirit of the difference principle itself. If we need inequalities to encourage the kind of performance by the talented rich that generates benefits for the poor, then as Cohen puts it, "it might be folly not to have them, but it does not follow that having them is a requirement of basic justice, where a *basic* principle of justice is one that has application in a society where, as in Rawls's, everyone always acts justly" (Cohen 1995, 393, his emphasis). The inequalities in wealth justified by the difference principle reflect the expectations of citizens in a liberal democratic society. Particularly because Rawls rejects justifications based on desert and entitlement, we need much more than Rawls provides to explain why these expectations of incentives are just.

If we apply this insight to Cohen's critique of the incentive argument, we bring the need for perspectives back into an account of what needs to take place in the original position for principles of justice to emerge. We need to be constantly aware that the perspectives of those in power are taken for granted, and we need to be vigilant in uncovering the assumptions that underlie these perspectives. We live in a society with large disparities in wealth, one in which the third-person impersonal utterances of the incentive argument seem neutral, unbiased, and true. Perhaps so much so in many contexts that the less well off also accept its validity to some extent. Cohen's interpersonal test for assessing justifications makes perspectives and biases apparent. In one place, Cohen tries out the following justificatory move made in a statement by a rich person to a poor person: " 'if you were in our shoes you would feel the same way' " (Cohen 1995, 369). The reply he imagines a poor person could give points to the significance of perspectives: " '[n]either of us really knows how I would behave. Not all rich people market maximize as a matter of course, and I hope that, if I were rich, I would not belong to the vast majority that do, especially if I retained a lively sense of what it is like to be in the condition I am now actually in' " (Cohen 1995, 370).

The interpersonal test as a justificatory mechanism gives each person responsibility, as a member of a community, for actions that affect other members. Interpersonal first-person justifications serve as tests for whether all people are treated as members of a community. Rawls's principles of justice are supposed to be the result of an agreement that all members assent to abide by because they are fair for everyone. Cohen's interpersonal test for comprehensive justification shows that the difference principle "requires a model of society in breach of an elementary condition of community" (Cohen 1995, 336). In conditions under which the poor really are out of community with the rich, it is easier to understand why Rawls might be right to suggest that it is not rational for the poor to envy the rich. If the rich really do make it the case that the poor will be worse off when the rich have no monetary incentives, then it is not irrational for the poor "to fall in with what the rich propose" (Cohen 1995, 374). But the interpersonal test creates a context that makes it possible for anyone in a community to demand justification from fellow members for principles and policies.

While Cohen uses the idea of justifications in interpersonal settings to test and reject the incentive argument for inequalities in wealth and thereby to strengthen the case for socialist egalitarianism, his account of comprehensive justifications can also be put to work in critical thinking about what equal concern and respect requires. The revised original position, where dialogue among multiple people with diverse perspectives takes place, is precisely the sort of interpersonal setting in which justifications and the assessment of them can play a central role in structuring the debate and testing principles and policies. When we include justificatory mechanisms in interpersonal settings as part of the methodology of wide reflective equilibrium, we provide a context for assessing claims by concrete persons of unjust treatment and for evaluating policies for eliminating various injustices. Because the assessment is grounded in a consideration of perspectives in the context of concrete lives affected by social practices and political contexts, the kinds of policies that emerge can stand as justified to every person and from every point of view. The interpersonal test, with its requirement for comprehensive justifications, ones that can stand as reasonable and fair to all parties and particularly to those whose perspectives have been absent or ignored, can answer Putnam's worries about an unwieldy and conflictual original position.

So far, however, I have said more about those principles that would not be selected than about those that would. In the light of Sen's and Cohen's critiques, it would seem that two things about the difference principle can no longer be retained: the focus on a distribution of material goods as the way to improve the condition of the least well off and an incentive-based justification for inequalities in wealth. I shall have more to say about what might emerge from the revised original position after I have developed more of the positive aspects of a relational approach to equality. For now, we can safely say that the *principles* that emerge in the revised original position would be the general ones I have already identified: treating everyone with equal concern and respect and respecting human diversity and ways of being. Beyond that there would be agreement to have justificatory mechanisms in place for allowing the diverse perspectives of various disadvantaged groups to be represented and for presenting and assessing justifications for policies that would be able to stand as reasonable to all members of the community. While the principles would be universal, the policies would not and could not be fixed for all time or for all contexts (even for particular contexts) but would be continually open to dialogue, up for negotiation, in need of justification, and subject to change.

Drawing Conclusions and Looking Ahead: Perspectives in and on Dialogue

It will prove useful to return to the problem presented in the concluding paragraphs of the previous chapter: the assumption in traditional theories of equality that the inequality suffered by aspiring builder B is simply an unequal opportunity to build. Both formal and substantive equality theorists assume that the task is to provide aspiring builder B and those like her with the same opportunities to compete for and win the positions and benefits enjoyed by those who are already in places of influence and power. But merely adding women to the existing structures will not provide them with substantive equality.[10] With the relational critique of liberal theory developed thus far, I can now explain clearly why initially describing the problem for women in the society of builders merely in terms of their aspiring to be builders already assumes quite a lot about norms and about assimilation into established and accepted structures.

Liberal theory has concentrated on what is required to provide aspiring builder B with an equal opportunity to compete for places in current and valued structures, but she may not really aspire to be a builder or she may aspire to be a builder but not if she has to give up commitments and responsibilities that she has come to value. We can now ask two kinds of questions with respect to the builders' community and the member we can now simply call "B." What happens when we treat B as a nonbuilder with a full identity and perspective and her own interests, projects, and goals? What happens when we treat her as not just an aspiring builder, but as someone with an identity and perspective that can shed light on current oppressive structures and help to change them?

Let us imagine entering into a dialogue with B in what is now a very changed original position, where critical thinking about what is required to treat people with equal concern and respect takes place. B and those like her will express concern that their own lives are defined or perceived as having less value than others. They will be concerned about the power relations that emerge when differences are identified and used to justify restricting or devaluing particular interests, projects, and goals. B shows that her perspective complicates an understanding of what it means to perceive things from another's perspective when that perspective is outside the norm. Taking the perspective of people like her into the original position illustrates the importance of considering the concerns raised by those in disadvantaged positions. That is not to say that every perspective will be relevant or that all inequalities will be unjustified, but we need an appropriate context for making judgments about relevant perspectives and justified inequalities, and Rawls does not provide it. That context contains the foundational principles of treating people with equal concern and respect and of respecting human diversity and ways of being. In addition, we can determine the conditions needed to meet these two demands in specific contexts by making justifications in interpersonal settings a requirement for presenting, formulating, and testing policies.

The exclusion of perspectives other than those of the dominant undermines the notion that the original position as formulated by Rawls is a neutral or objective "starting point for political philosophy" (Dworkin 1981b, 345). After all, the parties in the original position do know that we have emerged from a long history of treating difference as the basis for judgments of inferiority and unequal treatment, *and* they do not know what position *they* will be in. Emphasizing the relevance of difference highlights several conditions needed to accord equal concern and respect to all people: the need to be aware of the power relations that issue from the human capacities to differentiate and evaluate, the need to be concerned with how difference looks from the perspective of those identified as different, and the need to be sensitive to the effects on self-concepts and identities and on levels of self-respect of and respect for those grouped and defined as different.

In my account of the conditions needed to secure equal concern and respect, self-respect is still the "most important primary good," but it takes on a hue different from the one a liberal substantive account like Rawls's paints. Self-respect is undermined when there are assumptions and stereotypes about a person's capacities based merely on his or her membership in a group. Self-respect is also undermined when members of oppressed groups do not have conditions that support and respect their attempts to be considered and to contribute to and participate in social and political structures. This is why tests such as interpersonal justifications are essential to the methodology of wide reflective equilibrium in the original position. Finally, self-respect is undermined when members of oppressed groups have their freedom to develop capacities, meet basic needs, and pursue interests, projects, and goals restricted on a number of fronts and in various ways. Facts of diversity call for innovative means for satisfying the principles of treating people with equal concern and respect and respecting ways of being. Perspectives highlight this diversity and reveal that attention to the distribution of material goods will not be sufficient for meeting the demands of equality. We can now understand better why Rawls cannot fix his oversight in *A Theory of Justice* that gender is a relevant attribute by just adding gender to the list of features that the parties in the original position should imagine away. A substantive understanding of equal concern and respect for all people involves imagining oneself in another's place in a much more radical sense than Rawls allows in his version of the original position.

6

🔥 🔥 🔥

Conceptions of the Self:
The Significance of a Network
of Relationships

Introduction

Never far from consideration in the examination of liberal theory are questions about the coherency and adequacy of the liberal conception of the self. Most of what I have said thus far relies on an underlying conception of the self as relational. Chapter 2 outlines the relational features of language and of people. Chapter 3 offers insights about the importance of understanding the perspectives of those who are detrimentally affected by the relationships of inequality and powerlessness that they are in. Chapter 5 demands that the original position contain experiences of the widest possible variety of people in communication with others in social and political contexts. The idea that relationships are significant to equality analysis has been in the foreground, but their significance for personhood has not. We caught a glimpse of the self that underlies a relational approach in the description in Chapter 3 of the significance of the notion of moral personhood as the basis for equality and in the rejection in Chapter 4 of the libertarian self abstracted from social practices and political contexts. It is now time to confront metaphysical issues of selfhood head on. We need an adequate conception of the self from which to formulate a theory of equality. We can develop one by delineating how a relational conception differs from conceptions of the self prevalent in moral and political theory.

In this chapter, I set the stage for examining conceptions of the self and its relevance for political theory by confronting the well-known and prevalent belief that all liberal theory views the self as atomistic, individualistic, and possessive. Such charges would appear to flow from libertarianism's tendency to theorize about the self in abstraction from political contexts, a tendency not evident in liberal substantive theory's defense of positive measures. Yet, as communitarians point out and the discussion in the previous chapter reveals, there are other problems with the liberal self as Rawls conceives it. The Rawlsian self can stand apart from his or her ends and obtain a point of view that is impartial and unbiased about all perspectives. A relational theory of equality takes the many kinds of perspectives of people embedded in various sorts of relationships to be morally relevant to an analysis of equality. But how similar is this embedded and encumbered self to the account that communitarians give?

I need to distinguish my account of a relational self from the well-known and, at least on the surface, similar communitarian view. Unlike many communitarian projects that begin and end with descriptions of people embedded in social contexts, the relational approach I advance forms the base for developing a political theory. One feature of such a theory will be the attention given to the impact of relationships of power, of oppression, and of authority, on the people who are in them and to the inequalities such relationships generate. For communitarians, the unit of analysis is the community and not the individuals or the relationships they are in. If we want to begin with relationships to develop a conception of the self, then we cannot avoid discussing the ethic of care, an approach moral and political theorists associate with a contextualized concern for others and for the relationships moral agents are in.

While the relational self I delineate has more similarities to accounts implicit in an ethic of care than it has to either liberal or communitarian accounts, there are important differences too. As interpreted through Gilligan's work, care is an approach that focuses on interpersonal relationships and our responsiveness to the needs of others as a legitimate way of reasoning about morality and moral problems in general, an approach that is certainly compatible with my account so far. But Gilligan's focus on dyadic, personal relationships has resulted in a characterization of care as a moral approach that is and should be associated with women and applicable only to personal relationships in a private realm, not to issues of justice. I want to avoid the debates about whether women are more caring than men and whether care constitutes a legitimate approach to morality and focus on an aspect of the ethic of care that has received less attention: the basic insight that the "different voice" realizes the significance of being in a "web of relationships" and reasons about moral problems in terms of connection with, rather than separation from, others.

One of the main tasks in my critical examination of Gilligan, one necessary for developing a relational theory of equality that incorporates insights from both care and justice, is to highlight the impact that relationships of all kinds have on self-concepts, identity, and self-determination. I shall pursue this task by expanding the network of relationships from the personal and dyadic ones on which Gilligan tends to focus to include public as well as personal relationships. Even though Gilligan views relationships as central to an ethic of care, she is interested in relationships in order to illustrate and validate care as a moral response. She thereby fails to provide a critical analysis of relationships or to develop the moral and political implications of such an analysis. Gilligan is not a political theorist, but a political theory can be built up from the skeletal foundation she outlines in the extremely suggestive and insightful but mostly undeveloped examples in her research.

Examining Liberalism's Individualism

An account of the ontology of persons as relational fits with the descriptions of the interdependence and interconnectedness of people in communities that I have been emphasizing throughout. The builders learn the standards and rules of their community in relationships with others, and in the process they become members of a community. A relational approach provides an account of personhood at odds with accounts in the philosophical tradition that take self-determination to be merely a matter of recognizing and actualizing one's own interests, projects, and goals. A relational conception of the self suggests that we come to know ourselves and others only in a network of interactive relationships and that this shapes and is necessary for exercising self-determining capacities.

When we place the social features of moral personhood in the foreground, a new light is shed on the charge that liberals assume an individualistic, atomistic, and competitive conception of the self. First, a look at a few examples of the objection to liberalism: "the individual is 'self-made': identity is a function of individual desire, will and effort; freedom is simply the power to do or forbear according to one's subjectively determined appetites or aversions unconstrained by other human beings; and self-realization is nothing more than success in the competition for necessarily scarce goods. The individual alone is responsible for choices made, for effort invested and for the outcomes achieved, be they successes or failures" (Hawkesworth 1984, 297). Mary Hawkesworth attributes this picture of the self to liberal theory.

Or consider Lorraine Code's description of the liberal focus on individual freedom as a primary value: "[a]utonomous man is—and should be—self-sufficient, independent, and self-reliant, a self-realizing individual who directs his efforts toward maximizing his personal gains. His independence is under constant threat from other (equally self-serving) individuals: hence he devises rules to protect himself from intrusion. Talk of rights, rational self-interest, expediency, and efficiency permeates his moral, social, and political discourse" (Code 1991, 77–78). Or finally, there is Alison Jaggar's claim that "the liberal assumption [is] that human individuals are essentially solitary, with needs and interests that are separate from if not in opposition to those of other individuals" (Jaggar 1983a, 40). There are two points to be made concerning these kinds of objections. First, contrary to many liberal critics, such accounts of the self are not typical of and common to all liberal theory, and, second, the real objection is not that liberals deny the relational aspects of selves, but that they do not take these aspects to be relevant to an account of what it is to be a person or to treat people with equal concern and respect.

Will Kymlicka has been perhaps the most vociferous in making the first point against liberal critics. He rejects the sort of descriptions given above as inaccurate depictions of all liberal accounts. "It is a commonplace amongst communitarians, socialists, and feminists alike that liberalism is to be rejected for its excessive 'individualism' or 'atomism', for ignoring the manifest ways in which we are 'embedded' or 'situated' in various social roles and communal relationships" (Kymlicka 1989, 9).[1] Kymlicka begins with the classical liberal view of the self as a self-determining being and reemphasizes that liberal theory is concerned with setting up the structures needed to secure equal concern and respect for each individual. Kymlicka argues that liberalism holds that "government treats people as equals, with equal concern and respect, by providing for each individual the liberties and resources needed to examine and act on these beliefs. This requirement forms the basis of contemporary liberal theories of justice." He adds, "[t]hat may not be what people think of as liberalism, for it has become part of the accepted wisdom that liberalism involves abstract individualism and scepticism about the good" (Kymlicka 1989, 13).

Kymlicka answers the individualist charge by arguing that liberals focus on formulating conditions required for treating people with equal concern and respect and that this makes social conditions relevant to an account of what individuals need to flourish. There are two questions that I want to raise in connection with Kymlicka's response to the charge of individualism. First, in admitting that he is concerned with defending modern liberalism as exemplified "from J. S. Mill through to Rawls and Dworkin" (Kymlicka 1989, 10), Kymlicka leaves open the question of whether the charge of individualism applies to a purely formal conception of equality. The second and more important question is whether in acknowledging the relevance of social conditions, as Kymlicka claims, liberal substantive theorists still continue to ignore particular social relations that result in inequalities for many people.

With respect to the first question, one of the clearest statements that justifies applying the charge of individualism is given in Hobbes's social contract, which emerges out of a state of nature, where individuals, like "mushrooms, come to full maturity, without all kind of engagement to each other" (Hobbes 1941, 109). We have already identified aspects of Nozick's account that are similarly problematic. Nozick grounds his account of the inviolability of individual rights in a pre-social, state-of-nature view of individuals as separate, distinct, and free. Libertarians defend individual rights of noninterference by arguing that individuals can best exercise self-determining capacities when they are left on their own and not interfered with by the state or other individuals. In addition, we discovered that in defending the fans' choice to pay Chamberlain to play, Nozick expresses no concern for or awareness of how these actions will affect families, friends, or the society in general. Discussions of attachments and relationships are absent. They are not considered to be relevant to political theory and appear to be hindrances to self-determination. At the very least, all of this constitutes evidence that formal equality theorists do not consider relationships to be relevant to an account of whether equality obtains. The one relationship that is discussed, between the individual and the state, is one in which noninterference is advocated.

I would agree with Kymlicka that a defense of positive rights speaks against viewing liberal substantive theory as assuming a conception of the self as individualistic, atomistic, and competitive. Sypnowich, for example, ties her defense of positive rights to the rejection of any notion of people as isolated and distinct entities. Many people do not flourish or realize their full potential in a state that only guarantees rights to noninterference. When we acknowledge the moral significance of this, the move is made from duties of noninterference to responsibilities to others. "If we accept that human rights emerge in society, and not in a state of nature, as claimed by liberal theorists such as Locke and Nozick, then the idea of the human personality thriving in 'negative' conditions, without interference, must be rejected. Once we abandon 'atomistic' conceptions of the person, we are forced to include in the catalogue rights which require that the community actively participates in the development of the person, by providing, for example, education or health care" (Sypnowich 1990, 111).

Showing that liberal substantive theorists do not fall prey to the charge of individualism in the same way that formal theorists do does not answer the first question completely, as we will discover in the next section's discussion of the communitarian critique of Rawls. In the end, however, I think we can avoid engaging in the project of determining precisely what conception of the self underlies liberalism or which liberals fall prey to the charge of excessive individualism. When a relational approach is made the starting point for theorizing about the structures needed to secure equal concern and respect, certain inadequacies of liberal theory outside of these charges begin to manifest themselves. We can move straight to the second question about the aspects of social relations that liberals tend to ignore and the particular inequalities generated in and through these relationships. Whereas liberals have tended to begin with the individual and then move outward to draw conclusions about others, a relational approach begins with the individual in social practices and political contexts. At least on the surface, so too does communitarianism. If we examine communitarianism, we can discover just why metaphysical issues about personhood are relevant to moral and political theory.

Communitarian Objections: Rawls's Self Is Metaphysically Incoherent

In the most famous communitarian indictment of Rawls's theory of justice to date, Sandel argues that the self in the original position, a self unembedded, unsituated, and detached from the interests, projects, and goals that form its conception of the good, is a metaphysical incoherence. I have already noted that Rawls emphasizes that the original position is a hypothetical device, one that allows us to engage in critical thinking about equality and justice. So it may appear that Sandel's case against Rawls rests on a misunderstanding of the original position as an actual contract taking place between real people of the sort Rawls describes. But Sandel's critique cannot be so easily dismissed. The communitarian critique had an impact on Rawls's own thinking and resulted in a reformulation of the scope of his theory of justice, though not, as we will discover in the next chapter, of the original position itself or the principles of justice that emerge. But more importantly for my purposes, in addition to providing a critique of the liberal self, Sandel provides a positive account of the importance of community to self-concepts and identity, a communitarian conception of the self that does not appear at first glance to be so very different from the conception of the relational self I want to advance.

In his critique of Rawls, Sandel argues that the self in the original position is "a subject *so* shorn of empirically-identifiable characteristics as to resemble once more the Kantian transcendent or disembodied subject Rawls resolved to avoid. It makes the individual inviolable only by making him invisible, and calls into question the dignity and autonomy this liberalism seeks above all to secure" (Sandel 1982, 95, his emphasis). Sandel rightly undermines an account of the self that suggests that we can easily detach ourselves from either our commitments or our community. He argues that there cannot be a self as devoid of characteristics as the one he thinks Rawls asks us to imagine in the original position. The relevant point is not whether there is such a self, but that this self is incapable of meaningful choice and action and cannot possibly be in a position to bargain for principles: "[b]argaining in *any* sense requires some difference in the interests or preferences or power or knowledge of the bargainers, but in the original position there are none" (Sandel 1982, 128, his emphasis). I have been arguing that difference is relevant and that we need knowledge of the perspectives of the disadvantaged in the original position for critical thinking about equality and justice. Sandel, however, takes the insight about what happens in the original position in a different direction.

Sandel argues that "once *all* individuating characteristics are excluded, the parties are not merely *similarly* situated (as persons in real life with similar life circumstances and certain overlapping interests), but *identically* situated" (Sandel 1982, 131, his emphasis). Sandel uses this description of the indistinguishability of selves in the original position to argue that Rawls ends up in the place he most wanted to avoid, the Utilitarian position of failing to "take seriously the distinction between persons" (Rawls 1971, 27). While it seems as though the critique rests so far on what people in the original position are like, Sandel's concerns are metaphysical ones about whether the self is too thick or too thin to generate principles of justice at all. Ultimately, Sandel waivers between interpreting the Rawlsian self as so thin that it cannot be said to "possess" anything, including equal moral worth, or as so thick that it possesses the attributes and worth of all the individuals in its community—the intersubjective conception of the self.[2] But what does this attack on the self in the original position mean for political theory?

Charles Taylor correctly points out that Sandel "tries to show

how the different models of the way we live together in society—atomist and holist—are linked with different understandings of self and identity: 'unencumbered' versus situated selves" (Taylor 1989, 160). Taylor adds that although Sandel's work "is a contribution to social ontology, which can be developed in a number of directions" (Taylor 1989, 160), Sandel does not advocate or develop a political theory. My concerns, by contrast, are precisely moral and political ones about whether the original position is what Rawls took it to be: a vantage point both impartial and adequate for critical thinking about equality and justice. To that end, the previous chapter demonstrates the inadequacy of the conditions Rawls placed on bargaining in the original position. Those conditions cannot foster genuine critical thinking about equality or provide adequate principles of justice. What I ended up with by way of a radically revised original position, however, would seem to be compatible with Sandel's positive account of the embeddedness of selves in communities.

Sandel's communitarian conception of the self is of a being whose ends and goals constitute his or her identity and are formed in and through communities. People are not detachable from their particular conception of the good or from their attachments to others in a community. Our interests, projects, and goals are constitutive of our self-concepts and identity, and we make choices as encumbered selves who are situated and embedded in the communities we are born into. But the key question in this description of the communitarian self is what Sandel means by "constitutive." In examining this question, Kymlicka captures what I take to be a central criticism of communitarianism.

Kymlicka points out that when it comes to explaining how communitarian selves make choices about interests, projects, and goals, Sandel waivers between a strong and a weak view of a self constituted by his or her community (Kymlicka 1989, 52–58). On the weak view, Sandel describes a partially constituted "voluntarist self" able to reflect on and question its interests, projects, and goals. "[T]o be capable of a more thoroughgoing reflection, we cannot be wholly unencumbered subjects of possession, individuated in advance and given prior to our ends, but must be subjects constituted in part by our central aspirations and attachments, always open, indeed vulnerable, to growth and transformation in the light of revised self-understandings" (Sandel 1982,

172).³ The partially constituted self has ends defined by the community, but can think about and pursue different ends. "As a self-interpreting being, I am able to reflect on my history and in this sense to distance myself from it" (Sandel 1982, 179).

On the strong view, by contrast, Sandel describes a radically constituted "cognitivist self,"⁴ a self who is fully constituted by the community he or she is born into, who merely discovers his or her role and acts accordingly. "[C]ommunity describes not just what they *have* as fellow citizens but also what they *are*, not a relationship they choose (as in a voluntary association) but an attachment they discover, not merely an attribute but a constituent of their identity. . . . [W]e might describe this strong view as the constitutive conception" (Sandel 1982, 150, his emphasis). On the strong view of a constitutive self, individuals are just the interests, projects, and goals shaped for them in a community and self-knowledge is discovering and interpreting the roles defined and determined by one's community.

Kymlicka argues that depending on which account Sandel favors, his communitarianism is either inconsistent with our firm conviction that we choose rather than discover our roles or compatible with liberalism. "The strong claim (that self-discovery replaces judgement) is implausible, and the weak claim (which allows a self constituted by its ends can none the less be reconstituted), while attractive fails to distinguish his position from the liberal view" (Kymlicka 1989, 56). Kymlicka argues that the strong view of fully and radically situated and embedded selves is implausible because it has no fit with our firm conviction that we do and can question, revise, challenge, and change the roles set out for us in communities. If Sandel adopts the weaker view, however, he no longer has an argument against the Rawlsian project. In other words, on the weaker view, we are back to what is common to all theories of equality: valuing an individual's capacity for self-determination, and theorizing about the conditions required for treating people with these capacities with equal concern and respect.

People do step back from the rules and practices in a community and question, challenge, and change structures that support inequalities. To this extent, accounts of individual freedom and agency are necessary. We learned that Rawls disagrees with libertarians who argue that freedom is enhanced when the state does not interfere in individual lives and merely protects negative rights to noninterference. Liberal substantive theorists like Rawls argue that justice requires substantive measures, a necessary but not sufficient one being a redistribution of wealth, so that all people, and not just those advantaged by natural talents and social position, have real freedom to pursue their conceptions of the good. But while Rawls takes us in the direction of realizing how differences result in unfair disadvantages and unequal opportunities, he does not take differences seriously enough and fails to recognize the effect and significance of differences as they are defined in and by oppressive relations. And even if on a voluntarist account Sandel captures an adequate conception of people as having their identities and projects shaped by communities, we will discover that communitarian accounts fall prey to the same charge of failing to recognize that oppressive relationships shape identities in ways that result in inequalities for the many people who are in them.

A Relational Critique of the Communitarian Social Self

Communitarian thinkers "urge an alternative philosophical anthropology, which sees the human being as socially constituted, living a life in a context of shared meanings and understandings, in reference to a culture, or as MacIntyre puts it, a tradition or narrative" (Sypnowich 1993b, 486). With its focus on embedded agents, communitarianism seems to offer a more accurate account than does liberalism of how people are shaped by the social practices and political contexts in which they live. Our norms, rules, beliefs, values, goals, and conceptions of the good are shaped in and through communities. Such factors as friends, family, ethnic origin, local community, and nation give shape and content to our commitments, self-concepts, attachments, and identities in ways that would appear to be highly relevant to an account of what is needed to ensure that all people are treated with equal concern and respect. But this is not the direction communitarians take.

Taylor points out that Sandel does not provide a political theory. True; but worse, the description of *communities* that he does provide is inaccurate and could not form the basis for any political theory. Sandel invokes a model of community that describes like-minded members connected by sentiments of benevolence, respect, and goodwill in a context of agreed-upon rules and practices. "[I]n so far as our constitutive self-understandings comprehend a wider subject than the individual alone, whether a family or tribe or city or class or nation or people, to this extent they define a community in the constitutive sense. And what marks such a community is not merely a spirit of benevolence, or the prevalence of communitarian values, or even certain 'shared final ends' alone, but a common vocabulary of discourse and a background of implicit practices and understandings" (Sandel 1982, 172–173). We learned in Chapter 2, however, that even in such a simple language as that of the builders, "a common vocabulary of discourse and a background of implicit practices and understandings" can and do result in exclusions, inequalities, and injustices. We also learned toward the end of the previous chapter that Cohen makes it a condition of community that all the people in it be able to ask for and assess justifications because some policies are merely assumed to reflect "shared final ends." Sandel cannot accommodate either the first point about what communities are like or the second point about people from within who are excluded from them.

Sandel's description of communities held together by common goals and values does not describe any actual community. The notion of shared final ends and of common understandings of the rules and practices is a myth, as Kymlicka points out in his damning indictment of communitarianism. "Sandel and Taylor say that there are shared ends that can serve as the basis for a politics of the common good which will be legitimate for all groups in society. But they give no examples of such ends—and surely part of the reason is that there are none. They say that these shared ends are to be found in our historical practices, but they do not mention that those practices were defined by a small section of society—propertied white men—to serve the interests of propertied white men. These practices are gender-coded, race-coded, and class-coded, even when women, blacks, and workers are legally allowed to participate in them" (Kymlicka 1990, 226–227).

An examination of the few examples that Sandel provides of cohesive and unified communities ruled by benevolence and an identity of interests highlights the inadequacy of both his descriptions and his endorsement of the preservation of such communities. Sandel assumes that families are held together by love and an identity of interests and that justice has no place in the family. "[T]he questions of what I get and what I am due do not loom large in the overall context of this way of life" (Sandel 1982, 33). But families are also places where abuse, exploitation, and oppression are present and where the perspectives of those subjected to this treatment are suppressed. Similar assumptions about cohesiveness and unity are at work when Sandel defends the shared community goal of censoring pornography "on the grounds that pornography offends its way of life" (Sandel 1984, 17). Some feminists justify censoring pornography not because it offends a way of life, but because it endorses images of women as mere sexual objects, images that affect our understanding of sexuality and personal relationships and perpetuate inequalities in both public and personal relations. The recognition of the significance of different experiences and perspectives is a major theme in this work. In the context of evaluating communitarianism, an account of perspectives reveals facts of pluralism rather than cohesiveness within communities.

Nancy Rosenblum takes pluralism, not unity and cohesiveness, to be a characteristic feature of our communities and is puzzled that this is not recognized by communitarians. "The tendency of communitarians and individualists to disregard pluralism is remarkable, since two current themes in political thought—methodological and moral contextualism, and propositions about the 'situated' or 'constituted' self—could reasonably be expected to draw attention to it as an inescapable reality. After all, the context of moral and political practices is, on any description, pluralist; on any account of personal development, the self is formed from an array of relations in diverse spheres" (Rosenblum 1989, 208). The observation that pluralism is an inescapable reality rules out the communitarian description of cohesive communities as a model for moral or political theory, a model that does not permit the assessment of community practices and values that result in injustices for some members.

Sandel takes communities characterized by justice to be hindrances to moral development. "Not egoists but strangers, sometimes benevolent, make for citizens of the deontological republic; justice finds its occasion because we cannot know each other, or our ends, well enough to govern by the common good alone" (Sandel 1982, 183). Even if it is possible to imagine fairly cohesive communities with an identity of interests, we still need to ask if justice is irrelevant in such communities. Without justice, the very differences among people that Sandel accuses Rawls of failing to take seriously are either repressed or can form justifications for unequal treatment. Moreover, without justice, conflicts, when they do occur, would be settled in the communitarian "cohesive" society by reference to established ends or goals identified as common or good, goals that may very well ignore the experiences and perspectives of some members.

Even if Taylor is right that Sandel's goal is not to develop a political theory, communitarians such as Alasdair MacIntyre do want to. MacIntyre says that his reason for writing *Whose Justice? Which Rationality?* was to determine which understandings and what traditions could serve as models of comprehensive and developed communities held together by a common good. In *After Virtue*, he provides a picture of community living in which we enter society as characters in a narrative, a narrative centered on a virtuous life lived in the roles set for us by tradition: "[w]e enter human society, that is, with one or more imputed characters—roles into which we have been drafted—and we have to learn what they are in order to be able to understand how others respond to us and how our responses to them are apt to be construed" (MacIntyre 1981, 201). But the tradition and history MacIntyre invokes are nostalgic pictures of past traditions and communities in which discrimination was overt and explicitly justified in the rules and practices.[5]

Communitarian claims that self-knowledge and agency consist in discovering and living an identity set by a community ignore the facts of actual communities structured by oppressive power relations and dominated by particular groups. The identities to be discovered and lived by members of some groups are roles created and defined by those with the power to name difference and to circumscribe and limit the activities of those so labeled. This is why the focus needs to be on relationships and not on either individuals or communities as such. An examination of relationships can reveal the norms that result in exclusionary social practices and the perspectives of those who are ignored and detrimentally affected by communal norms and practices.

A relational approach begins with specific communitarian insights such as "the broad metaphysical conception of the individual, self, or subject as constituted by its social relationships and communal ties" (Friedman 1993, 234). But these descriptions of people and communities are mere starting points. The communitarian complacency about the moral values held in and expounded by communities, its disregard for differences within communities, and its obliviousness to relations of power and oppression make it a poor ally for any theory of equality.[6] We can credit communitarians with outlining the importance of the background institutions, practices, and community rules to self-concepts and identities. The communitarian insight is to reveal that human growth and agency are given content and meaning in and through social relations in communities. Communitarians fail to recognize, however, that some members of communities are restricted, constricted, and powerless in personal relationships and in public relations with those in power. Here is where we need justice, but it needs to be a justice that takes relationships to be relevant to an assessment of inequalities and unequal treatment. Some would describe what is needed as "justice tempered by care," the kind of care found in the extensive literature that Gilligan's work on an ethic of care has generated.

The Framework for Gilligan's Research on Care

Before I launch into my own view of Gilligan, I need to lay some groundwork by summarizing how Gilligan's work is generally understood. Gilligan's main contribution is taken to be the evidence she uncovers for women's "different voice." Her research is generally understood as attempting to show that men and women think differently about morality and approach the solving of moral problems differently. Men tend to reason about moral issues by using a justice approach in which they stress the ability to formulate abstract rules and principles as the way to solve moral problems. Women, conversely, tend to reason about morality and moral problems by using an ethic of care orientation that centers on the importance of caring for others. Gilligan is viewed as grounding these tendencies in object-relations theory, which explains how mothers "experience their sons as a male opposite" and begin a process in which boys "in defining themselves as masculine, separate their mothers from themselves" (Gilligan 1982, 8). Girl infants, in contrast, have an early identification with mothers, and this is the source of the value they place on connecting to others and maintaining relationships. While men fear intimacy and connection, women fear separation and feel threatened by the breakdown of relationships.[7] The relational element in Gilligan has been understood as consisting of her observations that women's moral orientation is centered on remaining connected with others and on the value they place on maintaining relationships.

To be sure, all of these observations about men's and women's different reasoning capacities and orientations are in Gilligan's work. Amy's and Jake's different responses to the Heinz dilemma, the interviews with women in the process of making decisions about abortion, and the many interpretations of college students' thoughts on morality can all be said to highlight the different patterns of moral reasoning of men and women. This research takes up a large part of Gilligan's work and a considerable portion of the enormous literature on Gilligan focuses on her ideas about the ethic of care, her view of women as predominantly caring, and her tendency to essentialize and universalize women's experiences.[8]

These areas of her work continue to dominate the literature even though Gilligan explicitly says in her famous disclaimers that she does not intend to establish either a strong link between the ethic of care and women or an explanation of the origin of the different voice. What follows is the complete list of disclaimers: the different voice is "characterized not by gender but theme"; "the association is not absolute" and the difference is meant "to focus a problem of interpretation rather than to represent a generalization about either sex"; "no claims are made about the origins of the differences described"; and no claims are made about the distribution of the voices "in a wider population, across cultures, or through time" (Gilligan 1982, 2). Critics have rightly pointed out that Gilligan does not always live up to her own disclaimers. Many of these criticisms are important correctives to these aspects of her research, and I shall return to some of them later. However, there is more to the relational aspects of Gilligan's work than is revealed in her account of a different voice that values and cares about relationships.[9] To make this clear, I shall now reintroduce Amy and Jake, characters who helped to elucidate the significance of perspectives in Chapter 3 and who will turn out to play a central role in the project of connecting care and justice in Chapter 7.

Much of the discussion of what Amy and Jake say when they are asked if Heinz should steal the drug to save his wife's life focuses on what these responses illustrate about care and justice, whether care can form the base for a moral theory, and which approach to moral problems is prior, more appropriate, or more comprehensive. I have a different starting point. I want to take a passage in Gilligan's interpretation of Amy's response to the Heinz dilemma, where she discusses relationships in general, and then develop the underlying ideas in the sections that follow. We will discover that this starting point reveals much more about the care perspective than is generally thought. In this passage, Gilligan presents a very broad picture of the reach of relationships: "[p]erceiving relationships as primary rather than as derived from separation, considering the interdependence of people's lives, she envisions 'the way things are' and 'the way things should be' as a web of interconnection where 'everybody belongs to it and you all come from it' " (Gilligan 1982, 57).

Gilligan's brief description of interdependence and her awareness of the significance of relationships is fully compatible with the account of moral personhood that I sketched in Chapter 3. There, I presented moral personhood as an ongoing process that takes place in relationships in communities, a process in which self-concepts and identity involve all aspects of a person's life and are shaped in relationships of all kinds, of compassion, care, dependency, power, oppression, and interdependency. In the end, however, Gilligan fails to develop the full significance of what remain as mere references in her work to "a web of interconnection." When we apply the insights of the relational approach developed thus far, a more developed, complex, and comprehensive picture of the relational self as a social and political being than is revealed in Gilligan emerges. One of the things that picture will show is that the "voice" is not "different" in the sense that, whereas Amy is situated in relationships, Jake is not. Amy is telling us how it is for all of us. What is different about the "different voice" is that it grasps the significance of relationships in our lives.

The Ontological Significance of Relationships

Although Gilligan makes numerous references to the self as part of a "web," "network," or "world" of relationships (Gilligan 1982, 17; 29; 30; 32; 33; 49; 59; 62; 147; 167), the relationships she most often describes are dyadic and personal ones of two sorts: relationships that have been unequal historically, between husbands and wives, boyfriends and girlfriends; and relationships of dependency, between parent and child, caregiver and cared-for. Most of the women in Gilligan's studies talk about dyadic relationships with mothers, fathers, boyfriends, husbands, and children and rarely about their relationships in a broader context of relatives, friends, policy-makers, or role models in institutions. An adequate conception of the relational self, by contrast, needs to take seriously the whole context within which we interact and relate to others. Relationships are inescapable features of our lives. They have an impact on our thoughts and feelings and structure our identities in ways that are unavoidable and imperspicuous. Our identities are structured merely by being members of purposeful and interactive social contexts.

Feminists have made vital contributions to an account of the self as essentially relational. Caroline Whitbeck argues that all kinds of relationships are constitutive of self-concepts and identity. "The relation is not fundamentally dyadic at all, and is better expressed as a self-others relation, because relationships, past and present, realized and sought, are constitutive of the self, and so the actions of a person reflect the more- or less-successful attempt to respond to the whole configuration of relationships" (Whitbeck 1983, 62). We live our lives in relationships; relationships of support, care, nurturance, power, authority, powerlessness, oppression, equality, and inequality; relationships we value, take for granted, maintain, struggle in, and end. As Minow aptly puts it, "[t]he social-relations view assumes . . . that people live and talk in relationships and never exist outside of them. . . . People live and perceive the world within social relationships, and people use these relationships to construct and express both power and knowledge" (Minow 1990a, 111).

Being in relationships with others is fundamental to being a person. "One becomes a person in and through relationships with other people; being a person requires that one have a history of relationships with other people; and the realization of the self can be achieved only in and through relationships and practices" (Whitbeck 1983, 68). As Lorraine Code puts it, "[a] human being could not become a person, in any of the diverse senses of the term, were she or he *not* in 'second person' contact from earliest infancy" (Code 1991, 85, her emphasis). Code borrows the concept of "second persons" from Annette Baier. "A person, perhaps, is best seen as one who was long enough dependent upon other persons to acquire the essential arts of personhood. Persons essentially are *second* persons" (Baier 1985a, 84, her emphasis). There are several separate elements in this account of second persons, which, taken together, shape essential features of a relational conception of the self.

First, the second-person account rests on a basic and inescapable aspect of human lives: each of us starts off in relationships, in fact, in relationships of dependency. Second, the second-person account is a conception of *personhood*. Similar to the justification I gave for replacing Rawls's "moral personality" with "moral personhood" as the description of moral equals, the second-person account emphasizes that a person is shaped in and through interaction with others. Personhood captures the idea that being a person is an ongoing process, the "arts" of which are learned and developed in relationships. Lastly, persons come to know themselves and their interests only in and through relationships. Persons are relational beings in social contexts "whose creativity and moral integrity are both developed and realized in and through relationships and practices" (Whitbeck 1983, 52). We may grow out of initial relationships of dependency, but we remain in relationships of interdependency whose ongoing influence throughout our lives makes us who we are.

Relationships are ontologically significant to what it is to be a person and to be the person that one is. Being in relationships with others is ontologically significant in the sense that it is the background against which content is given to that which is of fundamental value to liberals, an individual's freedom to plan and manage a life. In relationships with others in a community of relationships content is given to such basic human capacities as pursuing, questioning, exploring, developing, and actualizing interests, projects, and goals. Each of us is engaged in a constant and continual process of conflict, discovery, change, and self-realization—all in the context of relationships.[10] The view of personhood as an ongoing process that shapes self-concepts and identity emerges from realizing the significance of persons engaged in interactions with others in a network of relationships.

A relational conception of the self implies neither that relationships are entirely constitutive of self-concepts and identity nor that all kinds of relationships have a similar impact on people. With respect to the first point, relationships are neither one-way nor uni-dimensional. Lives are planned and managed in the broader context of networks of relationships, and this adds complexity and multidimensionality to the notions of self-concepts, identity, and self-determination. As Ann Ferguson puts it, "conscious selfhood is an ongoing process in which both unique individual priorities and social constraints vie in limiting and defining one's self-identity" (Ferguson 1987, 350). With respect to the second point, while close personal relationships may well have a greater impact on self-concepts and identity, it is within the whole configuration of relationships that one questions, revises, and pursues one's interests, projects, and goals.[11] So while I am undoubtedly more affected by the grief I feel at the loss of a loved one than I am about the death of a stranger, it is precisely on those occasions when I am indifferent about the death of a stranger that I am likely to question the kind of person I am, or have become, that I could come to care so little. The questioning, evaluating, and readjustment of my beliefs and attitudes in the light of interactions and reactions to others make me the kind of person I am, try to be, or want to become.[12]

Perhaps the places where the impact of relationships on people's lives is most apparent are in early nurturing relationships. As Code points out, without them, children would not survive, let alone thrive. "Left on their own to develop autonomous self-sufficiency, protected from interference, human infants and children would simply not survive. So there is something to the contention that it makes a considerable difference to how one thinks about selfhood and moral agency if one takes into account the centrality of care, responsibility and trust in early childhood development" (Code 1987a, 367). Of course liberals would not deny Code's point that infants cannot survive on their own without interference, but just to acknowledge this is to miss the point of Code's description. Her point is that a different account of personhood and moral agency emerges when we focus on the "centrality of care, responsibility and trust" in people's lives and in human development. As I understand it, her point is also that care, responsibility, and trust are not just features of early childhood relationships, but extend and ought to extend into relationships of all kinds throughout our lives, a point sometimes missed in the literature on the ethic of care.

It does not follow from an acknowledgment of the importance of care in nurturing relationships that these relationships can or should be given "paradigmatic status" (Code 1987a, 367) in moral and political theory. And an absence of an account in political theory of caring for dependents does not imply that we should view these kinds of relationships as entirely constitutive of the self or every self, or that these relationships should be models for political citizenship, or that they form the whole basis of an account of either relationships or personhood. As these relationships exist in current social practices and political contexts, in fact, they should *not* form a model of caring human relations, at least not without a critical evaluation. We shall discover in the next section that it is precisely the lack of such evaluation that counts as a deficiency in some feminist accounts of the self and of the role of care.

Caroline Whitbeck takes the conception of the self that views relationships as primary to personhood to be part of a "feminist ontology." She identifies her project as attempting to describe the "new view of the person and of ethics" that thereby emerges (Whitbeck 1983, 51). In this section, I have sketched this "new view of the person." An essential feature of this account of a relational self is that persons are in a complex and ever-changing network of relationships. My goal is to show how this "new view of the person" should affect our thinking about what is needed to ensure equal concern and respect for all people. In other words, my objective is to draw out the new view of ethics that emerges from the new view of the person.

While we can note that the relational self makes rare appearances in traditional moral and political theory (Marx is one example), as I said earlier we need not determine once and for all which liberals and what liberal theory assumes an individualistic conception of the self. What we need to do is sketch a relational conception of the self that demonstrates the moral relevance of all kinds of relationships, and not only caring ones, to conceptions of equality and justice. To that end, the rest of this chapter will be taken up with two major tasks: elucidating care as an orientation by making a case for the need to critically analyze care understood merely as an activity and a moral response; and, connected with the first, clarifying the concept of care by disambiguating several senses of care that are at work in Gilligan and the literature on her and thereby giving care a greater role than has been conceived for it so far. Both tasks can be achieved by examining different kinds of relationships and the sort of care that is demanded of them.

An Expanded Network: Relations of Oppression and Power

In advocating a place for the care perspective in moral and political theory, many turn to those places where the role of care is most obvious—in relationships between caregivers and those they care for. Despite Whitbeck's generalized account of the significance of relationships to personal identity and self-images, for example, most of the examples she uses to illustrate her account of the relational self are of the mother–child relation. Moreover, she develops her account of the new view of ethics that emerges from the new view of the self by focusing on the nurturing activities present in mother–child relations (Whitbeck 1983, 51–69). Writers such as Ruddick (1984) and Noddings (1984) also use the mother–child relation as a model for developing moral and political theory, but many have taken their accounts to be more a valorization of traditional feminine virtues than a critical analysis of these kinds of relationships as they exist in current social practices and political contexts.[13] While I shall return to an examination of the positive aspects of Ruddick's account of care in Chapter 7, here I want to explore the need for a critical analysis of care.

Merely advocating care as modeled on early nurturing relationships fails to acknowledge the dark side of such relationships—the abuse suffered by children and the damaging effect on the self-images of women who become the self-less, self-sacrificing mothers they are told to be.[14] Noncaring relationships have an impact on self-concepts and are as constitutive of identity formation as caring relations are. Mother-child relationships are places of care in the sense of nurturance, affection, responsibility, and concern for another, but they are also places of physical and psychological abuse. Mothers do not always know or understand the separate needs and interests of those they nurture, and it remains the case that "no matter how strong their biological and psychological bonds, mothers and daughters are also separate individuals. They have neither the same selves nor the same interests" (Keller and Moglen 1987, 500). And yet, it is through these very relationships of dependency where children are "taken care of" that they acquire their separate identities, grow out of unequal relationships with parents, and enter into and form relationships with others; whether the care is good or bad.

Children need to be in caring relationships where self-realization and self-development are promoted and enhanced, but so do caregivers. Sypnowich points out that "[o]ne need not be an atomist to suggest that personal identity comes not just from the forces that constitute the self but from one's efforts to distance the self from such forces" (Sypnowich 1993b, 494). Mother-child relationships, far from being some form of ideal, may be places where caregivers crave and need privacy and separation, and where a child's total dependency puts a caregiver's separate interests, projects, and goals on hold. As Anita Allen notes, caregivers "have a special privacy interest in a solitude that affords them the possibility of the full development of their unique personalities" (Allen 1983, 244).[15] Caregivers need not, are not, and should not be entirely submerged in dependency relationships.

So far, I have paid attention to early nurturing relationships to argue that the care that is provided in them needs to be critically analyzed. There are two points to be made in connection with this. First, care in nurturing relationships cannot be analyzed in isolation from relationships in the broader social and political context within which they are situated. Nurturing relationships are nested in a network of relationships. Whether children are and can be nurtured properly so that they flourish as separate and unique human beings depends not only on the level of care that caregivers receive in other personal relationships but also on the level they receive in public relationships.[16] What we need is a critique of the social and political conditions that force or permit people who have the task of nurturing others to live and function in relationships of power, control, and oppression. Second, nurturing is not the only kind of care or the only kind of caring relationship. Nurturance in the sense of "taking care of" someone is one place where care happens and, significantly, it happens in an unequal relationship. Moreover, a focus on mother-child relationships limits not only the range of relationships in general but also the range of nurturing relationships. An example will serve to illustrate both points and show that public relationships affect personal relationships and the very capacity that people have to nurture children.

In a political context where same-sex relationships are not only not sanctioned by the state but are also viewed as deviant and immoral, it is not difficult to imagine some of the consequences for those who want to care for children in these relationships. It may not even be viewed as a viable option for many because there is no state-financed support or because of the real fear that the children will suffer discrimination. Those who decide to raise children may be detrimentally affected by tax and inheritance laws or workplace legislation designed for heterosexual couples and their families. Same-sex couples will need to worry about what kind of neighborhood they live in, what schools their children go to, and even what sorts of answers to questions about their lives their children will bring home. This brief discussion of one sort of relationship shows why we need to broaden our analysis from an examination of nurturing relationships between a mother and child to an examination of how relations of power, inequality, and oppression affect people, social relations, and even a society's capacity to provide care. While Gilligan describes personal relationships in addition to nurturing ones, the sort of critique I am proposing is missing in her rather limited analysis of even this broader range of relationships. If we are to provide a critical analysis of the effects of all sorts of relationships on people's lives and on care itself, we need to expand the network.

In uncovering the biases in theory that result in the devaluation of care in relationships, Gilligan argues that a moral orientation centered on relationships in human life "could lead to a changed understanding of human development and a more generative view of human life" (Gilligan 1982, 174). Yet, the different voice that Gilligan hears is one that is predominantly concerned about a failure of communication and is motivated by a desire to maintain relationships and a fear of separation, all with respect merely to personal relationships. In the process of describing the ethic of care, Gilligan has been understood as being mainly concerned with examining care as a viable moral orientation and advocating care as a valuable moral stance without questioning its construction or manifestation in current structures.[17] Claudia Card, for example, points out that "Gilligan's writings portray everyone as basically honest and of good-will" (Card 1991, 17) and wanting to improve communication.[18]

Perhaps in selecting the issue of abortion, Gilligan does not succeed in giving sufficient emphasis to the need to question care or to move beyond personal relationships of a particular sort. It is obvious that there are times when greater efforts to communicate and maintain relations are inappropriate or even misplaced, as issues other than abortion can illustrate. Imagine, as Michele Moody-Adams does, what women would say if they were asked not about moral decisions within personal and caring relationships, but about sexual harassment or sexual assault. These examples make us think differently about advocating care and the maintenance of relationships. In these contexts, it is more likely that the justice approach would prevail, an approach that emphasized the value of separation and of individual rights of noninterference (Moody-Adams 1991). I shall return to a discussion of this example in the context of exploring the connections between care and justice in Chapter 7, but here I want to examine care itself.

I do not think the problem with Gilligan's account is that she advocates care unquestioningly. She does, after all, defend the decisions of women in the abortion study who assess and then sever noncaring or self-sacrificing relationships with their boyfriends or husbands (note that all the relationships are heterosexual). In fact, we shall discover in the next section that Gilligan interprets these decisions as ones that demonstrate a developed understanding of care as a moral orientation. "Care" in the sense that Gilligan uses when she is describing women who have developed a critical perspective on care at stage three reasoning is appropriately described as "being concerned," or "feeling responsible for," or "having compassion," or "being sympathetic" and not as self-less and self-sacrificing "taking care of" others. The sense of care I consider Gilligan to be advocating might be captured if we shift from understanding the approach as one that cares to understanding it as one that reasons about care in a web of relationships. But there is much more to care as an orientation that is still missing in Gilligan.

The brief discussion of the examples of sexual assault and of same-sex relationships illustrates that the question of whether Gilligan is guilty of advocating care unquestioningly is subordinate to two other problems with her account of the ethic of care: she provides virtually no account of how relations of power and authority have implications for an understanding of care as a moral orientation, and she fails to grasp the significance of the multiple effects on self-concepts and identity of being in a network of relationships, a network of various kinds of ever-changing relationships. Both problems have their source in a general failure to place care into broader social practices and political contexts in which diverse people differentially affected by the structures of power interact in multiple ways in a variety of relationships.

In claiming that Gilligan fails to take account of the social practices and political contexts where care is given or withheld, we confront the now common objection that despite her disclaimers, Gilligan is guilty of universalizing women's experiences. Gilligan conducts interviews with mostly white, heterosexual, middle-class, educated women and tends to take these experiences as representative of all women's moral development and thinking. Even in the context of the abortion study, where Gilligan describes the women as "diverse in ethnic background and social class" (Gilligan 1982, 71), she makes no observations about how factors of race and class affect women's thinking. Yet, it is not difficult to realize that such factors are important, particularly in the American context where abortion is legal, but there is no universal health care. Without financial resources, the kind of weighing of options that Gilligan focuses on as representative of every woman's reasoning about abortion is a luxury that many women would not have.

We could imagine that things would be different again in a context where abortions are illegal or in a context like that in Canada where there is universal health care and no abortion law. In 1988, the Canadian Supreme Court struck down as unconstitutional the abortion law that required that decisions on abortion be made by a committee of three doctors in an accredited hospital. One of the issues examined by the justices in the Supreme Court decision was how this law had received different interpretations and unequal application in various regions in Canada. In those regions where people had strong moral objections to abortion, for example, hospitals just did not set up the required committee of three doctors. We can imagine that this would have an effect on how different women in different regions with different resources would think about the issue of abortion.[19]

These kinds of observations about how factors other than gender affect self-concepts and deliberations are absent in Gilligan. Her studies are fairly contained, and we do not find out, for example, how women might or would relate to servants, employees, service people, or street people. Even in the relationships she does describe, those between psychologists and research subjects, the role played by power and authority is not fully recognized by her.[20] The psychologist is in a position of authority, one that requires that he or she interpret and judge what research subjects say and do. Even Gilligan must do this and do it from her perspective as a white, middle-class, female academic. Amy and other women in her studies are presented as having enough confidence to "come to question whether what they have seen exists and whether what they know from their own experience is true" (Gilligan 1982, 49). In more extreme cases of differential power and authority, however, we can easily imagine that research subjects would not even have this level of confidence in their answers or that they might adopt a stance of compliance and cooperation when faced with blatant discrimination in the interview process. The effects of these kinds of relationships and interactions on self-concepts, identity, and ways of thinking about the world and others are missing in Gilligan.

Research subjects who are disabled or on welfare, for example, and who are dependent on the state for survival may be inclined to anticipate the desired answers and then to play along as a means of coping with structures that they rely on for their survival, but that systematically exclude them. Consider, for example, the significance of Gilligan's own position of authority and advantage in her interpretations of Betty's responses, one of the research subjects in the abortion study. Betty is "an adopted adolescent who had a history of repeated abortions, disorderly conduct, and reform school" (Gilligan 1982, 109). Gilligan tells us that Betty was referred to her study after being denied an abortion. She views Betty as "demonstrating life lived at the extreme" (Gilligan 1982, 109) and proceeds to disparage her lack of effort in obtaining contraception for herself at the same time as she reports Betty's state of poverty. Now consider an interpretation of the same interview process radically at odds with Gilligan's view of Betty as "illuminat[ing] the potential for change in a seemingly sparse life" (Gilligan 1982, 109): "Gilligan is incensed with Betty's 'preoccupation with her own needs and her struggle to ensure her own survival in a world perceived as exploitative and threatening, a world in which she experiences herself as uncared for and alone.' After saying the right things to Gilligan, Betty gets her abortion. What Gilligan sees *and approves* as a change in reasoning, Betty might well see as empowerment through manipulation: 'I feel like I can change a lot of things that I thought before I would never be able to change.' In this instance, Betty has learned to speak Gilligan's discourse, but Gilligan has not learned Betty's" (Code et al. 1991, 18, their emphasis).

The example shows that stereotypes, perceptions, self-concepts, and identities are created around differences other than gender and these other factors have a differential impact on members of groups who are other than white, middle-class women.[21] Many critics are justifiably critical of the tendency in feminist theory to take the experiences of white, middle-class women as representative of the experiences of all women.[22] In much of her work, bell hooks describes the effects of factors outside of sex, while maintaining an account of common features of oppression around which members of oppressed groups can organize to change oppressive structures.[23] Her account provides a needed corrective to some of Gilligan's own tendencies (despite her disclaimers) to speak as though there is only one other kind of "voice," the "voice" socialized by gender. I would add to this call for examining multiple factors, the various intersections of them, and their effects on individual lives, the need to examine the diverse ways these factors differentially shape public relationships of all sorts; those between members of specific oppressed groups and the state, or the medical profession, or bank managers, or school teachers, or business people, and so on.

Feminist critiques of the multiplicity of factors of oppression are valid and important, but they need not result in a rejection of Gilligan's core insight about the importance of thinking about people in relationships. Rather, they call for a greater sensitivity to the social construction of difference, a greater awareness of the particularity of kinds of relationships, and a specification of different social and political contexts within which unequal and damaging relationships are formed. These elements parallel the features that I have been referring to as relational insights about language and about people, a dynamic whole of interconnected and interrelated relationships.

The more robust conception of the relational self as embedded in a complex and ever-changing network of relationships gives us a base to analyze how relationships can be both positive and negative, conducive and damaging, to self-concepts and growth. Such analyses are necessary for showing how individuals and their interests, projects, and goals can be totally subsumed by and consumed in relationships of dominance, dependence, power, and control.[24] A critical analysis of the effects of relationships on self-concepts and perceptions of difference raises questions about the political implications of relationships of inclusion-exclusion, power-powerlessness, and oppressor-oppressed. When self-concepts and identities are constructed in these kinds of relationships, issues of restrictions on freedom and opportunity emerge and the move is made to issues of justice.

We now have a much richer account of the relational self than is provided in Gilligan's descriptions of people functioning mostly in personal relationships. I used Gilligan's research as a starting point, but then expanded the network of relationships and showed the multiplicity of ways in which relationships can be oppressive, discriminatory, and damaging to the freedom and flourishing of some members of communities. Examining the kinds of relationships that the excluded and powerless are in and placing these relationships in the context of oppressive structures now raises the need to reevaluate an ethic of care understood merely in terms of concern, sympathy, and responsibility for others. We need to bring to the surface another aspect of care as an orientation, one that can be extracted from a discussion of the network of relationships that the marginalized, powerless, and oppressed are in and then developed through an examination of their perspectives. In the process, we shall explore answers to a question about perspectives raised by Putnam in the previous chapter. Does taking perspectives seriously inevitably lead down the slippery slope to considering the perspective of each and every person?

Generalizing the Care Perspective's "Concrete Other"

In an insightful article called "The Liberation of Caring: A Different Voice for Gilligan's 'Different Voice,' " Bill Puka suggests that Gilligan is talking less about an equally viable and valuable moral orientation that women happen to prefer than about the effects of discrimination on women and the strategies they adopt for coping with oppression. He reinterprets Gilligan's three levels in an ethic of care as different ways that women respond and orient themselves to the structures that exclude them. What Gilligan interprets as an approach that responds to the breakdown of personal relationships, Puka interprets as women's reactions to a general condition of oppression. To understand the force of Puka's critique of Gilligan, we need a brief outline of the stages in Gilligan's ethic of care and Puka's reinterpretation of them. Note, however, that I shall not discuss the dissimilarities and will deal only briefly with the similarities between Gilligan's and Puka's descriptions of the levels of care. I am interested in Puka's basic idea that women are responding to their oppression and want to examine and extend the implications of this insight for care as an orientation relevant to issues of justice.

Gilligan's description of the first stage as one of selfishness, "an initial focus on caring for the self in order to ensure survival" (Gilligan 1982, 74), is reinterpreted by Puka as women adopting a stance of protection against harm to ensure "psychological survival in the face of ongoing domination through strategies of self-protection and self-concern" (Puka 1990, 223). Gilligan describes the second stage as emerging from a transition phase in which the first stage comes to be perceived as selfish and a response of selflessness in which "the good is equated with caring for others" (Gilligan 1982, 74) is embraced. Puka reinterprets this second stage as one in which women adopt a stance of accommodation as a way of overcoming their "ongoing powerlessness." At this level, women gain a sense of fulfilment and self-esteem by achieving competency in playing the roles that are assigned to them by those in power.

Gilligan describes third stage moral reasoning as a resolution of the tension between the first two stages in terms of a focus "on the dynamics of relationships" (Gilligan 1982, 74). Stage three reasoning exhibits an awareness that the self and other are differentiated and equal and an understanding that the needs and interests of the self count too and ought to be respected within relationships. The third and final stage is reinterpreted in Puka's scheme as women responding to oppression by embracing the "competencies of those oppressed roles one cannot avoid" and recognizing their different perspective as a "source of evolving strength and pride" (Puka 1990, 223). At stage three, a balance is achieved between the awareness that the needs, expectations, and demands of others have structured self-concepts and identities and the knowledge that this difference ought to be treated with equal concern and respect.

Disappointingly and perhaps surprisingly, Puka views his analysis as merely providing a framework with which to *describe* the phenomena of women's oppression. He takes his generalized account of women's strategies for coping with oppression to be a reason to reject care as a viable orientation and argues that his model of the care orientation is a cognitive developmental explanatory theory, not a political one. But this will not do for two reasons. First, Puka's rejection of care depends on an understanding of it as caring for oppressors in the sense of being concerned about or feeling responsibility toward them. Obviously, if this is how care is understood in a context of examining women's responses to oppression, care needs to be questioned. But we need to disentangle this notion of care from what is going on in the important case that Puka describes, a case that not only reveals much more about the care perspective than he thinks, but one that can also help to articulate a feature of the ethic of care that is highly relevant to political theory.

The second reason connects with a point made in connection with Hacking's account of two vectors of influence, the naming and defining from above and the "pressing from below." In Chapter 2, I argued that it will not do to separate out and ignore the moral and political implications of the model of two vectors because moral and political consequences flow from the naming and defining and structure relationships between oppressors and those who are oppressed. This argument is all the more relevant in the context of Puka's depiction of care as women reacting to their oppressors. In describing the three levels, his account allows that the "pressing from below" happens in various social and political contexts of women's oppression and that the severity of the oppression determines possible responses. Surely, this not only makes it possible to examine the interactive relationships between women and their oppressors, but it calls for a critical analysis of the social practices and political contexts that create and maintain these kinds of relationships. It also reiterates the need to reexamine care understood only in terms of an approach of concern for or responsibility toward others. We now move beyond an analysis of both care and relationships in terms of either women or women's oppression.

In expanding the network of relationships beyond those considered in current work on care ethics, we realize that differences such as race, class, disability, and sexual orientation have multilayered impacts on self-concepts and identity, affect life plans and opportunities in a variety of ways, and result in different sorts of inequalities in freedom, capacities, needs, and opportunities. But once we acknowledge the kinds of relationships that are perpetuated in oppressive structures and the multiplicity of ways in which these relationships can be oppressive, discriminatory, and damaging to self-concepts and identity and to individual freedom and flourishing, two things become apparent. First, an ethic of care needs to be dissociated from close or exclusive ties to women, their personal relationships, and their condition of oppression. Second, we need to develop the aspect of an ethic of care that is distinct from *concern* or *feeling responsible* for others. With respect to the first point, Puka suggests but does not develop the idea that his account of care in terms of women's coping strategies can be applied to oppressed groups in general when he writes, "[c]are levels bear a strong resemblance to patterns of attitudinal assimilation and accommodation commonly observed among poor and oppressed groups, or in oppressive situational contexts" (Puka 1990, 223).

When we put to use the suggestion that care is linked to all oppressed groups, we address some of the shortcomings of Gilligan's failure to live up to her own disclaimers and then begin the task of reconceiving care. With respect to the disclaimers, the suggestion that factors other than gender better explain who adopts the care perspective corresponds more closely to recent research. Second, it avoids the tendency of assuming a point of view from which to generalize about all women.[25] Third, it undermines object-relations theory as the sole explanation for or source of the different voice.[26] Because my concern is with showing the significance of all kinds of relationships to equality theory, I shall briefly summarize some of the results of research mentioned in the first point: the connection between care and oppressed groups, a connection to which a number of critics have drawn our attention in recent literature on the ethic of care.

Joan Tronto argues that the bias of which Gilligan is guilty is linking care to women. "[T]he differences Gilligan found between men and women may also describe the differences between working and middle class, white and ethnic minorities, and that a gender difference may not be prominent among other groups in the population besides the relatively privileged people who have constituted Gilligan's samples" (Tronto 1993, 82; Tronto 1987, 243–244). Patricia Hill Collins argues for the resemblance between female and black characteristics (Collins 1990, 206–207). Sandra Harding draws out the parallels between African moral thinking and an ethic of care (Harding 1987a, 296–315).[27] Carol Stack's studies of African Americans in the rural south "suggest that under conditions of economic deprivation there is a convergence between women and men in their construction of themselves in relationship to others. . . . [B]lack women's and men's contextualization of morality and the meaning of social ties [is] a cultural alternative to Gilligan's model of moral development, with a different configuration of gender differences and similarities" (Stack 1986, 322–323).

Finally, in a rather nice description, Susan Sherwin draws together the results of this research. "The dichotomy of values that Gilligan identifies between men and women is paralleled by a dichotomy between Europeans and formerly colonized peoples. Whatever positive value these common traits may hold, the virtues to which women have been shown to aspire seem to be virtues of subordination. Further, the African data reveal that the perspective that Gilligan associates with men is actually held only by some men, specifically those of European descent" (Sherwin

1992, 50). Once we tie care to an orientation adopted by oppressed groups in general, it is difficult to limit the understanding
of an ethic of care to "taking care of" or "being concerned
about" or "feeling responsible for others." Care is more appropriately described as an "orientation to other," a perspective that
emerges in structures of power when those who are oppressed are
forced to situate themselves in relation to their oppressors.

The concept of orientation to other begins from a simple descriptive point that those who are in relationships of oppression,
at the level of both the personal and political, have to situate
themselves in relation to those in power. As a descriptive device,
the notion of orientation to other explains that women, for example, care about relationships because they need to care that they
and those they care about will be cared for. Sherwin provides an
explanation for why women are other oriented. "Within dominance relations, those who are assigned the subordinate position,
that is, those with less power, have special reason to be sensitive
to the emotional pulse of others, to see things in relational terms,
to be pleasing and compliant. Thus the nurturing and caring at
which women excel are, among other things, the survival skills of
an oppressed group that lives in close contact with its oppressors"
(Sherwin 1992, 50).[28]

The notion of orientation to other captures a feature of the care
perspective that needs to be acknowledged: those who adopt the
care perspective need not and in many contexts should not be
caring or concerned; particularly about their oppressors. The orientation I am describing has more to do with an awareness of
others and describes those who pay attention to others because
they are in relationships with powerful others and they and those
they care for are detrimentally affected by those relationships. The
notion of orientation to other is not intended to replace or exclude care in either sense of taking care of or nurturing someone
or of being concerned for others. Rather, the notion of orientation to other shifts the focus away from care in and of itself and
onto power relationships, the contexts within which care functions. It moves us from moral responses in personal relationships
to relations of inequality, power, and oppression as they exist in
social practices and political contexts and affect all sorts of care—
including the care or lack thereof that policy-makers provide for

those who suffer oppression in different ways and on various fronts.

Expanding the ethic of care to describe aspects of awareness of and paying attention to others in contexts of oppression has several consequences, all of which help to highlight features of care conceived as an orientation to other: it results in a greater sensitivity to the social construction of difference, it creates a greater awareness of the particularity of kinds of relationships, and it provides a critical perspective on the social and political contexts within which unequal and damaging relationships are formed and perpetuated. Assembling these insights underlying the orientation to other also permits us to examine the perspectives that members of oppressed groups have on the structures that create and maintain oppressive relations. By turning to another criticism of Puka's analysis by Joan Tronto, we can reintroduce the important idea of the significance of perspectives for an analysis of equality.

Tronto argues that Puka fails to perceive his model as anything but a descriptive account of women who respond in different ways to a condition of oppression because he assumes a certain perspective. "The notion that an ethic of care is nothing but a response to subordination makes some sense if the ethic is viewed from the standpoint of the powerful. It also makes sense if the relatively powerless conceive of what they do from the standpoint of the powerful" (Tronto 1993, 89). Tronto suggests that Puka describes oppression and makes judgments about the (in)effectiveness of women's responses to oppression from a particular perspective and that things are different from the perspective of those actually "pressing from below" and aware of the impact of their actions on their oppressors.

If judgments about the actions, beliefs, and commitments of members of oppressed groups were suspended in favor of really learning what things are like from these perspectives, we could better understand what would be needed to change oppressive conditions and structures. If we are to realize the full significance of an idea central to the orientation to other, that those who are oppressed need to respond to those in power, then we must not only limit our examination to how those responses are received by those in power. We also need to take seriously the possibility that those responses are valid and valuable ways of being in their own right. Perspectives, we shall discover, are relevant to an understanding of the ethic of care as an orientation that can be both a basic awareness of and a concern for others or either one of these by itself. I have already argued for the central role of perspectives in an analysis of the inequalities generated by oppressive relationships. With a clearer idea of those perspectives in the outline of the orientation to other, let us now examine briefly the interactive dimensions of these relationships in the social practices and political contexts in which they are situated, to uncover their potential for changing oppressive structures.

Political Implications of an Orientation to Other

Unlike communitarianism, relational theory merely *starts* from descriptive facts about people in communities. It advocates the evaluation of oppressive relations and employs the interactions between oppressors and those who are oppressed as political strategies for challenging and changing oppressive structures. Political issues of exclusion and of lack of power and authority emerge when we view those who are oppressed as necessarily in relation with and needing to respond to the discourse and actions of the dominant and powerful. I used this basic feature of the orientation to other, that those who are oppressed need to react to and interact with the dominant and powerful, to argue that the care orientation is also about the oppressed person's need to be aware of relationships of all kinds and about the impact of their interactions with the dominant and powerful. Those who are in relationships of oppression need to be aware of the dominant discourse, the social practices, and the political context within which their speech and actions are interpreted and judged. They need to notice and be sensitive to the effects of their struggle and resistance on the dominant and powerful. They need to make decisions about whether and what sorts of change and challenge will be possible by being aware of and assessing the particular social practices and political conditions in which they are situated.

We can now better explain what is only implicit in the Gilligan and Puka account of the levels of care. In social and political contexts of entrenched and intransigent oppression, oppressed groups may be forced to adopt the coping strategies in the first two levels of mere survival and of assuming the roles assigned to them. Such mechanisms of survival are forced on those whose perceived inferiority is backed by rules and laws that specify unequal treatment for unequals. Laws of apartheid backed by strict punishment for violations, for example, make successful challenge and struggle difficult, if not impossible. While we no longer accept that equality can mean unequal treatment for unequals, the lingering effects of entrenched and intransigent perceptions of difference as inferiority continue to make the survival strategies of the first two levels necessary means of interacting with oppressors in some personal relationships and in particular political contexts. Now apply this to the alternative interpretation offered of the relationship between Gilligan and the respondent Betty discussed earlier. Betty reacts to Gilligan and those who have the authority to decide her fate by saying and doing what she interprets as expected of her in order to cope with being pregnant and in poverty in that social and political context. In a society where women need funds to procure abortions and where child care is considered a private responsibility, this may be the only way for Betty to do what she needs to do to survive. But notice that we are not merely describing Betty's responses but pointing to the social practices and political contexts that make those responses necessary.

We can begin to discover how changes to political structures are implicated in accounts of the processes involved in "pressing from below" and in the interactions between those who are oppressed and the dominant and powerful. The concept of orientation to other captures the idea that oppressed groups have a particular vantage point that can contribute to a greater understanding of how structures maintain and perpetuate oppression. By beginning with the simple insight that "the more marginal we feel in the world, the more likely we are to glimpse a contrast between some people's perceptions of reality and our own" (Minow 1990a, 379), Minow and other feminists have argued that the world is perceived and structured differently from different perspectives and that these perspectives can provide vantage points for a better understanding of social relations.[29] The concept of orientation to other suggests that oppressed groups have particular perspectives that can contribute to a greater understanding of how social and legal structures maintain and perpetuate oppression. These are the perspectives that enter the dialogue about what justice requires and stop the slide Putnam worries about, a slide to considering each and every person's perspective.

bell hooks captures some of the complexity of perspectives and of relationships between those who are oppressed and those who have power and authority:

> Within any situation of colonization, of domination, the oppressed, the exploited develop various styles of relating, talking one way to one another, talking another way to those who have power to oppress and dominate, talking in a way that allows one to be understood by someone who does not know your way of speaking, your language. The struggle to end domination, the individual struggle to resist colonization, to move from object to subject, is expressed in the effort to establish the liberatory voice—that way of speaking that is no longer determined by one's status as object—as oppressed being. That way of speaking is characterized by opposition, by resistance. It demands that paradigms shift—that we learn to talk—to listen—to hear in a new way (hooks 1988, 15).

One of the strategies throughout has been to shift the focus to those who are categorized and judged as inferior as a way of exploring the validity and value of different perspectives. Relational insights about language and about people provide shifts in perspective that can help to unsettle fixed ways of thinking about social relations. Relational theory engages in the process of questioning the unstated points of reference underlying the familiar standards of comparison, drawing out hidden relations of power, and establishing the relevance of the perspective of the "different" as a way of reconceptualizing the meaning of a right to equal concern and respect. The notion of orientation to other plays an important role in giving us information about the kind of orientation adopted by members of oppressed groups and the value of the perspectives they have on the structures of power.

But in arguing that different perspectives are relevant, I want to clarify that it is not difference per se that needs to be validated and valued. In describing the creation of categories of difference and critically analyzing the devaluation of difference, I have been situating these activities of categorization and judgment in their social contexts because this makes certain inequalities and injustices apparent. Attention to commonalities in the experiences of those whose differences have mattered to life prospects can explain why all perspectives are not equally viable and valuable. Again the focus is on the inequalities that emerge from damaging and oppressive relations, relations that are structured when people are categorized into groups and treated as inferior and unequal. Perspectives that themselves create or perpetuate damaging and oppressive relationships would thus be rejected. This kind of account can explain why, for example, the Ku Klux Klan is not an oppressed group.[30]

Learning things from the perspective of oppressed groups has implications for unsettling social and political structures that support oppression. Because those who are oppressed need to be constantly aware of the particularities of the perspective of the dominant and powerful, they are engaged in ever-changing adjustments to their strategies of resistance. They need to be sensitive to the dominant discourse and the dimensions of legislation, policy, and social and economic conditions in order to advocate and implement effective strategies for changing oppressive structures. Moreover, their situatedness in a network of complex and ever-changing relationships suggests that the strategies available for politicizing difference are varied, controversial, and in a constant state of process and change. We shall return to some of these ideas about the ways in which the perspectives of oppressed groups can contribute to challenging social practices and changing oppressive conditions in the latter half of Chapter 7 and in Chapter 8.

Drawing Conclusions and Looking Ahead:
Interactive Relationships in Action

What has emerged through the relational critique of Gilligan's limited focus on dyadic and personal relationships is an expanded understanding of the range and reach of relationships. Relations of power, oppression, dominance, exploitation, authority, and justice form identities and self-concepts just as much as relations of dependency, benevolence, care, self-sacrifice, and friendship do. This chapter's examination of relationships tells us two things relevant to equality analysis: the norms, standards, and practices representing the perspective of the dominant and powerful set up relationships of inequality, relationships in which those who are oppressed and powerless need to respond to the discourse and actions of the dominant; and the perspectives of those who are in relationships of oppression, perspectives that reflect an orientation to other, are vantage points that can contribute to an understanding of what is needed to treat all people with equal concern and respect.

To grasp the relevance of relationships to equality analysis, we need to switch the focus from care in personal relationships to a responsiveness to others in a network of complex and ever-changing relationships. To draw out the implications for equality theory of these relational insights, we need to make use of the aspect of an orientation to other that has us examine interactions between oppressors and those who are oppressed. Notice that the need to examine these interactions also emerged in the call for a revised original position in which dialogue among multiple kinds of people about the effects of social practices and political conditions on freedom and opportunity takes place.

Once again, the example of the builders' community can serve to assemble insights and arguments: this time in the context of highlighting the relevance of a relational conception of the self for an account of what is needed to treat people with equal concern and respect. So far, the discussion shows that B is not only embedded in an interactive social context that has determined the activities deemed appropriate for someone like her; she has also had her identity and self-concepts structured around nonbuilding activities. Yet, we learned in Chapter 5 that liberal theory assumes that what is wrong with the treatment given to B is that she is either denied the opportunity to build or her "equal" opportunity to build is not sufficiently substantive or real. We also learned that this predominant tendency in equality theory to think in terms of removing barriers in the way of B's opportunity to build comes from thinking about her inequality from the perspective of the norm of male builder and the standard of building activities.

Now that I have drawn out the ontological significance of relationships and expanded the care perspective to an orientation to other, a variety of inequalities emerges. B's activities, relationships with others, identity, and place in a community are shaped by the social practices and political context in which she lives. B is nested in a network of relationships in which the particularities of her experiences and of her membership in various groups will affect her personal and public relationships. If we imagine not only that B's role in caring for children, say, is devalued, but that this role also determines for her a relationship of dependency on the state, we highlight the need for a critical analysis of what it means to take care of others not only at the level of personal relationships but also at the level of public relationships. If her dependency on the state results in a condition of poverty, then perceptions and judgments about this difference will circumscribe her activities and relationships in yet other ways.

We learned in the example of the Poverty Game that discovering the actual details of living on welfare also opens the door to examining questions of restricted access both to information and to the people who are assigned the task of "taking care of" hundreds of "similar cases." The relationships B is in circumscribe her activities, her needs, and her level of freedom for satisfying such basic preferences as what she and her children eat or where they live. The inequalities that become apparent when we focus on the network of relationships she is in are further and further removed from the standard liberal analysis of her inequality in terms of an unequal opportunity to build. The main insight from this chapter is that B has a vantage point on the structures that can give us information about and knowledge of the inequalities perpetuated by those structures. She has had to live her life needing to pay attention to her relationships with the state, welfare workers, those who perceive her as lazy, and so on. These relationships shape her day-to-day activities in ways that affect her and all those she takes care of or is concerned about. She will need conditions that allow her perspective to count in the determination of what justice requires.

What will enable B, and members of other oppressed groups, to perceive themselves as contributing and valuable members of a community? What social and political conditions will allow them to have their interests, projects, and goals treated with equal concern and respect? How will it be possible to use their insights into the structures that exclude and oppress people to change those structures? So far we have a framework for answering these questions in the argument that different perspectives are as potentially viable and valuable as those representing the taken-for-granted standards and norms of activity. This uncovering of the function of unstated standards of comparison moves the discussion away from assumptions about what is valuable activity and what needs to be done to accommodate and assimilate difference into current and existing structures. Thinking about difference from the perspective of the different brings equality discourse into the context of relations of power, authority, oppression, and disadvantage, relations that limit and restrict the freedom and opportunities of some people.

We will discover in the final two chapters that those who are oppressed achieve recognition of their difference as equally valuable and become effective agents for change when particular social and political conditions prevail: a basic constitutionally articulated commitment to the moral equality of all people and to a respect for human diversity and ways of being; mechanisms for testing current and proposed policies that enforce the giving of justifications and allow an assessment of them through dialogue among people with different points of view; an affirmative effort to include members of groups that are discriminated against within current positions of power and influence; and legislative support for various positive rights and measures beyond those that provide basic income. We shall discover in the next chapter that many liberal substantive equality theorists endorse at least some of these conditions, but do so in the context of expecting assimilation into current oppressive structures rather than promoting the inclusion of different perspectives as a way of changing those structures. Applying relational insights to liberal theory's limited and problematic treatment of difference can unveil fresh and interesting policy options.

7

❧ ❧ ❧

Resolving the Dilemma
of Difference: Intertwining Care
and Justice

Introduction

In Chapter 5, we learned that liberal theorists like Rawls fail
to consider the full significance of different perspectives and
thereby ignore certain inequalities experienced by those in
relations of power, oppression, and dependency, relationships we
then examined in Chapter 6 in the process of expanding an understanding of the care perspective. We shall discover in this
chapter that these failings show the limitations of policies offered
by liberal theory for dealing with those who are different. Martha
Minow uses the phrase "dilemma of difference" to describe the
dilemma created in a liberal framework that structures debates
about equality in terms of two policy options, either formal or
substantive equality of opportunity (Minow 1987; 1990a, 20–21;
25–39; 79–93).

We learned that formal equality theorists defend the removal
of rules and laws that prohibit some people from having equal
opportunities. They argue that equal treatment in the form of
individual liberty rights to noninterference satisfies the requirements for equality. Substantive equality theorists argue that the
commitment to equal concern and respect requires positive mea-

sures in the form of differential treatment for those whose unequal starting positions result in unfair disadvantages and unequal opportunities. Dworkin distinguishes the two conceptions by calling formal equality "the right to equal treatment" and substantive equality "the right to treatment as an equal" (Dworkin 1978, 227).[1] The distinction is particularly clear in the case of policies with respect to persons with disabilities.

The right to equal treatment concentrates on equality as sameness of treatment. In a world where able-bodied people are the norm, a person in a wheelchair, for example, has her right to equal treatment respected even if nothing is done to accommodate her difference. She is being given the same treatment as everyone else. The right to treatment as an equal, on the other hand, focuses on the differential effects her disability has on her opportunities. Treating her as though she is the same as the able-bodied person creates unequal opportunities since she cannot get into a building that has only stairs and may not be able to take notes in a class the "same" way able-bodied people can. Her formal equal right of access is without substance. Substantive equality theorists argue that respecting her right to treatment as an equal requires special measures to accommodate her difference, measures such as building ramps.

Minow argues that the two options of same treatment or different treatment create a dilemma because each risks further disadvantaging members of oppressed groups: "when does treating people differently emphasize their differences and stigmatize or hinder them on that basis? and when does treating people the same become insensitive to their difference and likely to stigmatize or hinder them on *that* basis? . . . I call this question 'the dilemma of difference' "(Minow 1990a, 20, her emphasis). When policies concerned with erasing the effects of historical facts of overt discrimination attempt to minimize the significance of difference by treating all people the same, then differences that really do matter are ignored. But highlighting difference and singling out members of groups for "special treatment" also risks perpetuating stereotypes associated with difference and having those identified as different and needing special treatment internalize messages about their difference as inferiority and inequality. We shall discover in Chapter 8 that arguments in the debate on affirmative action reflect both horns of this dilemma.

This chapter consists of two parts: the first examines the dilemma of difference and the second attempts to resolve it by exploring the intersections of care and justice. The chapter begins by using relational insights about language and people to reveal the underlying assumptions and structure of a framework that casts difference as a dilemma. When we discover that liberal options catch us in the dilemma by assuming the "solution" to difference is assimilation into current structures, new light is shed on attempts to come to grips with a dilemma that has been particularly vexing and problematic for feminist theory. Feminist arguments that attempt to validate different perspectives as valuable ways of structuring and being in the world run the risk of being misappropriated and misinterpreted within liberal theory. We need to understand this as a function of the framework and then apply the twofold strategy of evaluating feminist opposition to equality analysis and applying relational insights to liberal theory's treatment of difference, to highlight the connections between care and justice, connections that in turn open a way to resolving the dilemma of difference.

Setting the Stage: The Logic of the Sameness/ Difference Debate

A first step in solving the dilemma of difference is to understand it. By recalling the relational features of the language of equality discussed in Chapter 2, we realize that the logic of language creates the underlying structure that casts difference as a dilemma. Judgments of sameness and difference, equality and inequality, assume standards of comparison from which similarities and differences are identified. When we categorize people, we identify some descriptive feature or features that differentiate them from an established standard. We learned that hand in hand with the categorization of particular people as different go descriptions of appropriate activity for those who are identified as different from the norm. These aspects of language are so much a part of our stream of life that we assume and rarely question the norms that are already embedded in social practices and political contexts. By asking a simple question, Minow makes the standards apparent and unsettles their presumed fixity. "A reference point for comparison purposes is central to a notion of equality. Equality asks, equal compared with whom?" (Minow 1990a, 51). The notion that differences are defined relationally undermines the idea that there are essential differences that justify unequal treatment for all those who fit under these categories. It also opens the way to exploring the role that power plays in creating and maintaining the standards, rules, and practices that support the perception of differences as inferior.

A second crucial step in understanding the dilemma of difference is to reveal the logic underlying prescriptive statements of equality. Statements prescribing equality logically presuppose the existence of agreed-upon standards and rules for determining inequalities and judging injustices. Claims of inequality presume a standard of comparison from which one differs and assume a state of equality that one ought to have. Once these standards and rules for treatment are in place and familiar, a reasonable strategy is to deny difference and demand the same treatment as those in power. This strategy, however, leaves the norms in place and un-examined. "A notion of equality that demands disregarding a 'difference' calls for assimilation to an unstated norm. To strip away difference, then, is often to remove or ignore a feature distinguishing an individual from a presumed norm—such as that of a white, able-bodied, Christian man—but leaving that norm in place as the measure for equal treatment" (Minow 1990a, 51). The strategy of denying difference assumes the validity of the norms that are in place and vindicates the goal of assimilation into current structures.

Assimilation, as Young points out, "always implies coming into the game after it has already begun, after the rules and standards have already been set, and having to prove oneself according to those rules and standards. In the assimilationist strategy, the privileged groups implicitly define the standards according to which all will be measured" (Young 1990, 164). Once we understand the central role that unstated standards of comparison play in the perpetuation of difference as inequality and inferiority, we can begin to find a way out of the dilemma of difference. Shifting to the perspectives of those identified as different, a key strategy throughout, works to unsettle the idea that standards are universal and neutral. Questioning the objectivity and neutrality of standards can uncover the role of power and authority and give validity and value to the perspectives of those identified as different. The shift in focus to what things are like from the perspectives of the different allows us to understand the dilemma as a problem within the framework underlying the dilemma.

A different light is shed on the framework and on the policy options within that framework when we imagine how that framework appears from the perspective of those who are outside the norm. "Short of a total revolution, the relatively powerless have to persuade the powerful to allow them to enter into the circle of power that already exists. In trying to make such a persuasive case, the powerless have only two options available to them to try to change the distribution of power. The two options are: to claim that they should be admitted to the center of power because they are the same as those already there, or because they are different from those already there, but have something valuable to offer to those already there" (Tronto 1993, 15).

Difference becomes a dilemma in a framework that creates two options with the same end goal of assimilation into current valued structures. Either the different person denies the difference and performs the activity in the same way according to the same rules or the different person affirms the difference and is judged less capable or incompetent. Either the different person denies the difference and struggles in a world not built to accommodate the difference or the different person affirms the difference as grounds for positive measures and risks being perceived as undeserving and in need of special treatment. But "[w]hen participation is taken to imply assimilation the oppressed person is caught in an irresolvable dilemma: to participate means to accept and adopt an identity one is not, and to try to participate means to be reminded by oneself and others of the identity one is" (Young 1990, 164). The allowable options from both perspectives, of those in power and those without power, leave the structures in place and unexamined. This account of the underlying logic of the creation and maintenance of difference in social and political contexts of power provides a framework for examining alternative approaches to theorizing about difference. One way out of the dilemma will be to examine the structures that set up and perpetuate relationships of power, inequality, and oppression.

Joan Tronto uses the insights about the dichotomous choices of equality or inequality, inclusion or exclusion, power or powerlessness, and sameness or difference to make a point about how these choices make the feminist task of theorizing about the conditions for eliminating women's oppression inherently complex and difficult. "Thus, the great sameness/difference debate is inherent in feminist theory not because feminists are too dense to get beyond this issue, but because the strategic problem of trying to gain power from the margins necessitates the logic of sameness or difference in order to persuade those with power to share it. Once this framework for analysis is accepted, then there is no logical way to escape from the many dimensions of the difference dilemma. The outsiders, who must on some level accept the terms of the debate as they have been historically and theoretically constructed by those in the center of power, must choose from that starting point one of two positions on the question of difference" (Tronto 1993, 15). But feminists have begun the work of recasting the dilemma by uncovering the biases underlying the unstated standards of comparison, and they have been instrumental in questioning the framework within which the dilemma of difference is maintained. The solution, as Deborah Rhode suggests, is to recast the dilemma. "If women are to obtain adequate recognition of their distinctive experience, they must transcend its constraints. The difference dilemma cannot be resolved; it can only be recast" (Rhode 1989, 312–313). In the process of recasting the dilemma, however, feminist theory has also fallen prey to having its arguments in support of difference misinterpreted and misappropriated.

Abandoning the Strategy of Denying Difference

Historically, as we realized in Chapter 3's discussion of classical liberalism, the principle of equal concern and respect for all people has been enormously important for achieving the goal of eliminating unequal treatment based on morally irrelevant discriminations. Although the revolutionary implications were slow in being realized, the classical liberal ideal of equality created a forum allowing the formally excluded to argue for inclusion in the community of equal citizens it described and espoused. As Iris Young so aptly puts it, "[t]he ideal of universal humanity that denies natural differences has been a crucial historical development in the struggle against exclusion and status differentiation. It has made possible the assertion of the equal moral worth of all persons, and thus the right of all to participate and be included in all institutions and positions of power and privilege. The assimilationist ideal retains significant rhetorical power in the face of continued beliefs in the essentially different and inferior natures of women, Blacks, and other groups" (Young 1990, 159). The rhetorical power of being able to assert that one shares the same relevant features as those in the center makes it easy to sympathize with theorists who take difference theory as dangerously supportive of a status quo of unequal spheres of influence. Within the liberal framework, equal treatment is assumed unless and until morally relevant differences can be shown to justify unequal treatment. In this context, members of disadvantaged groups apply the logic of treating like cases alike, assert their fundamental similarity to those in power, and use this as a strategy for securing equal treatment. Liberalism's espousal of equal rights for all individuals has made possible such gains as the right to vote and to hold property and continues to provide arguments for entry into white male-dominated professions. It is easy to comprehend how arguments that appeal to the moral relevance of any differences fall prey to being misappropriated as justifications for unequal treatment or misinterpreted as expressions of one's freedom to choose different roles and activities.

Karen Offen describes the danger of misappropriation of arguments for women's differences. "It is no secret to those who study women's history that certain aspects of arguments grounded in women's special nature, physiological and psychological distinctiveness, the centrality of motherhood, and a sharp sexual division of labor within the family and society have in the past been co-opted by those hostile to women's emancipation to fuel arguments for their continued subordination" (Offen 1988, 154). The second danger of misinterpretation is evident in arguments by those who charge that theories such as Gilligan's that describe traditional caring roles "tend to perpetuate the status quo, to affirm the established division of labour, and to foreclose the possibility of radical transformation" (Broughton 1983, 130). This response to difference theory reflects a real fear that reclamations of difference are politically dangerous, a fear that was realized in practice in *EEOC v. Sears, Roebuck, & Co.*

The Equal Employment Opportunity Commission charged that Sears was guilty of discriminating against women because women were underrepresented in higher-status and higher-paying jobs at Sears. The lawyers for Sears argued that the statistics of underrepresentation did not reflect discriminatory hiring policies, but instead reflected women's free choices to make family and children their priority. Lawyers for Sears cited Gilligan's research in support of their argument that women just have different interests, projects, and goals and that these differences explained their underrepresentation in jobs that required more time and travel.[2] In other words, by using a libertarian-type defense of the right to choose without interference, Sears argued that female employees, who were merely choosing to avoid jobs that took them away from their families, ought to have their free choices respected. Women at Sears were being treated equally with men because they had the same right to compete for better jobs and to choose not to do so too. The case exemplifies the complexity of the arguments and the many dimensions that make difference a dilemma in a liberal framework.

The solution, as I take it, is not to abandon descriptions of difference because they are politically risky. As I have been illustrating throughout, one of the positive features of the relational approach I have been advancing is that it provides more coherent and robust descriptions of people in social contexts than do traditional accounts in liberal theory. These descriptions are at the base of what I have argued is necessary for critical thinking about equality and justice. What we need to do is to find our way out of the constraints of liberal conceptions that cast difference as a dilemma. I think a good starting place for understanding the major tensions around difference theory is to explore how and why work by Gilligan and other feminists that validates difference has generated a huge industry of criticism. With this understanding, we can then work to resolve the tensions by considering anew the value of the "different voice" in terms of its links to justice.

In an interesting examination of the phenomenon of the Gilligan debate, Kathy Davis provides an overview of the diverse and contradictory interpretations that Gilligan's work has generated and argues that "it is unlikely that any amount of explicitness on the part of Gilligan would enable her to control how her claims are put to use in a wider context of argumentation" (Davis 1992, 227). One such example of Gilligan's explicit claims about her intentions is the following: "I am well aware that reports of sex differences can be used to rationalize oppression, and I deplore any use of my work for this purpose" (Gilligan 1986b, 333). Davis's point is that finding a few passages in which Gilligan states her intentions or achievements will not reduce misunderstandings about her research or change the underlying fears of adopting a strategy that validates and values difference. The Gilligan debate has taken on a life of its own in a literature that draws in scientific, epistemological, political, philosophical, psychological, and sociological methodology and argument. At the same time as critics insist that their opposition to Gilligan is based on factual and scientific evidence that contradict her findings, critics belie their real concerns by stating their fears about the political implications of her research.[3] At the same time as some feminists admit a "shock of recognition" with respect to Gilligan's descriptions of difference,[4] they express worries about adopting strategies that validate difference.[5]

In the previous chapter, I purposely avoided the debates about statistical data regarding how many women actually adopt the care approach and about interpretations of whether what they say is truly indicative of care, and moved the discussion beyond both women and care. I shall continue to avoid the debates in this chapter by taking up a suggestion by Davis that a more productive engagement with the Gilligan debate is to explore "what it is about the project of a female morality of care that is so attractive or frightening to feminists at this particular juncture in history" (Davis 1992, 228). The project is frightening in a liberal framework that casts difference as a dilemma. Valuing difference raises legitimate fears because it is risky and politically dangerous in a context that has made disregarding difference the criterion for equal treatment.

But the feminist strategy of denying or ignoring difference, while perhaps politically expedient, is also fraught with difficulties and pitfalls, as Barbara Houston points out. "We need to consider what happens if we fail to address issues of sex difference and the gender relatedness of certain morally relevant characteristics or kinds of moral thinking. The landscape from this point of view is also bleak. If we simply ignore gender differences, we run the danger of continuing to induce in girls and women a state that Kathryn Morgan eloquently describes as 'moral madness.' Those who reject an account of difference are issuing what Louise Marcil-Lacoste has called an 'imperative of silence' on a description of sex differences" (Houston 1988, 183–184).[6] We need to be cognizant, as is Gilligan herself, of the dangers inherent in an approach that values difference, and then we need to take care that our theories more accurately reflect the complex construction of difference than Gilligan herself recognizes. The reworking of an ethic of care into an orientation to other, a basic awareness of relationships and the impact of them on people's lives, provides elements for accomplishing this task by allowing us to examine the relationships that are formed when difference is constructed as inequality and inferiority.

Differences, the Network of Relationships, and the Orientation to Other

It became clear in the previous chapter that Gilligan falls into generalizing about experiences shared by all women and fails to grasp the complexity of the interlocking factors of oppression and its multiple effects on self-concepts and identity. Difference is constructed as inequality and inferiority in various ways, has multilayered impacts on self-concepts and identity, and affects life plans and opportunities in diverse ways. In the critique of the ethic of care in Chapter 6, I expanded the network within which care exists and argued that an expanded network of relationships calls for a reevaluation of care as an orientation uniquely associated with women or relevant only in personal relationships or captured merely as a moral stance of concern for others. Care is better described as an orientation to other adopted by oppressed groups who need to be aware of the relationships they are in, both at the personal and the public levels. Once we acknowledge the significance of all sorts of relationships to identity and self-concepts and to the levels of freedom one has to satisfy needs and achieve capabilities, the resulting account of care provides a new perspective on justice and on what is needed to treat people with equal concern and respect.

The idea of orientation to other switches the focus from care in and of itself to relationships, of which relationships of care are but one kind. It explains that those who are oppressed and excluded from spheres of power and influence need to adopt stances and strategies in relation to those in power that are sensitive to the effects and implications of their relationships to the powerful. They need to know about the laws and decisions made in the public sphere because they are affected by them. Think again of the case of same-sex couples whose income, benefits, and life choices are affected by tax laws and workplace legislation. They also need to know about the implicit rules and practices that create and support perceptions of them as inferior or more suited to particular roles because such stereotypes limit the freedom to question, revise, and pursue interests, projects, and goals. Think again of the example of the women on welfare who are faced with specific hardships in a political structure that "deals" with their cases by limiting their interaction with welfare officials and by scrutinizing and questioning their daily activities. These social practices with respect to welfare recipients restrict their access to information, information that could allow them to change self-concepts and the structures that reflect and perpetuate stereotypes of them as lazy. Relationships with the law and with public officials affect the relationships people in each of the cases just discussed have elsewhere and even their ability to create, sustain, or end relationships.

I argued in Chapter 5 that treating all people with equal concern and respect requires empathy, a dialogic approach in which we learn the factual details of inequalities experienced by particular others and the effects of those inequalities on particular lives. Knowing the details and experiences of particular disadvantaged lives makes the injustices of these inequalities vivid. We obtain this knowledge of particular inequalities and injustices when we validate and value the perspectives of those who are oppressed. As the orientation to other illustrates, these perspectives are privileged vantage points for acquiring that knowledge. The poverty game illustrates the effects of a dialogic approach that takes perspectives seriously. By experiencing what women on welfare do (even if only imaginatively through a game) and learning from them what their lives are like, we confront stereotypes and reduce the potential for biased judgments about the lives of others. We learn how particular structures restrict one's capacity to meet basic needs and to make choices that improve life prospects for oneself and future generations. The elimination or reduction of bias in judgment actually requires not that we imagine our differences away, but that we attend to the detail of the particularities of people's lives as they live them.

The arguments emerging from these relational critiques of Gilligan's account of care and of liberal theories of equality can now be used to reexamine the connections between care and justice and to explore the possibility of bridging the gap between the two. But to do this, we need to place two reminders in front of us about care as reconceived in the previous chapter. First, orientation to other highlights care in the basic sense of being aware of and paying attention to others, and this is an orientation that members of oppressed groups need to adopt. Second, within and under this more general notion of the ethic of care is the specific sense of care as being concerned about and feeling responsibility for others. The two can be distinguished in the way I have just outlined, but they are also inextricably connected. Members of oppressed groups have valuable insights into what caring for and being concerned about others requires because they have had to be aware of how the actions of the powerful prohibit or diminish the provision of care for them and those they care for and about. Much of the discussion that follows builds from important feminist work on care as a concern for others. But the notion of orientation to other is always close at hand in the work I do to demonstrate the importance and significance of taking the perspectives of those who are in relationships of oppression into account.

Now let us turn to the task of building a bridge between care and justice. Once again, particular insights in Gilligan's work will serve as a springboard—this time in the context of exploring the connections between justice and care: "[m]y critics equate care with feelings, which they oppose to thought, and imagine caring as passive or confined to some separate sphere. I describe care and justice as two moral perspectives that organize both thinking and feelings and empower the self to take different kinds of action in public as well as private life. Thus, in contrast to the paralyzing image of the 'angel in the house,' I describe a critical ethical perspective that calls into question the traditional equation of care with self-sacrifice" (Gilligan 1986b, 326–327). Gilligan characterizes her work as providing a critical analysis of care. While we discovered that Gilligan falls far short of achieving what she intends or thinks her work achieves, this quotation does contain the germ of a very valuable insight: a connection between justice and care in the idea of a critical ethical perspective on inequalities. But to develop this idea, we first need to clarify and correct some misrepresentations of liberal conceptions of equality and justice common in both the feminist literature in general and Gilligan.

Misconceptions about Equality in Feminist Theory

Many feminists hold that equality is an inappropriate goal because the achievement of it will not eliminate particular aspects of women's oppression. Mary Hawkesworth provides an account of these feminist suspicions of, and hostility toward, equality as a goal. "The commitment to difference that grows out of a belief in women's specific moral endowments and the value of women's traditional activities typically is accompanied by a wariness of the notion of 'equality.' Fear of assimilation to alien principles and dread of being reduced to a level of tawdry 'sameness' generate suspicions about the uncritical pursuit of equality. Within the rhetoric of difference, women are forewarned that in unreflectively attempting to imitate men, they may well destroy the best in themselves" (Hawkesworth 1990, 115). Underlying Hawkesworth's description is the feminist critique of male norms and values assumed in current structures. The argument is that if the goal of equality means giving up differences and embracing the same values and aspirations as men, then the goal needs to be questioned and even abandoned. But it is too quick a move to associate equality with sameness of treatment or formal equality *simpliciter*. This understanding of equality and the concurrent association of formal equality with all liberal theory create the dichotomy that "has led some feminist legal theorists to reject the concept of equality and argue that women should demand something else—perhaps justice, perhaps special rights based on special needs. It has led others to reject the critique itself and continue to promote the similarity of women to men in the name of equality" (Littleton 1987, 1310).

There are a number of feminists who opt for rejecting the concept of equality in favor of what they think are more useful categories of analysis. Merle Thornton argues that as a goal for feminism, equality is "stretched beyond its usefulness" (Thornton 1986, 96) and supports instead a feminist analysis of liberation.[7] Elizabeth Gross argues that feminist theory has shifted from "a politics of equality to a politics of autonomy" (Gross 1986, 193). Although she acknowledges that "the aspiration towards an equality between men and women was nevertheless politically and historically necessary," she considers the goal of equality as merely a "prerequisite to the more far-reaching struggles directed towards female *autonomy*—that is, to women's right to political, social, economic and intellectual self-determination" (Gross 1986, 192–193, her emphasis).

Catharine MacKinnon argues that "sex equality" is a "contradiction in terms, something of an oxymoron" (MacKinnon 1987, 33) and proposes instead that policies be examined from the "standpoint of the subordination of women to men" (MacKinnon 1987, 43). She considers what she initially called the "inequality approach" (MacKinnon 1979, 102) and now refers to as the "dominance approach" to be an approach that focuses on issues of the distribution of power and of male supremacy rather than on the perpetual issue of whether women are the same as or different from men and deserve equal or unequal treatment. Ann Scales agrees with MacKinnon that "[l]aw must embrace a version of equality that focuses on the real issues—domination, disadvantage and disempowerment—instead of on the interminable and diseased issue of differences between the sexes" (Scales 1986, 1394). Most of these feminist analyses can be said to fit into what Karen Offen depicts as approaches supportive of "equity as distinct from equality" (Offen 1988, 139).

I am not prepared to jettison the language of equality. While I agree that concepts such as domination, autonomy, and disempowerment are useful categories of analysis, even these concepts, which are taken to be rejections of equality analysis, rely on the logic of equality discourse. The analyses rest on judgments of the different and unequal life prospects, amounts of power, and opportunities of women as compared with men. Appeals to the injustices of the various aspects of women's oppression assume agreements that women's *inequalities* in power, in autonomy, in opportunities, and so forth, are unjust. Moreover, for the purely strategic reason that working within the accepted discourse and structures to effect change is effective, the language of and arguments for equality and equal treatment should not be abandoned.[8] As Hawkesworth astutely remarks, "[a]t a moment when the preponderance of rational and moral argument sustains prescriptions for women's equality, it is a bit too cruel a conclusion and too reactionary a political agenda to accept that reason is impotent, that equality is impossible" (Hawkesworth 1989, 351).[9] One of the basic relational insights to be drawn from Chapter 2 is that judgments of equality and inequality are fundamental aspects of social relations. They are embedded in social practices and cannot be avoided.

Perhaps most fundamentally, I am not convinced that what these feminists are doing is rejecting equality in favor of something else, autonomy, say, or liberation. Rather, the dissatisfaction with equality theory has its source in a misrepresentation of all liberal theorists as supporting a purely formal conception of equality. In the next two sections, I shall provide a multilayered critique, one that both rejects and builds on aspects first of Gilligan and then of liberal theory. The goal in the next section is to use Gilligan's descriptions of justice and equality to illustrate her mischaracterization of all conceptions of equality as purely formal and thereby make room for exploring some of the connections between care and justice that Gilligan fails to recognize. The goal in the section after next is to use the notion of perspectives to show why justice needs care and vice versa. To that end, I shall again move the focus from care to relationships and thereby make room for elucidating how the perspectives of people in all sorts of oppressive relationships are needed for understanding what equal concern and respect requires.

Care As Justice and Justice As Care

One of Gilligan's respondents says of equality, " '[P]eople have real emotional needs to be attached to something and equality doesn't give you attachment. Equality fractures society and places on every person the burden of standing on his own two feet' " (Gilligan 1982, 167). We have encountered these sentiments before in the familiar depiction of liberal theory as excessively individualistic. Gilligan uses this understanding of equality to contrast justice and care. "The morality of rights is predicated on equality and centered on the understanding of fairness, while the ethic of responsibility relies on the concept of equity, the recognition of differences in need. While the ethic of rights is a manifestation of equal respect, balancing the claims of other and self, the ethic of responsibility rests on an understanding that gives rise to compassion and care" (Gilligan 1982, 164–165). "A recognition of differences in need" would seem to be exactly what underlies Rawls's fair equality of opportunity: it is not fair that differences such as race and class continue to result in disadvantages. That Gilligan associates equality with a purely formal conception of the right to equal treatment is most evident in her statement that "an ethic of justice proceeds from the premise of equality—that everyone should be treated the same" (Gilligan 1982, 174).[10] But not even Kohlberg's interpretation of justice in the Heinz dilemma fits the conception of equality as purely formal.[11]

For the formal equality theorist, the commitment to equal concern and respect is satisfied when individuals have equal liberty rights. Conflicts are adjudicated by determining unjust infringements on these rights of noninterference. Under Nozick's scheme, the druggist in the Heinz dilemma is entitled to do what he wants with the drug, provided that the conditions underlying "the principle of justice in acquisition and the principle of justice in transfer" are satisfied (Nozick 1974, 150–153). What this amounts to is that unless the drug was stolen by the druggist, the druggist, like Wilt Chamberlain, is entitled to whatever proceeds he determines for himself. Presumably, Nozick would condemn stealing the drug as an infringement of the druggist's inviolable rights. But Kohlberg's version of the Heinz dilemma does not fit this conception of equality.

In Kohlberg's account, Jake's "correct" moral reasoning in the Heinz dilemma reflects the ability to recognize that the positive right to life has priority over the negative right of noninterference with property. Heinz's wife is dying, and the choice to steal the drug is carrying out the positive duty to save the life of another.[12] In fact, there is a sense in which we understand the Heinz dilemma as a moral dilemma only on an ethic of care: a moral response is called for because caring relations such as those between Heinz and his wife are threatened. There is also a sense in which theories of justice already assume a realm of social relationships, as Nielsen points out when he writes, "it may not be an exaggeration to say that if there were not such caring, such concern with human suffering, the meeting of human needs and the establishing of certain human relationships, there would be little need for justice or for a concern for rights" (Nielsen 1987, 389). Realizing that the Kohlberg framework need not be viewed as supporting a libertarian strict adherence to negative rights of noninterference forces us to reevaluate Gilligan's understanding of the ethic of justice.

Gilligan describes the ethic of justice as a morality that "ties moral development to the understanding of rights and rules" (Gilligan 1982, 19). It differs from the ethic of care in that it is based "on the primacy and universality of individual rights" (Gilligan 1982, 21). One respondent, whom Gilligan takes to exemplify justice reasoning, answers the question about what morality is by saying, "I think it is recognizing the right of the individual, the rights of other individuals, not interfering with those rights" (Gilligan 1982, 19). In summary, Gilligan tends to interpret the justice approach in terms of the libertarian argument that respect for individuals requires merely negative rights of noninterference. But we know that justice can be dissociated from this libertarian interpretation of equality as the mere right to equal treatment.

Once it becomes clear that the justice approach is supportive of, or at least, not necessarily hostile to, an account of positive rights, the contrast between care as a responsibilities approach and justice as an individual rights approach is no longer tenable.[13] Gilligan distinguishes the care and justice perspectives in the concerns expressed by one woman she interprets as exemplifying the care perspective: "[T]hus while Kohlberg's subject worries about people interfering with each other's rights, this woman worries about 'the possibility of omission, of your not helping others when you could help them'" (Gilligan 1982, 21). At least on the surface, depicting care in terms of a responsibility to help others is not so obviously different from liberal substantive theory's support for positive measures as a recognition of different people's needs for different treatment in order to achieve equality. I say "on the surface" because there are still features that differentiate the care perspective from substantive justice, and these become apparent when we pay attention to the kinds of relationships that care understood in the broad sense of orientation to other high-lights. But before we examine these, it will be useful to assemble additional similarities between care and justice.

Contrary to Gilligan's own understanding of the tenets of equality as in deep opposition to care, an ethic of care and equal-ity theory have similar starting points. Construing responsibilities in the care approach as responsibilities to avoid harm and to re-spect others as moral equals makes it evident that the care Gilligan describes assumes two of the foundational principles of classical liberal theory. To depict care as a moral injunction to refrain from hurting others and to advocate a responsibility to "look out for each other" assumes the moral principle that each person deserves equal concern and respect. To adopt a stance of care and compas-sion is to be committed to treating people with equal concern and respect.[14] Moreover, in depicting care as "the recognition of differences in need" (Gilligan 1982, 164), Gilligan is applying the classical liberal precept that because we value self-determining ca-pacities, we ought to enhance people's unique capacities to man-age and pursue their goals and life plans. After all, Gilligan is critical of situations in which the self is totally consumed by and subsumed in self-less and self-sacrificing care.

As with liberals, so too with Gilligan, disagreement then re-volves around different accounts of what is needed to treat people who have a capacity for self-determination with equal concern and respect. We can now note that Gilligan and liberal substantive theorists agree that the purely formal right to equal treatment is not sufficient to meet the demands for equal concern and respect for others. So far, we have what might be described as a "caring justice." But will a substantive interpretation of equality and jus-tice address all of the concerns raised by a care perspective? We already know from our examination of justice that a recognition of the significance of difference called for radical revisions to the origi-nal position and the principles that emerge from it. I argued in Chapter 5 in the section entitled "Dialogue: Eliminating Bias and Achieving Impartiality," for principles that take on a hue different from classical liberal principles and interpretations of them in the liberal tradition. I then made the reformulated principles founda-tional to my account of what emerges from the revised original position: we ought to treat everyone with equal concern and re-spect, and we ought to respect human diversity and ways of being.

We also know that care as Gilligan depicts it does not live up to its full political potential. What is distinctive and positive about the care perspective becomes apparent when we again make relationships rather than care the focal point for theorizing about equality. As in the previous chapter, we do this in stages. We begin by moving away from thinking of care as an uncritical response to helping or taking care of others. We then elucidate and develop care in its orientation as concern for others. Finally, we determine what concern for others requires by examining the relationships members of oppressed groups are in and the perspectives they develop on social structures; care as an orientation to other. What we now need is a "just caring."[15]

In the previous chapter's critique of conceptions of the self in both liberal theory and care ethics, we learned that liberal theory has not said very much about the basic fact that people begin their lives in relationships of dependency, where needs are met and identities are formed. I noted that it would seem that these relationships are the clearest cases of just how significant relationships are to human lives. The point was meant to highlight the idea that different focal points result in different accounts of personhood and moral agency, but I also issued warnings about focusing exclusively on the relevance of these early nurturing relations for political theory. The absence of an account of nurturance in political theory does not imply that we should view these kinds of relationships as entirely constitutive of the self or every self, or that these relationships should be models for political citizenship, or that they form the whole basis of an account of either relationships or personhood. Nurturing relationships as they manifest themselves in current social practices and political contexts are not always models of caring human relations and, at the very least, they need to be subjected to critical analysis. Once we acknowledge that these nurturing relationships are themselves nested in a network of relationships, two things become apparent: it is the network that tells us how and whether particular social practices and political contexts allow early nurturing needs to be met, and these early relationships are not the only sorts of dependency relations.[16]

Beginning with the fundamental fact that at points throughout our lives we all require care, whether in the form of parental care, health care, educational care, or care in old age, allows us to acknowledge that most of us are neither totally dependent nor independent, but are more accurately described as interdependent.[17] In contrast to the liberal tendency to focus on what individuals need to be independent, autonomous beings, a focus on our interdependence in relationships shows how precarious our independence from others is and how inevitably intertwined the notions of autonomy and responsibility for others are, a responsibility evident when people depend on us in the most general sense of trusting in our concern for them.

A relational approach does not call for a rejection of liberal notions of autonomy and responsibility but a reconception of them in terms of the fundamental significance of all sorts of relationships.

> This approach shifts the focus from protection against others to structuring relationships so that they foster autonomy. Some of the most basic presuppositions about autonomy shift: dependence is no longer the antithesis of autonomy but a precondition in the relationship—between parent and child, student and teacher, state and citizen—which provide the security, education, nurturing, and support that make the development of autonomy possible. Further, autonomy is not a static quality that is simply achieved one day. It is a capacity that requires ongoing relationships that help it flourish; it can wither or thrive throughout one's adult life. Interdependence becomes the central fact of political life, not an issue to be shunted to the periphery (Nedelsky 1993, 8).

The notion of interdependence puts relationships in the foreground and begins to show how the focus and thrust of both justice and care theory changes when relationships of all sorts are the central concern.

The idea of the fundamental significance of human interdependence returns us to the arguments of the previous chapter about the ontological significance of all kinds of relationship to self-concepts and identity and the moral and political significance of being in a network of complex and ever-changing relationships. Relational insights about our embeddedness in a network of relationships provided a critique of justice in Chapter 5 that generated a requirement for dialogue among multiple people with diverse perspectives in order to determine what justice requires. Those relational insights also provided a critique of care in Chapter 6 that related care to the orientations adopted by members of oppressed groups who need to be aware of those in power and to pay attention to the effects of their relationships with them on their lives and the lives of those they care for and about. In both cases, attention turned to the significance of the perspectives of people in all sorts of relationships as a way of understanding what is needed for equality. Perspectives can reveal what is required for "just caring."

Gilligan explains a respondent's care perspective "as the capacity 'to understand what someone else is experiencing' as the prerequisite for moral response" (Gilligan 1982, 57). Sympathizing, having concern, being responsible, or feeling attached are all important aspects of caring about others and are central to the capacity to understand what someone else is experiencing, but a moral response to another person's needs requires more than this. It requires knowledge about that person as a distinct and unique being. It is not the sort of knowledge that issues objective and neutral judgments about people's needs or a mere sympathetic response to another's feelings. Knowing what our responsibilities to others are means being attentive to what particular persons say they need in order to pursue their individual interests, projects, and goals. These descriptions of care as a moral response to the needs of others should be reminiscent of the empathy that I defended as a requirement for treating people with equal concern and respect, a requirement that is part of the morality of even purely personal relations.

When we move beyond interpersonal relationships to social contexts and human relationships in general, we realize the fundamental importance of acquiring knowledge about others from their perspectives, if we are to understand inequalities and injustices. It will be useful to return to the examples of sexual assault and sexual harassment, examples, as we learned in the previous chapter, that Gilligan's critics have used to defend justice as prior to or more important than care and to separate out contexts where care is appropriate from ones where justice is appropriate. As I take it, a more adequate response to these sorts of examples is to construct a notion of "just caring" that moves away from exclusive attention to care as concern for others in interpersonal relationships.

The approach I advance is to show how considering relationships and people's perspectives on them as a focal point for analysis rather than care in and of itself can shed new light on both care and justice. In the examples of sexual harassment and sexual assault, we need to look at the social practices of a society that define these actions in ways that circumscribe relationships and perpetuate inequalities. Not only do we realize why care as "concern for others" is not sufficient for addressing injustices at the level of political and public relationships, but we also learn that women's perspectives on sexual harassment and sexual assault need to form the base for understanding these inequalities and changing institutional structures. These perspectives generate an account of our responsibilities to others that has not been evident in liberal theory so far, an account that needs to be sensitive to differences with respect to people, positions, social practices, and political contexts.

On the one hand, a critical perspective on care is needed to know what justice requires because it is needed to know what treating people in all kinds of relationships with equal concern and respect requires. On the other hand, justice cannot be assessed without a focus on relationships and a capacity to empathize with a variety of perspectives. We need to be more attentive to different people's perspectives on the structures of power, in particular to those people who continue to be on the margins or outside those structures. Justice theory needs to take account of the diverse needs of different others, how they perceive their needs and how all this affects what is required to treat them with genuine concern and respect. But what sort of impact will attention to particular perspectives have on principles, structures, and policies, the very things with which justice concerns itself?

Justice Needs Care and Care Needs Justice

In *Contemporary Political Philosophy*, Kymlicka argues that political theory has failed to acknowledge the significance of dependency and care and that an incorporation of these issues is likely to radically alter accounts of autonomy, responsibility, and justice. "Can we meet our responsibilities for dependent others without giving up the more robust picture of autonomy, and the notions of responsibility and justice that make it possible? It is too early to tell. Justice theorists have constructed impressive edifices by refining traditional notions of fairness and responsibility. However, by continuing the centuries-old neglect of the basic issues of child-rearing and care for dependants, these intellectual achievements are resting on unexamined and perilously shaky ground. Any adequate theory of sexual equality must confront these issues, and the traditional conceptions of discrimination and privacy that have hidden them from view" (Kymlicka 1990, 285–286). This quotation is the very last paragraph of the book so Kymlicka provides no solutions to the problems he raises. We first need to remember, as we discovered in the previous section, that dependency extends beyond relations with children and is also only one sort of relationship that is ignored in political theory. But once we uncover why the dependency relations Kymlicka identifies are significant, we establish the case for making relationships of all kinds the focal point for equality analysis. So what is missing in political theory when it fails to take into account issues of caring for dependents?

We have one answer to this question in Okin's critique of Rawls. While Rawls does provide a lengthy discussion of how a sense of justice grows out of the family (Rawls 1971, 462–479), Okin locates a contradiction in his position. On the one hand, Rawls holds that justice emerges from early nurturing and caring relations, yet, on the other hand, he neglects to submit these kinds of relations to tests of justice. Rawls assumes that matters of justice are not applicable to the private sphere of the family, which is characterized instead by sentiments of benevolence, care, and mutual dependence. Okin's solution is to bring justice into the family and to open up participation in the original position to individuals rather than to heads of households. The end result in Okin's account is that women, who are primarily responsible for caring for dependents, will have the same access to Rawls's primary goods as do men. "Until there is justice within the family, women will not be able to gain equality in politics, at work, or in any other sphere" (Okin 1989, 4).

Eva Feder Kittay argues that Okin's call for having individuals rather than heads of households represented in the original position makes urgent another question, a question about "whether the parties representing individuals will represent the interests of both dependents and caretakers. If human dependency counts among the general facts to which representatives in the OP have epistemic access, they know that when the veil is lifted they may find themselves dependent or having to care for dependents" (Kittay 1997, 229).[18] Unlike Okin, Kittay favors bringing care into the realm of justice. "[A] justice that does not incorporate the need to respond to vulnerability with care is incomplete" (Kittay 1997, 237). Kittay highlights what is missing in justice theory and in Okin's revisions to it by focusing on cases of "utter dependency" where care is most apparent and an individual's interests are not independent of others: "[t]he dependency care I want to spotlight centers on the most acute moments of human dependency: helpless infancy and early childhood, frail old age, and incapacitating illness and disability" (Kittay 1997, 220).

Kittay works out the implications of her dependency critique for Rawls's principles of justice by arguing that the social positions of the dependency worker and the dependent need to be added to the original position. When these perspectives are represented, a third principle of justice is the likely result. Kittay formulates it as: "*To each according to his or her need for care, from each according to his or her capacity for care, and such support from social institutions as to make available resources and opportunities to those providing care, so that all will be adequately attended in relations that are sustaining*" (Kittay 1997, 252, her emphasis). But because there seems to be no "natural way of converting such a principle to either of Rawls's two principles of justice," Kittay concludes that the theory of justice as fairness "falls short of meeting dependency concerns" (Kittay 1997, 252).

I think that Kittay is right to suggest that a genuine consideration of "utter dependency" would not fit well with either the first principle of equal liberties as Rawls conceives it or the difference principle that justifies inequalities in wealth if it is to the benefit of the least well off. But I think that this gives us reason to revise Rawls differently, by making the principles the general ones I have suggested of treating people with equal concern and respect and respecting human diversity and ways of being. At a second level, we then worry about formulating policies for specific social and political contexts and cases. It also gives us reason to return to the idea of the need for a dialogue among many different kinds of perspectives as a forum for testing and formulating policies, and the perspectives of those in various dependency relations will be one sort among many perspectives. Using Sara Ruddick's work to expand Kittay's idea that dependents and those who care for dependents have "epistemic access" to what it is to care will emphasize the relevance of the many diverse perspectives and of all sorts of relationships to equality analysis.

Ruddick lends support to the idea that caregivers develop ways of being, feeling, and relating that are sources of knowledge for promoting and enhancing the moral development and growth of citizens, a proper goal for any political theory. The maternal thinking she describes requires a configuration of cognitive and emotional capacities similar to those required for empathy. "[A] mother caring for children engages in a discipline. She asks certain questions—those relevant to her aims—rather than others; she accepts certain criteria for the truth, adequacy, and relevance of proposed answers; and she cares about the findings she makes and can act on" (Ruddick 1989, 24). In Ruddick's terms, a mother develops these ways of thinking and knowing in the context of the three demands for preservation, growth, and social acceptability that the responsibility of caring for children places on them. Maternal thinking, as Ruddick develops it, happens in precisely a place where the goals are to protect, preserve, and enhance the well-being and moral development of concrete others. We can say, then, as Jay Drydyk does, that "within every culture, there is at least one pervasive subculture that cultivates authentic knowledge of what is good for others" (Drydyk 1995, 22).[19]

We have reason, then, to have the perspectives of those who have been traditionally responsible for caring for and nurturing others enter the dialogue about equality and justice. What can political theory learn from a "maternal thinking" perspective? Annette Baier suggests that a genuine consideration of this kind of perspective can result in structural changes to basic institutions. "A more realistic acceptance of the fact that we begin as helpless children, that at almost every point of our lives we deal with the more and the less helpless, that equality of power and interdependency, between two persons or groups, is rare and hard to recognize when it does occur, might lead us to a more direct approach to questions concerning the design of institutions structuring these relationships between unequals (families, schools, hospitals, armies) and the morality of our dealings with the more and the less powerful" (Baier 1987b, 53).

We can extend this insight about the design of institutions that provide care for dependents to institutions in our social context that prohibit some people from providing this kind of care. If such basic goods as income and self-respect cannot be provided in a context that makes it difficult for same-sex couples, for example, to care for dependents, then we need to examine the legislation and institutional structures that make it difficult for some people to provide such basic care for others. Same-sex couples can present perspectives on nurturing that challenge traditional models of mother–child relationships and are relevant to issues of care and justice. In general terms, a conception of equality that takes our relationships seriously, both those that succeed and those that fail, might view the relationships of temporary inequality between parent and child or teacher and student, for example, as places for learning how power and authority can be used to foster moral development and transform inequality into relationships of equal concern and respect.

Ruddick's project of developing care in personal relationships of dependency into a critical perspective shows why justice needs care. However, maternal thinking is but one of many perspectives. As a perspective, perhaps even as an aspect of a variety of perspectives, of one kind of oppressed group, it can provide insights about caring and nurturing roles that show that these relationships are relevant to political theory in the ways just sketched: they can reveal the inequalities that particular legislation and institutional structures create for some people, and they are fundamental to providing knowledge about enhancing moral development and ways of being. By relating the care perspective to an orientation adopted by oppressed groups in general, I want to expand the network of relationships that are significant to critical thinking about equality and justice. There are all sorts of public and political relationships of dependency and inequality that do not have the positive features of personal ones and are also ignored by political theorists; namely, relationships of power and oppression. The need to subject relationships to critical analysis is most apparent when we turn to these relationships of inequality, but we already have the tools for doing this. We begin with the basic insight about needing to take seriously the perspectives of all sorts of people in relationships of oppression, inequality, and disadvantage. We then make use of the idea of care as an orientation to other.

When differences are defined in relation to those with power and authority, they shape the kinds of relationships into which one enters and determine the level and scope of possible interactive engagements between oppressors and those who are oppressed. We can recall in this context the inadequacies both in Hacking's account of these interactions in his model of the "two vectors of influence" and in Puka's account of the care perspective as simply women's responses to their oppression. I noted that what is missing in both accounts is an awareness of the perspectives of those "below" as well as a recognition of the actual dynamics of the relationships between oppressors and those who "press from below." Now is the time to use the notion of orientation to other to extract the implications of these perspectives and interactions for policy initiatives. This, we will discover, allows us to explore the intertwinings of care and justice, to answer perplexing questions about Gilligan's complementarity thesis, and to move beyond a framework that casts difference as a dilemma.

Politicizing Difference and Promoting Inclusiveness

The basic insight of the notion of orientation to other, that those who are oppressed need to take account of the dominant and powerful, can now be used to explain how change can take place. In interactive engagements and dialogue with the dominant and powerful, familiar and accepted categories are challenged and structures that support oppressive relations can be transformed. But the possibility for enabling and enacting change rests on permitting genuine interactions, ones in which the dominant and powerful recognize the validity and value of the different perspectives of those who are other oriented. These interactions are the places where complex intertwinings between the different approaches to morality can and do take place. The relationship between care and justice, then, does not have to be in terms of the assimilation of one perspective into the other, but can be in terms of each perspective informing the other and transforming the whole.[20] In the process of realizing that genuine respect for the perspectives of all those who are oppressed results in challenges to the norms assumed by liberal structures, we find a way of escaping the dilemma of difference and thereby strengthen the case for inclusion, not assimilation.

In a number of places in her work, Gilligan experiments with the idea that the two moral approaches of care and justice provide entirely different, all-encompassing ways of perceiving and structuring the world. She uses the famous example of the ambiguous figure of the duck-rabbit in Wittgenstein's *Philosophical Investigations* (Wittgenstein 1953, 194) to illustrate that the approaches of care and justice are each important in their own right, an idea reflected in Wittgenstein's notion of "seeing as."[21] In the case of the duck-rabbit, we can see the figure either as a duck or as a rabbit, but not as both at once. Gilligan has been interpreted as saying that we can "see moral conflicts in terms of either justice or care but not both at once" (Hekman 1995, 9). But this interpretation runs the risk of lending support to attempts to prioritize justice or care in terms of either their comprehensiveness or their suitability in particular contexts. What I have been arguing is that justice, properly conceived, and care, properly conceived, are much closer than is generally thought and that each needs the other.

Susan Hekman argues that Gilligan switches her earlier version of justice and care as complementary in *In a Different Voice* to a version of justice and care as "focus phenomena," "different ways of organizing the basic elements of moral judgment" (Hekman 1995, 9), in her later work. I agree, but I am not sure that this represents a rejection of the complementarity thesis. If by complementarity, one means that the concerns of care perspectives can be assimilated into a justice approach, then I support any move to undermine this kind of interpretation. If one means that there are no similarities or connections between a care and justice approach, then this obviously contradicts my attempts in the last two sections to bring care and justice closer together. A relational approach supports the idea that the two approaches are not always or entirely in opposition and that they inevitably interact and intertwine in ways that allow new possibilities and ways of being in social relations to emerge.

Gilligan's example of two children disagreeing about what game to play can illustrate how an interaction between two people with different approaches can create new relationships and structures. This is the upshot: "the girl said, 'Let's play next-door neighbors.' 'I want to play pirates,' the boy replied. 'Okay,' said the girl, 'then you can be the pirate that lives next door.' " (Gilligan 1986a, 242). Gilligan calls the girl's suggestion the "inclusive solution" and contrasts this with the boy's "fair solution," which is the familiar and expected resolution of the conflict: to keep the games separate, take turns, and play each game for an equal period of time. In the inclusive solution, the girl combines the games in such a way as to change the identity of the game and the nature of their relationship. Through its interaction with another perspective, the inclusive solution brings new possibilities into being. In the process of playing a new game altogether, the identities and relationships of the participants are transformed.

Contained in Gilligan's seemingly simple and nonpolitical example are features of relational theory that can move us out of the dilemma of difference. The dilemma of difference, cast as either playing the standard and accepted game in the same way or playing a different and inferior game and being excluded from the standard game, is recast in terms of exploring the radical potential in genuine interaction and dialogue between those who are oppressed and the dominant and powerful. In these interactions, changes to self-concepts and identities for both oppressors and those who are oppressed can begin to effect changes to the structure as a whole just as it changes the game and the participants in the example. The familiar liberal framework for understanding the activity and the rules is transformed. The idea of the dynamics of interaction reflects the features I have advanced as central to care as an orientation to other: the value of the perspectives of those who are oppressed and the significance of their interactions with the dominant and powerful. It also fits with my argument for the need to have interactive dialogue among different points of view in order to achieve critical and unbiased thinking about equality and justice.

An example more complex and serious than that of the next-door neighbor game is provided by Minow's discussion of a deaf girl, who communicates in sign language (also coincidentally called Amy), faced with exclusion from mainstream educational facilities. In a world where the norm is the ability to speak, this is the kind of difference that has had and continues to have a significant impact on opportunities and treatment. Leaving aside the question of what formal equality theorists would say about Amy, liberal substantive theorists have tended to "deal" with Amy from the perspective of the assumed norm of the able-bodied person.

Because she cannot assimilate by learning a language in the same way, the question for liberal substantive theorists is one of justifying special treatment beyond what is required for people who fit the norm. A relational approach allows us to move outside the framework of the dilemma of difference and perceive Amy as a concrete person with unique and creative capacities.

Amy can interact and communicate in relationships—only very differently. While her inability to speak in the same way as those viewed as "normal" prevents her from engaging in most relationships with those who are not like her, it can also be viewed as the occasion for setting up new relationships and changing institutional structures. Minow considers what everyone could gain in an integrated school where special efforts are made by everyone to learn Amy's language. In imagining an inclusive solution, she thereby shows how structures can be transformed and perceptions changed. "[W]hat if the teacher instructed all the students in sign language and ran the class in both spoken and sign language simultaneously? This approach conceives of the problem as a problem for all students. After all, if Amy cannot communicate with her classmates, they cannot communicate with her, and all lose the benefit of exchange. . . . If her classmates learned to communicate with Amy, they could also learn how much of their understanding of disability rests on social practices that they themselves can change" (Minow 1990a, 84–86).

Living and being immersed in oppressive relationships is damaging to self-concepts and to levels of freedom to meet basic needs and develop capacities. Inclusive solutions apply the principles of treating people with equal concern and respect and respecting human diversity and ways of being by exploring and validating different perspectives and allowing these to inform and challenge current institutional structures and social practices that continue to perpetuate inequalities. In the next chapter, I shall apply these insights to the issue of affirmative action and show how these measures work to transform current institutional rules and practices and the damaging perceptions of members of oppressed groups supported by them. But there are a few issues yet to discuss before we get there.

In emphasizing aspects of the social construction of identities and self-concepts, a relational approach raises questions about how it can be possible for the girl in the next-door neighbor game or Minow's Amy to make changes to the structures that restrict or oppress them. So perhaps I have moved too quickly in discussing possibilities for change. How do people with identities structured by their difference perceived as inequality become agents of social and political change? How can women, socialized into caring and nurturing roles as they are constructed in patriarchy, free themselves of the oppressive effects of these roles? Certainly women do so, as Gilligan notes in her later work when she writes, "[a]s I have continued to explore the connections between the political order and the psychology of women's and men's lives, I have become increasingly aware of the crucial role of women's voices in *maintaining or transforming* a patriarchal world" (Gilligan 1993, xii, my emphasis). However, Gilligan tells us more about the ways in which women "maintain" patriarchal structures than about how women can "transform" them.[22] We need to know about "how women who are socialized into subordinate gender roles nonetheless can develop the sense of self-respect and the personal power necessary to be strong feminists able to effectively change institutional sexism" (Ferguson 1987, 341). What makes "pressing from below" possible at all?

In Chapter 2, I criticized Hacking for failing to note that categories and their meanings are not only determined "from above," but sometimes new possibilities and ways of being are actualized "from below." I noted that the idea of moral imagination or creativity captures this phenomenon, but how is creativity possible in contexts of severe oppression? Susan Hekman provides an answer to this kind of question about change that fits very nicely into my complex of relational insights about language and people. She likens creativity to language acquisition processes. "Speakers who acquire languages are restricted by the vocabulary, rules, syntax, and grammar of the languages they speak. Yet any competent speaker of a language is capable of creativity, of devising unique sentences out of the discursive mix available to her. The same is true of subjectivity. Subjects have a diverse array of subjectivities available to them" (Hekman 1995, 111). But I want to expand this insight.

It is not only subjects choosing from available and diverse subjectivities, but subjects making choices in the context of engaging with others in a network of complex and ever-changing relationships shaped by social practices and political contexts. This picture of a network of interaction complicates an account of creativity, but it takes seriously the idea that a context in which differences continue to matter to life prospects itself creates human diversity and ways of being by expanding the possibilities for reaction, interaction, and change. An examination of the social practices and political contexts in which members of various oppressed groups need to respond to those in power provides access points for understanding and evaluating the effectiveness of particular kinds of strategies not only from above but also from below and in various kinds of relationships.

At the level of personal relationships, for example, removing oneself from relationships of inequality, abuse, and exploitation may be a necessary strategy—sometimes for survival and sometimes for gaining an understanding of the social practices that perpetuate such relationships. In relationships removed from the damaging effects of structures that support difference as inferiority, people can gain a better understanding of the processes and effects of socialization on self-concepts and identity. This understanding is one of the outcomes of consciousness-raising, a method of analysis that many take to be fundamental to feminist theory.[23] Consciousness-raising begins with personal experiences as the raw data for understanding how differences are constructed as inferior and unequal and then moves to a critical analysis of the social and political contexts within which these differences are understood.[24]

Through the seemingly simple process of describing and analyzing personal experiences, feminists have revealed the lack of fit between women's experiences and the understanding of those experiences in traditional theory and in practice. Consciousness-raising groups provide a safe environment for discovering shared experiences of oppression, for coming to understand how structures create and perpetuate unequal and oppressive relations, and for acquiring confidence and strength. The importance of developing these critical perspectives on the structures is evident in an analysis of the relevance of women's experiences of sexual harassment for workplace policies. The methodology of consciousness-raising, a "shared and participatory practice" (Held 1993, 181) of interactive dialogue and critical thinking, makes it possible for members of oppressed groups to understand the structures, to imagine new social relations and ways of being, and to become effective agents for changing oppressive structures. But notice that this interactive dialogue at the level of shared experiences and personal relationships happens in a broader network of relationships. Not only does the analysis of personal relationships rest on the understanding of how those relationships are created and maintained in social practices and political contexts, but strategies for change bring in the broader network of public relationships.

I cannot entirely remove myself from a social and political context that defines and circumscribes the category I am placed into, that creates and defines the rules and practices that affect the choices I have and make, and that sets the framework for policy initiatives and strategies in terms of assimilation into current institutional structures. Even if I choose to separate myself from the dominant and oppressive structures and create a separate community of like-minded people, for example, I am still forced to be cognizant of and sensitive to the rules, structures, policies, and stereotypes that affect me or my community.[25] This is an awareness and sensitivity that is a central feature of the orientation to other. Political concepts, ideas, and arguments all become part of the interdynamics of relationships in which those who are oppressed interact, communicate, and struggle with their oppressors and resist and challenge understandings of difference as inferiority and inequality. When we focus on the interactions between oppressors and those who are oppressed in the broader context of a network of relationships, we create an opening for reconceptualizing the function of rights and for restructuring legal institutions that adjudicate inequality claims. We return to the task of articulating elements central to justice: principles, structures, and policies.

A Relational Interpretation of Rights Discourse

In interpreting the respondent Kate's reflections on the two approaches of justice and care, Gilligan writes, "she sees the limitation of the 'individually-centered' approach of balancing rights and claims in the failure of this approach to take into account the reality of relationships, 'a whole other dimension to human experience.' In seeing individual lives as connected and embedded in a social context of relationship, she expands her moral perspective to encompass a notion of 'collective life.' Responsibility now includes both self and other, viewed as different but connected rather than as separate and opposed. This cognizance of interdependence, rather than a concern with reciprocity, informs her belief that 'we all do to some extent have responsibilities to look out for each other' " (Gilligan 1982, 147). In one place, Gilligan discusses responsibility "[i]n a world that extends through an elaborate network of relationships" (Gilligan 1982, 147). She describes Amy as situated in "a world of relationships . . . where an awareness of the connection between people gives rise to a recognition of responsibility for one another, a perception of the need for response" (Gilligan 1982, 30). For Gilligan, what joins people in a network of relationships is the fact of interdependence, a recognition that "it is the collective that is important . . . and that collective is based on certain guiding principles, one of which is that everybody belongs to it and that you all come from it" (Gilligan 1982, 160). These comments about responsibility to others make the network of relationships very broad indeed.

Earlier, in bringing care closer to justice, I argued that care conceived this broadly incorporates the foundational principles of treating people with equal concern and respect and of respecting human diversity and ways of being. So I defend a broad application of a "caring justice" understood in terms of these foundational principles reconstituted from classical liberal insights. A broad application reflects the infiltration of classical liberal principles the world over, an infiltration brought about, as Benhabib puts it, through "a situation of world-wide reciprocal exchange, influence, and interaction" (Benhabib 1995, 251). Before I go on to apply these insights about the universality of the principles to a discussion of rights discourse, I want to digress long enough to comment on what I view as a mistake in Rawls's revisions to justice theory in his later work.

I mentioned earlier that Rawls makes no changes to the principles of justice or the original position that generates them in his later work. I shall leave the task of evaluating the complexities of Rawls's later work, and in particular of *Political Liberalism*, to other people.[26] But I do want to discuss briefly one revision that matters to my analysis: Rawls's rejection of that part of *A Theory of Justice* that either explicitly argued or implicitly assumed that there can be principles of justice that are universal or absolute. In his later work, the language of "equal concern and respect for all individuals" is replaced with "citizens as free and equal" and Rawls takes his principles to emerge from and apply to a liberal democratic society that views its citizens in this way.[27] There is no longer "an Archimedean point from which the basic structure itself can be appraised" (Rawls 1971, 260) and no longer principles for structuring any and every society.

Rawls explains in "Justice as Fairness: Political not Metaphysical" that in the face of communitarian objections that his theory operates with metaphysical assumptions about the self and the principles, he wants to *clarify* the scope and status of his theory of justice: "it may seem that this conception [of justice] depends on philosophical claims I should like to avoid, for example, claims to universal truth, or claims about the essential nature and identity of persons. My aim is to explain why it does not" (Rawls 1985, 223). Rawls's answer to communitarian objections about the liberal self and the status of the principles is in effect to acknowledge that there is something to the criticism that tradition and history form the person and to retreat to a position that argues that the liberal tradition has formed in its citizens public tolerance for different conceptions of the good.[28] In a sense, then, the moral personality that Rawls describes is itself shaped by relationships, relationships in a liberal structure that allows different comprehensive conceptions of the good by protecting certain liberties and promoting tolerance.

Consider Rawls's rather nice description of the fundamental importance of personal relationships to the growth and development of political citizens:

> Citizens may have, and normally do have at any given time, affections, devotions, and loyalties that they believe they would not, and indeed could and should not, stand apart from and objectively evaluate from the point of view of their purely rational good. They may regard it as simply unthinkable to view themselves apart from certain religious, philosophical, and moral convictions, or from certain enduring attachments and loyalties. These convictions and attachments are part of what we may call their "nonpublic identity." These convictions and attachments help to organize and give shape to a person's way of life, what one sees oneself as doing and trying to accomplish in one's social world. We think that if we were suddenly without these particular convictions and attachments we

would be disoriented and unable to carry on. In fact, there would be, we might think, no point in carrying on (Rawls 1985, 241).

Rawls argues, however, that having the principles of justice as a background institutional framework is sufficient for allowing such relationships to flourish. It seems to be simply assumed that the background institutions structured by equal liberties and the difference principle will provide moral development and growth for citizens, implant moral ideals of tolerance in them, and ensure equal concern and respect for all conceptions of the good.[29] If Rawls's two principles of justice that structure institutions are supposed to do all this work, we have many reasons for questioning whether they can.[30] We also have reasons for agreeing with Rawls that his principles that specify certain liberties and delineate inequalities in wealth do not have universal application. But are these reasons for rejecting the universality of principles of justice as such?

Rawls has very little to say about the principles that would be generated in societies that do not view their citizens as free and equal other than to state that conceptions of different political selves will generate different principles. "[T]he contrast with a political conception which allows slavery makes clear why conceiving of citizens as free persons in virtue of their moral powers and their having a conception of the good, goes with a particular political conception of the person. This conception of persons fits into a political conception of justice founded on the idea of society as a system of cooperation between its members conceived as free and equal" (Rawls 1985, 243). Perhaps Rawls answers Sandel's objections that he "imagines an event that never really happened, involving the sorts of beings who never really existed" (Sandel 1982, 105) by restricting the application of his theory of justice to a liberal democratic society, but it is at too great a cost: the loss of the foundational and universal principle of equal concern and respect.

The two principles of treating people with equal concern and respect and respecting human diversity and ways of being are foundational to justice. By examining rights discourse, something that has had influence the world over, we can reveal the kinds of policies and mechanisms that a relational theory of equality incorporating these principles generates. The aim is to provide a relational interpretation and reconception of rights. The first point to make is that a relational approach rejects the idea that rights are fixed entities attachable to separate and autonomous individuals. Rather, rights emerge in relationships in social contexts and create a forum for dialogue among community members. "Human rights are components of a moral discourse that owes its existence to social life. . . . Human rights emerge in society, but they give vent to social criticism and reform, pointing to the need to transcend the boundaries of a society's existing norms and conventions in order to achieve justice" (Sypnowich 1990, 113). Let us examine the effect of rights discourse in action in relational terms in the case of negative rights to freedom of choice. We will then move to an examination of positive rights with a view to broadening the range of them.

In "Letter to Readers, 1993" (Gilligan 1993, ix–xxvii), Gilligan discusses the effects on women's self-concepts and reasoning of the Supreme Court decision in *Roe v. Wade*. While the decision still cast the issue of abortion in the framework of a conflict of individual rights, the right to life of the fetus versus the right to choose of the mother, Gilligan argues that the decision was important because it "made it legal for a woman to speak for herself and awarded women the deciding voice" (Gilligan 1993, ix). Gilligan interprets this legal decision and validation of women's decision-making capacities as a factor that made it possible for women to speak for themselves in other areas. "In the immediate aftermath of the *Roe v. Wade* decision, many women were openly questioning the morality of the Angel in the House . . . the woman who acts and speaks only for others. . . . [W]omen were exposing the morality of the Angel as a kind of immorality: an abdication of voice, a disappearance from relationships and responsibility" (Gilligan 1993, x).

In the context of debates concerning abortion, the right to choose has been understood as an individual liberty right. A discussion of the impact of the validation of this right on women's thinking and development casts a different light on the function of these rights. Emphasizing the dynamic features of relationships between the dominant and the disadvantaged, between those who espouse rights and those who challenge the structures that fail to provide the kind of equality espoused by those rights, permits a reconception of rights. When rights claims are placed in a broader context, as this interpretation of events surrounding *Roe v. Wade* illustrates, rights discourse becomes part of the political struggles of those who are oppressed to achieve the equality idealized in that dominant discourse.

In practice, the sort of positive rights defended by liberal substantive theorists have been held out as moral ideals rather than as legitimate demands by people for rectification, compensation, or redistributions of social goods. Like the human rights set out in international charters, claims to rights have status as moral injunctions and all too rarely as legitimate legal claims. Yet, even as moral ideals, rights are powerful and effective devices for legitimating claims of inequality. The discourse of equality and rights articulates a community's commitment to treating people with equal concern and respect and makes it possible for marginalized and disadvantaged group members to challenge legislation and policies that violate that commitment.

Rights register a commitment to moral equality and can be viewed as aspirations for an ideal of inclusion in a global community. "Rights discourse can express human and communal values; it can be a way for individuals to develop a sense of self and for a group to develop a collective identity. Rights discourse can also have a dimension that emphasizes the interdependence of autonomy and community" (Schneider 1986, 515). A relational approach views rights as expressions of commitments by a community to include all people. They stand as agreements by all members of a community or polity that inequality claims will be considered and adjudicated. In claiming unequal status and treatment, those who are oppressed "signal and strengthen their relation to a community" (Minow 1990a, 294).

The tradition of rights "sustains the call that makes those in power at least listen" (Minow 1990a, 297). As an ongoing, creative, and developmental process, rights discourse creates new possibilities.[31] The perspectives of the disadvantaged need to serve as sources of knowledge for challenging constructions of difference that perpetuate disadvantage and inequality. Dialogue and interaction with the powerful can be effective strategies for highlighting the inconsistencies and contradictions in equality discourse purporting to speak to and for all people and for extending and legitimating ever more substantive understandings of equality.

Incorporating insights about the need to understand different perspectives in order to reveal and eliminate intransigent inequalities calls for a set of positive rights in addition to and distinct from liberal substantive theory's distributional rights to welfare, health, and education. In the last part of Chapter 5, I called for strengthening the process of reflective equilibrium by allowing dialogue among multiple perspectives about the social practices that perpetuate inequalities in specific political contexts. Such a process is structured by the principles of equal concern and respect and respect for human diversity and ways of being, but the dialogue needs the mechanisms discussed in Chapter 5 to ensure that policies that emerge from the dialogue will be just. We can now present these mechanisms in the form of positive rights: the right to "introduce new points of view, questions, and criticism" (Benhabib 1995, 251), to protest, to demand justifications for policies, and to give assessments of them.[32] Such positive rights can provide the kind of interpersonal tests that allow us to assess the impact of policies, both current and proposed, on members of disadvantaged groups and to do so in the context of particular social practices and political conditions.

Drawing Conclusions and Looking Ahead: Shifting to Perspectives

The very features that make equality analysis so complex are also the features that give the language of equality its rhetorical force and power. We notice differences, draw comparisons, and make determinations of inequalities all within the context of relationships. Relational theory brings equality discourse into the context of relationships where relations of power, authority, oppression, and disadvantage limit the opportunities of some people.[33] Learning that inequalities and disadvantages emerge in and through relationships in which only some people have the power to define difference undermines the idea that there is one correct standard and only a few proper solutions. Understanding difference from the perspective of the different undermines assumptions about what is valuable activity and what needs to be done to achieve the inclusion of difference in current structures.

The institutions and policies that reflect the norms and perspectives of those in power have consequences for the lives and relationships of those who are oppressed. In needing to be aware of and sensitive to these structures and policies, the disadvantaged provide perspectives that can challenge assumptions about them that result in inequalities. At the base of the notion of orientation to other are descriptive facts about how members of various oppressed groups are in particular relations of inequality, oppression, and dependency with those at the center of influence and power. Their perspectives on the structures and policies provide valuable insights for revealing specific inequalities and finding ways to eliminate them. From their points of view, inclusive rather than assimilationist strategies almost always appear to embody greater equality. I will use more example, one that brings B back into the discussion and allows her to make an exit in this chapter.

Suppose that B is now engaged in interactive dialogue with people of all sorts and she is someone whose differences have been made to matter with respect to her life prospects and choices. We already imagined the possibility that her activities are restricted to caring roles that are devalued in her community. We also imagined that a condition of poverty in which she and her children depend on the state for survival circumscribes her activities, her needs, and her level of freedom for satisfying such basic preferences as what she and her children eat or where they live. Now imagine B, and many others like her, with mechanisms in place that allow them to present perspectives on the various effects of poverty on their lives. They reveal that their children have low levels of self-esteem and self-respect in a social context that judges people's worth by the expensive items one possesses. Taking these perspectives into account might allow us to question a capitalist structure that ties moral development and growth to property, to challenge advertising campaigns that promote these as proper goals, to organize boycotts to reduce the power of large corporations, and to understand and prevent the higher incidences of suicide in the teenage population that lives in poverty. Imagine too how the structures could change if mechanisms allowed them to ask for and assess justifications for policies that make every medical consultation life-threatening for their families but not wealthier families in a context without universal health care. These implications of putting institutions in place that make perspectives count in the determination of policies are just a small reflection of the kind of changes that can be conceptualized and put in place.

Relational insights have implications for identity and self-concept formation, moral personhood, autonomy, responsibilities, and communities, all of which ground political theory and practice. In this chapter, we explored the implications of relational theory for care and justice. A central feature of the care perspective, expanded and reconceived, is an awareness of others that comes from needing to pay attention to what those in power are saying and doing. Conditions of oppression force people to devise various ways of responding; sometimes of merely surviving, of consciousness-raising, of organizing and protesting, of forming caring attachments or ending uncaring ones, of developing self-respect, and so on. The perspectives of oppressed groups on the structures of power need to be treated as sources of knowledge for understanding inequalities and addressing injustices. "Just caring" can inform theories of equality and justice, theories concerned with identifying conditions that treat people with equal concern and respect.

In the next chapter, I explore the potential of relational theory to illuminate questions of equality further by applying its insights to an issue of practical policy, namely, affirmative action.[34] A relational approach opens the way to new and powerful arguments in favor of affirmative action as a means to providing conditions of equal concern and respect for all people. These measures literally place members of disadvantaged groups in positions of influence and power. As such, they hold the potential for actualizing the principle of respect for human diversity and ways of being by allowing these diverse perspectives to reshape current structures. As in this chapter, so too in the next, relational theory can break free of liberal arguments that cast issues like affirmative action in the framework of the dilemma of difference and offer new arguments and approaches to equality issues. Assumptions about how members of disadvantaged groups assimilate into current structures are radically altered when we assemble the insights of relational theory and apply them to the issue of affirmative action.

8

❦ ❦ ❦

Relational Perspectives and Affirmative Action

Introduction

Affirmative action is an ideal policy issue for examining practical applications of liberal theories of equality. It highlights the contrasts between formal and substantive equality and powerfully depicts the various dimensions of the two horns of the dilemma of difference. Michel Rosenfeld writes, "the affirmative action debate is not between persons who are 'pro-equality' and others who are 'anti-equality'. Both the most ardent advocates of affirmative action and its most vehement foes loudly proclaim their allegiance to the ideal of equality" (Rosenfeld 1991, 2–3). Both proponents and opponents of affirmative action claim a respect for and adherence to equality of opportunity and to treating people with equal concern and respect. As we discovered before, so here too, the debate centers on disagreements about the conditions for satisfying the requirement.

Formal equality theorists are critical of affirmative action measures and view them as unjust violations of negative individual liberty rights of noninterference. They argue that opportunities are equal when all people have the same formal right to compete. Ian Hunter, for example, holds that equal opportunity "means that there are no artificial barriers put in the way of a qualified man or a qualified woman." He then adds, "to specifically impose artificial barriers for men, or to create artificial advantages for women, in the name of equality is to debase both logic and language" (Hunter 1985, 202). Yet, liberal substantive theorists certainly view their defense of affirmative action as supporting and promoting equality. They argue that a commitment to equal concern and respect requires positive measures in the form of differential treatment for those whose unequal starting positions result in unfair disadvantages and unequal opportunities.

Affirmative action is "any positive action to recruit members of minority groups into jobs, schools, training programs, or whatever. That is, it is action which goes beyond the purely negative agreement not to discriminate" (Chegwidden and Katz 1983, 193). While this general definition shows that affirmative action can take many forms, the term has been closely associated with preferential hiring practices and with such controversial policies as setting quotas. I prefer the broader definition, but many of the examples I shall use in this chapter follow a literature that tends to discuss affirmative action in the context of preferential hiring policies. These policies are controversial because they appear to violate liberal principles of open competition for educational and employment positions in a free-market structure where places are awarded on the basis of talent and merit.

Some formal equality theorists defend restricted affirmative action measures, and some substantive equality theorists are opposed to certain kinds of affirmative action. The literature is massive and complex, and the arguments on both sides are not always clearly delineated. I shall outline the debate in very general terms and concentrate on providing a relational critique of two consequentialist arguments used by liberal substantive theorists to defend affirmative action in the context of hiring practices: affirmative action is discrimination that is justified by its goal of substantive equality, and affirmative action serves a role-modeling function. For reasons that will become clear later, I will examine these liberal defenses of affirmative action in the context of discussing the equality provisions set out in the *Canadian Charter of Rights and Freedoms*.

In the previous chapter, I used Minow's phrase "dilemma of difference" to describe the way in which both the approach of ignoring difference by formal means and that of highlighting difference by substantive means have effects on opportunities for members of disadvantaged groups. In this chapter, we will again discover that a shift in focus from established norms and standards to the perspectives of those who are oppressed offers a way out of the dilemma. By acting and interacting in contexts from which they were formerly excluded or underrepresented, members of disadvantaged groups can challenge stereotypes and change perceptions of difference as inferiority. A relational critique of the liberal understanding of role modeling shows affirmative action to be more subversive, and to lend more support to a radical restructuring of society, than is generally thought.

The Dilemma of Difference in Liberal Approaches to Affirmative Action

As we said, affirmative action is so controversial because it appears to violate liberal commitments to individual rights to open competition and to meritocratic principles. As Hawkesworth puts it, "[c]ompetition is supposed to establish equality of opportunity by ensuring that all individuals start on an even footing, are considered solely on the basis of merit, and are awarded jobs on the basis of demonstrated superiority over all other candidates" (Hawkesworth 1990, 55). By virtue of their commitment to the primacy of individual liberty rights of noninterference, libertarians have been affirmative action's most persistent opponents. With an emphasis on individual freedom and limited state interference, most sorts of affirmative action programs, which discriminate in favor of some people and thereby limit the freedom of others, become extremely difficult to defend under the libertarian understanding of equality. Robert Sasseen argues that equal opportunity "does not mean that men are equal at the starting line in the race of life, or that government should attempt to make them so. . . . Equal opportunity consists in, as it arises from, equal treatment under the law" (Sasseen 1976, 277–278). For libertarians, formal equality is both necessary and sufficient for achieving equality.

All formal equality theorists are committed to the impermissibility of discriminating against people on the basis of morally irrelevant features such as race, gender, class, ethnic origin, and so on. But, they argue, affirmative action measures violate this commitment by using the very same grounds to justify unequal or preferential treatment for those identified on that basis. For libertarians, who defend formal equality as sufficient, the disapprobation of discrimination works both ways. Discrimination is morally wrong whether individuals are singled out because they are women or men, black or white. Affirmative action is unjust discrimination because it singles out individuals for preferential treatment based on an individual's membership in a group. All people have the right to nondiscrimination—including white males.[1]

Peter Westen contrasts the decisions in two United States Supreme Court cases, *Sweatt v. Painter* and *DeFunis v. Odegaard*. In the first, the University of Texas Law School denied admission to Sweatt because he was black. In the second case, the University of Washington Law School denied admission to DeFunis because he was white. In the case of *Sweatt*, the Supreme Court argued that "a black applicant's race is not a difference that is constitutionally allowed to make a difference and that Heman Sweatt was the same as his white counterparts" (Westen 1982, 582). In the same way, in *DeFunis*, the Supreme Court argued that "since a black applicant like Heman Sweatt is the same as his white counterparts with respect to law school admission, it necessarily follows that a white applicant like Marco DeFunis is the same as his black counterparts and hence must be treated the same" (Westen 1982, 582). In both decisions, the purely formal right to equal treatment, in this case a right to compete for places in law school, was upheld as sufficient.

Peter Westen explains that the cases ought to be regarded as different because the intent and goal of the admissions policies are different: "Texas sought to perpetuate racial segregation whereas Washington sought to end it" (Westen 1982, 583).[2] The Supreme Court decision in *DeFunis* decontextualized the activity of discriminating among people and took it to have the same meaning before the law no matter who was identified as unequal. My analysis emphasizes the need to place the activity of discriminating among people into social and political contexts where such discriminations have meaning for the lived lives of persons. We need to take seriously the insights from Chapter 2 that the activity of identifying differences is entrenched in rules and practices that circumscribe the opportunities of those so labeled and described.

In a social and political context in which discrimination against blacks is entrenched and intransigent, to argue that the formal right of admission into law school is the same for all people just illustrates once again the inadequacy of theorizing about the self in abstraction from social and political contexts. Depicting the situations for DeFunis and Sweatt as the same utterly fails to capture the effects of group membership on self-concepts and identity and, contrary to the libertarians, these things *are* relevant to what counts as genuine equality, a point made repeatedly in many of the previous chapters. These kinds of barriers are not the external and formal ones set out in the law, but they have an insidious and detrimental effect on opportunities. People are embedded in social practices and historical contexts that perpetuate systems and structures of discrimination even when the rules and practices are legally condemned. While the removal of legal barriers is necessary and can begin to change practices, it is not sufficient for addressing the systemic and systematic effects of a history of entrenched discrimination.

By itself, formal equality permits the justification of compensatory measures for those individuals who can *prove* that they are the victims of direct and deliberate discrimination. Discrimination is dealt with case by case, individual by individual, as backward-looking compensation for proven unjust discrimination. However, individual fault-based accounts of discrimination do not support justifications of compensation based only or mainly on the criterion of membership in a disadvantaged group.[3] Arguments for compensatory justice as redress for individual harm illustrate the limitations of pure formal equality. In practice, the burden is on individuals who were discriminated against and treated unequally to prove discrimination.[4] Unless the discrimination is overt and blatant, it is notoriously difficult for individuals to prove that they lost a competition for a job or a place in an educational institution merely because they belong to a disadvantaged group.[5] In practice, compensation for proven discrimination has also tended to be monetary, an obviously inadequate response to valuing an individual's freedom to pursue interests, projects, and goals.[6] Most importantly, defending strict adherence to proof of deliberate and direct discrimination assumes that accounts of harm to particular persons as a result of unjust discrimination are clearly separable from accounts of harm to all people who are members of disadvantaged groups, an assumption that I shall challenge in the next section.

Members of groups who have suffered a history of disadvantage, marginalization, and exclusion have unequal opportunities through no fault of their own. Liberal substantive theorists argue that equality of opportunity requires positive measures for the disadvantaged as a means of equalizing starting positions in the "race of life." Rawls does not deal directly with affirmative action but we can use his inclusion of fair equality of opportunity in the second principle of justice to argue that he could defend affirmative action as a measure for equalizing the chance to develop one's talents and abilities to the fullest. But rather than deal with the complicated issue of what implications a defense of affirmative action under the second principle would have for the priority of liberty in the first principle, I shall turn instead to L. W. Sumner's explicit defense of affirmative action on the consequentialist grounds that it helps eradicate discrimination and promote substantive equality of opportunity.

Sumner identifies five types of affirmative action policies: special recruitment, tiebreaking, handicapping ("preferring female applicants to more qualified male applicants" [Sumner 1987, 208]), lexical assessment ("ignoring male applicants altogether unless there is no suitably qualified female applicant" [Sumner 1987, 208]), and numerical goals or quotas. He argues that the first, special recruitment measures, are nondiscriminatory because they merely "offset informational and motivational advantages traditionally enjoyed by men" (Sumner 1987, 208) and expand the pool of applicants without contracting the pool of advantaged white male applicants. He calls a tiebreaking hiring policy "a rather anodyne form of discrimination" because it does not authorize hiring a less qualified woman, for example, but only uses gender to break a tie. Contrary to common perceptions of quota hiring as the most controversial policy, Sumner identifies handicapping and lexical assessment as more controversial because they allow advantaged white males who are more qualified to be passed over altogether. He argues that quota hiring "might well result in less discrimination overall than would a straightforward policy of either handicapping or lexical assessment" (Sumner 1987, 210) because "a quota provides an employer with a goal to be achieved but does not stipulate the means to be used in achieving it. If the target can be hit by means of scrupulously nondiscriminatory procedures such as special recruitment, or mildly discriminatory procedures such as tiebreaking, then no one will have any serious ground for complaint" (Sumner 1987, 210).

Sumner defends a version of quota hiring in which he assumes for the sake of argument that it leads to some actual discrimination against men. He argues that there are then two strategies open to proponents of affirmative action for addressing the objection that affirmative action is a violation of antidiscrimination rights: they can admit that affirmative action is discrimination and then distinguish just from unjust discrimination, or they can deny that affirmative action is discrimination and argue that being a member of a disadvantaged group is a qualification for whatever is at stake. Summer rejects the second strategy on the grounds that arguing that affirmative action is not discrimination is too much like trying to revise the meaning of an already established concept. He holds that a settled reaction to affirmative action as discrimination makes it inadvisable to argue that the very same grounds for unjust discrimination (gender, race, etc.) should now be viewed as qualifications in hiring procedures. I turn now to Sumner's defense of the first strategy to show that this defense misses aspects of the effects of affirmative action hiring that can be addressed by arguments using the strategy he rejects, namely role modeling.

Sumner distinguishes between the morally reprehensible discrimination involved in traditional justifications for unequal treatment for unequals and the discrimination involved in affirmative action measures that have as their goal the elimination of the lingering effects of such discrimination.[7] He argues that "taking account of the social context in which these different forms of discrimination are practised" allows us "to plan the most effective strategy for promoting greater equality in the future" (Sumner 1987, 222). To identify those who deserve special consideration, substantive equality theorists turn to statistical data, which show that members of groups discriminated against in the past continue to have a disproportionately small share of the distribution of economic, social, and educational benefits.

Statistics show that members of traditionally disadvantaged groups are underrepresented in higher-status and higher-paying jobs relative to their numbers in the general population. Moreover, because they are underrepresented relative to their numbers in the qualified pool of applicants, they are underutilized.[8] Substantive equality theorists use the data both as evidence that more subtle forms of systemic or systematic discrimination are still at work and as a yardstick to measure progress toward substantive equality of opportunity. In addition, Sumner addresses charges that less-qualified or even unqualified candidates are hired through affirmative action practices by arguing that in a context of historically entrenched discrimination, perceptions of the merits and qualifications of individuals who are members of traditionally disadvantaged groups will be biased by beliefs or stereotypes about these individuals. Affirmative action measures can serve as a means of leveling out the effects of discriminatory attitudes.[9] Sumner's defense of affirmative action as justified discrimination is similar to the reasoning underlying the equality provisions in Section 15 of the *Canadian Charter of Rights and Freedoms*.

A Substantive Interpretation of Equality: Legislation and a Court Case

At the end of the previous chapter, I argued in favor of using the discourse of equality and rights as mechanisms for changing and expanding our understanding of the conditions needed for treating people with equal concern and respect. It can be said that the fairly recent entrenchment of equality rights in the *Canadian Charter of Rights and Freedoms* makes equality so much a part of the dominant discourse in Canada that rejecting equality in favor of supporting or advocating other values such as autonomy or empowerment is no longer a viable option in the Canadian context.[10] This makes the examination of the Canadian context particularly relevant to an analysis of equality. The equality provisions in the *Charter*, set in the Constitution in 1982 and in effect in 1985, represent Canada's attempt to define a conception of equality for its citizens. As a concrete example of legislation grounding affirmative action programs, it provides a unique opportunity to examine actual court cases challenging the legitimacy of mandated affirmative action measures.[11] My discussion of the *Charter* and of a case challenging affirmative action has four objectives: to assemble the main points of disagreement between the purely formal approach to equality and the liberal substantive approach; to contextualize and make concrete the arguments in the previous chapter about the effectiveness of using the dominant discourse and legislation to effect change; to elucidate the complex concept of systemic discrimination; and to set the stage for developing an account of the relational aspects of affirmative action hiring.

Section 15 of the *Charter* specifies in Subsection (1) that "every individual is equal before and under the law and has the right to the equal protection and equal benefit of the law, without discrimination and, in particular, without discrimination based on race, national or ethnic origin, colour, religion, sex, age or mental or physical disability." At the very least, Section 15(1) articulates a strong commitment to formal equality. In Section 15(2), however, affirmative action measures are specifically singled out as policies that do not fall under the class of discriminatory actions listed in Section 15(1). "Subsection (1) does not preclude any law, program or activity that has as its object the amelioration of conditions of disadvantaged individuals or groups including those that are disadvantaged because of race, national or ethnic origin, colour, religion, sex, age or mental or physical disability."[12] Implicit in the Charter is a distinction between two kinds of discrimination: the discrimination in affirmative action programs, which has as its object or goal the amelioration of conditions of disadvantage, and the discrimination specified in Subsection (1), which perpetuates conditions of disadvantage. The distinction is similar to the one made by Sumner between just and unjust discrimination.

The equality provisions in the *Charter* favor a substantive interpretation of equality. Formal equality is necessary, but not sufficient. To achieve genuine or substantive equality, we need positive measures. As Anne Bayefsky puts it, "the *Charter* explicitly provides for the legitimacy of affirmative action programs. . . . The goal in such cases must be the amelioration of actual conditions, not only an equal chance to strive for success. The aim is sufficient to reduce present inequalities so as to erase handicaps in the competition" (Bayefsky 1986, 111).[13] Implementing measures to reduce the effects of unequal initial starting positions is viewed as promoting, not violating, the antidiscrimination rights set out in 15(1). This is precisely the reasoning used by liberal substantive theorists to justify positive measures.

The Canadian Supreme Court decision in *Action Travail des*

Femmes v. Canadian National Railway Company Co. et al.[14] (CN) and the decisions that precede it provide a good illustration of both the inadequacy of the strict adherence to formal equality and the justification for positive or affirmative action measures. A discussion of this case also makes concrete what systemic discrimination involves and begins to take us beyond substantive theory's defense of affirmative action.

Action Travail des Femmes, a private organization promoting the participation of women in occupations traditionally dominated by men, brought a complaint before the Federal Human Rights Tribunal charging that CN discriminated against women. Evidence was collected that showed significant underrepresentation of women at CN (0.7 percent, well below the national average of 13 percent for women's participation in blue-collar jobs across the country); widespread discrimination in recruitment, hiring, and promotion policies that prevented or discouraged women from applying for or remaining in jobs at CN (CN restricted its career information promotions to trade schools, encouraged women applicants in interviews to consider traditional secretarial work as a more suitable alternative, and created an environment for women in which hostility and open insults were rampant); and job requirement skills unrelated to the job (experience in welding, for example, for any position at CN). All of these factors had the effect of excluding women from CN in large numbers.

The Human Rights Tribunal ordered first that CN "cease certain discriminatory employment practices and alter others; second, that CN hire one woman in every four employees hired until it reached a goal of 13 per cent representation by women in the targeted job positions; and, third, that CN file periodic progress reports with the Canadian Human Rights Commission" (Vizkelety 1990, 295). In other words, the Human Rights Tribunal mandated quota hiring as an effective method for changing a situation of entrenched and systemic discrimination against women, a situation that the evidence overwhelmingly verified. The evidence gathered at the trial required an understanding of discrimination and its effects that went well beyond perceiving it as discrimination against individuals. Action Travail des Femmes presented a strong case for recognizing the harm and the limitations on opportunity as affecting all members of a group because the discrimination was systemic and entrenched in CN's workplace environment.

Canadian National Railway appealed the Tribunal decision to the Federal Court of Appeal in 1985, arguing that the "Tribunal erred in its findings regarding systemic discrimination" and that it was not within the powers of the Tribunal to enforce mandatory affirmative action measures on CN. The Federal Court quashed the mandated affirmative action hiring of women as beyond the powers of the Human Rights Tribunal, but it accepted the findings regarding systemic discrimination. In its interpretation of the relevant sections of the Canadian Human Rights Code, Sections 41(2) and 15(1), which allow affirmative action measures, the Federal Court of Appeal argued, "[t]he text requires that the order look to the avoidance of future evil. It does not allow restitution for past wrongs." The court "concluded that the Tribunal exceeded its powers by issuing an order which had more to do with 'curing' past discrimination than preventing or avoiding future evil" (Vizkelety 1990, 296). The Federal Court recognized the effects of prolonged and entrenched discrimination, but advocated the purely formal solution of reiterating and reinforcing to CN officials and employees that they cease discriminatory practices.

So while the Federal Court of Appeal agreed with the analysis of the detrimental effects of systemic discrimination on women as a group, it opposed positive remedies as a way of reducing its effects, even though the legislation allowed for such special measures or programs. Under this defense of purely formal equality, affirmative action measures are only justified if they adhere to strict compensatory rectification of wrongful discrimination. While it is one thing to compensate individuals who are the victims of blatant and overt discrimination, it is quite another to extend compensation to all individuals who are members of discriminated groups and to have the burdens fall on all individuals who are advantaged. What is unusual about the Federal Court of Appeal decision is that the justices accepted the evidence that women at CN were systemically discriminated against at all levels: from recruitment procedures, to job qualifications, to treatment of women on the job. They did not contest the evidence that the discrimination formed a whole pattern of reactions and behavior toward women that had entrenched and systemic effects on the whole workplace environment at CN and on all women. In other words, their understanding of discrimination did not fit the individualistic picture of discrimination as intentional and overt violations of individual rights to noninterference. Yet, though admitting this evidence, their decision still opted for a rigid, blinkered, and uncompromising adherence to the formal and negative requirement of nondiscrimination against individuals.

In a dissenting opinion, Mr. Justice MacGuigan argued that the "prevention of discrimination has to be effective for women as a group" (Vizkelety 1990, 297) and thus departed from the reasoning underlying the majority's adherence to a purely formal equality requirement. The Federal Court of Appeal decision was taken to the Supreme Court of Canada and in a unanimous decision in 1987, the Supreme Court restored the mandatory affirmative action order by the Human Rights Tribunal. In its decision, the Supreme Court emphasized that the specific references to affirmative action programs in Sections 15(1) and 41(2)(a) of the Canadian Human Rights Code were intended to save affirmative action programs from "attack on the ground of 'reverse discrimination' " (Vizkelety 1990, 300). Whereas discrimination against members of disadvantaged groups prevents or restricts achievement of equal opportunity for those individuals, discrimination in favor of members of disadvantaged groups is designed to promote equality for those same individuals. Not only are affirmative action measures intended to prevent the same or similar discriminatory practices from occurring in the future, they are intended to address the effects of entrenched discriminatory behavior on members of disadvantaged groups and to provide them with fair equality of opportunity.

Mandating positive measures acknowledges the full impact that systemic discrimination has on the opportunities for the disadvantaged as members of groups. Arguments like those used by the Supreme Court begin with an analysis of the effects of discrimination on groups and are forward-looking in their goal of ameliorating conditions of disadvantage. The evidence provided by Action Travail des Femmes, for example, showed that perceptions and stereotypes of women as unable to handle blue-collar jobs were so entrenched that women could not successfully compete for or perform well in CN jobs. On a formal interpretation of equality under the law, women had an equal opportunity. The Supreme

Court rendered a substantive interpretation of equality and determined that women at CN were not treated equally in the substantive sense.

Affirmative action is an effective way to provide people, formerly excluded from areas traditionally dominated by the advantaged, with the means for exercising equal opportunity. Affirmative action literally places members of disadvantaged groups in positions from which they were excluded. We shall discover that such placement at least holds the promise that entrenched perceptions and beliefs about the proper role and function of members of disadvantaged groups can begin to change. But this kind of justification for affirmative action as respect for what disadvantaged groups can offer is not evident in the liberal arguments we have examined. Substantive equality theorists justify special measures that single out and benefit members of disadvantaged groups as a quicker way (some argue the only way) of reaching the goal of substantive equality in the sense of providing an equal opportunity to compete for positions in current structures, ones that are already established and valued. We encounter once again the intractability of the dilemma of difference, a framework in which established norms are assumed and policies take the form of assimilationist options.

In the various rulings concerning the affirmative action hiring of women at CN, there is no recognition that factors such as caring for children might present further challenges to CN's training procedures or that programs educating CN employees about the effects of sexism might be necessary. These sorts of questions about workplace structures tend to go unanswered when the goal is set as proportional representation in current structures. When the basic structures go unchallenged, affirmative action measures may only succeed in further stigmatizing members of disadvantaged groups by perpetuating a belief that they receive different treatment, not because of their qualifications or merit, but merely because they are members of disadvantaged groups.[15] This worry is an instance of the second horn of the dilemma of difference, a concern that affirmative action may allow stereotypes and perceptions about difference to become more entrenched and may succeed in having members of disadvantaged groups internalize messages about their lack of merit and their perceived inferiority.

As we discovered in the previous chapter, both the liberal approaches, of providing the same formal treatment or permitting different and special treatment, end up on one or the other of the two horns of the dilemma of difference. As in the previous chapter, so in the next few sections as well, the twofold strategy of examining feminist critiques and applying relational insights will reveal the limitations of the liberal understanding of affirmative action and the inadequacies of the underlying conceptions of equality. Once again, we will discover that the key to escaping the horns of the dilemma of difference is to understand that "the dilemma appears only when the background assumption is that the status quo is neutral and natural rather than part of the discriminatory framework that must itself be changed" (Minow 1990a, 76).

Feminist Theory and the Affirmative Action Debate

In explaining the underlying structure of the dilemma of difference at the beginning of the previous chapter, I argued that judgments of inequality assume norms, norms that are so entrenched in social practices and political contexts that they go unchallenged. Within this framework of familiar and established structures, policies dealing with those who are identified as different presume the goal of assimilation into current structures; those who are different assert either their similarity to or difference from those already in positions of power. The dilemma would appear to be particularly acute in the case of affirmative action policies, where the expectation is that members of disadvantaged groups will assert their similarity to those in positions of power and assimilate into current and established structures. We shall learn here with affirmative action what was revealed in the previous chapter: many feminists are critical of this framework that casts the debate in terms of either equal or different treatment. However, in uncovering the biases and assumptions underlying the framework, feminist criticisms of affirmative action, like those of equality examined in the previous chapter, can be, and sometimes have been, misinterpreted.

Michel Rosenfeld argues that Gilligan and her supporters, who value the virtues traditionally associated with women, have a difficult time defending affirmative action because their position calls for a radical restructuring of society and not an acceptance of the status quo of competition in current workplace structures. "[W]omen who oppose affirmative action as inconsistent with a program of radical transformation would have no reason to be part of any consensus or compromise on the legitimacy of affirmative action" (Rosenfeld 1991, 320 and 281). The arguments we have examined thus far for and against affirmative action do appear to accept background conditions of hierarchical workplace structures, competition for scarce jobs and promotions, and rewarding individuals for qualifications taken to be neutrally determined and objectively measurable. A defense of affirmative action by feminists who want to undermine the male norms and values assumed in these background conditions appears inconsistent because affirmative action seems merely to place members of disadvantaged groups into the competitive, hierarchical, and meritocratic workplace structures that they view as problematic.

The first important observation to make is that feminists are obviously not disputing the basic idea that the underrepresentation and underutilization of members of disadvantaged groups represent systemic and entrenched discrimination and that this is an injustice that limits freedom and opportunity. A similar observation can be made of the kind of critique feminists brought to the *Sears* case discussed in the previous chapter. Feminists who charged Sears with discriminatory hiring policies argued that women's underrepresentation in higher-paying, higher-status jobs is an injustice that needs to be addressed, but that it needs to be addressed in terms of questioning the structures within which women are forced to make career choices. Women's choices and opportunities are limited by the assumptions underlying the established norms: women are responsible for or more suited to child-rearing roles than are men, women need to adjust to a workplace designed for people without child-care responsibilities, and what constitutes higher-status and higher-paying jobs is neutrally and objectively determined. Feminist concerns about affirmative action reflect these sorts of criticisms of the norms that are in place.

To deny the real difference that child rearing has on women's opportunities for equality in a workplace structured with the male as the ideal worker, the norm, is to reinforce a disrespect for difference. Minow captures the problem when she writes, "[t]he very phrase 'special treatment,' when used to describe pregnancy or maternity leave, posits men as the norm and women as different or deviant from that norm. The problem was not women, or pregnancy, but the effort to fit women's experiences and needs into categories forged with men in mind" (Minow 1990a, 58).[16] Although this sort of criticism has been misinterpreted as feminists valorizing experiences common to women of having or wanting children and reinterpreted as women freely choosing to take on child-care responsibilities, the crux of the critique is that current workplace structures support the view that caring for children is not a political and public concern, but a private and personal one.

A questioning of the framework is also evident in other reservations about affirmative action expressed by various feminists: fears that these measures are mere token gestures, criticisms that in targeting some groups for special treatment disadvantaged groups are set against each other, concerns that these measures succeed in further stigmatization of those perceived as different, and worries about the unreasonable demands put on the few people who are expected to be representatives for their groups. Common to all these reservations is a criticism of arguments for affirmative action that assume a perspective from which members of disadvantaged groups are judged according to established standards, given special treatment, allowed in, and expected to conform to and assimilate into, the current structures. This questioning of assumptions is at the base of Sandra Harding's question about affirmative action hiring in the sciences, for example: "[w]hat is progressive about organizing heroic campaigns to 'add women and gender' to the social structure and subject matters of the sciences without questioning the legitimacy of science's social hierarchy and politically regressive agendas?" (Harding 1991, 55).

Questioning the assimilationist assumption then raises deeper questions about common beliefs regarding the objectivity and neutrality of selection procedures, of merit, and of the hierarchical division of labor. "Since impartial, value-neutral, scientific measures of merit do not exist, I argue that a major issue of justice must be who decides what are the appropriate qualifications for a given position, how they will be assessed, and whether particular individuals have them. If objective, value-neutral merit evaluation is difficult or impossible, the legitimacy of a hierarchical division of labor is called seriously into question" (Young 1990, 193).[17] What is criticized are those justifications for and implementation of affirmative action that ensure that these measures have only a "minor effect on altering the basic structure of group privilege and oppression" (Young 1990, 198).[18] And the effects of keeping the basic structures in place can be highlighted in numerous ways. A brief discussion of two examples, workplace designs and privileging some groups over others, will show the ways in which a whole system of disadvantage is left intact under assimilationist assumptions.

While there have been changes to physical environments, such as building ramps and washrooms to accommodate persons with disabilities, there have been fewer changes in the areas of job descriptions, flexible work hours and spaces, and provision of instructional or communication aids for disadvantaged groups in general, but particularly for persons with disabilities. Genuine inclusion of persons with disabilities would radically alter our conceptions of work and our perceptions of disability, including the perception that people with various kinds of disabilities constitute "a disadvantaged group" with "a perspective" and similar self-concepts and identities.[19] Taking the diversity of perspectives on disability into account would provide deep challenges to established ideas about what constitutes talent or qualification, for example. Minow's Amy can teach us just how changed both our educational structures and our attitudes and perceptions about various disabilities could be if we were open to communicating with her through sign language.

The second example, of setting target numbers for members of particular disadvantaged groups, shows how benefits to some do not challenge or alter a system of class structure. As bell hooks points out, "[i]t is evident that large numbers of individual white women (especially from middle class backgrounds) have made economic strides in the wake of feminist movement support of careerism, and affirmative action programs in many professions. However, the masses of women are as poor as ever, or poorer" (hooks 1984, 59). Young argues that "since these programs require that racially or sexually preferred candidates be qualified, and indeed often highly qualified, they do nothing directly to increase opportunities for Blacks, Latinos, or women whose social environment and lack of resources make getting qualified nearly impossible for them" (Young 1990, 198). Young sums up what underlies these reservations about affirmative action. "The terms of the affirmative action debate define a set of assumptions that accept the basic structure of the division of labor and the basic process of allocating positions. . . . To the degree that the affirmative action debate limits public attention to the relatively narrow and superficial issue of the redistribution of positions within an already given framework, that debate serves the function of supporting the structural status quo" (Young 1990, 200).

Underlying these feminist critiques is a call for reassessing the debate on affirmative action, and consequently, liberal conceptions of equality assumed by the debate. Critics are not calling for an outright rejection of these measures, but rather for a questioning of what they are expected to achieve, and a critical analysis of the limitations of particular affirmative action policies. To abandon affirmative action is to accept a status quo of inequalities that rests on perceptions of differences as inferior and as justifications for unequal treatment. As was revealed in the previous chapter, neither denying difference nor uncritically valorizing difference are appropriate strategies for challenging the liberal framework that casts difference as a dilemma. As we also discovered in the previous chapter, one way out of the dilemma is to show how the perspectives of members of disadvantaged groups present valuable points of view from which to understand how difference is constructed and to change the structures that support oppression.

But given feminist reservations about affirmative action, the question remains as to why validating and valuing different perspectives provide a defense rather than a rejection of affirmative action policies. After worrying that affirmative action can be mere "window dressing" and raising concerns that, some would say, should press feminists to abandon affirmative action altogether, Rhode turns to the familiar defense of affirmative action in terms of the importance of increasing numbers. "If its consequence is merely token representation, perfunctory interviews, or entry-level positions for the most upwardly mobile women, affirmative action may help more to legitimate than to challenge existing organizational values. . . . The danger of token representation is especially pronounced for minorities, where the presence of a few highly visible successes may obscure the remaining barriers. To minimize that risk we need more comprehensive policies, which receive strong governmental and managerial backing and which are designed to employ a critical mass of underrepresented groups.

Affirmative action is not the only strategy necessary to secure workplace equality, but it is one of the most critical" (Rhode 1989, 190).

Why is it important to achieve a "critical mass of underrepresented groups," and what will this provide in the way of change to current structures? Why settle for achieving the goal of proportional representation when the critique of entrenched discriminatory practices in current structures calls for more revolutionary strategies? The first step to take in answering these questions is to reemphasize that among other things, a relational approach shifts attention from those who have the power to name difference to those who have been so named and concentrates on the actual and potential interactions between the "two vectors of influence." I shall use relational insights about the significance of the interactive relationships between members of oppressed groups and the dominant and powerful, depicted in the concept of the orientation to other, to provide a reconceptualization of the reason for increasing members. We will discover that affirmative action measures can no longer be viewed as merely achieving a goal of proportional representation and are more appropriately defended as strategies that work from within to effect change. Attention to these strategies turns us to role models, but in the context of calling for a reconception of their function and of traditional role-modeling arguments for affirmative action. Let me clarify two things before proceeding. First, using relational insights to illustrate the effectiveness of strengthening affirmative action policies does not undermine other strategies for changing structures. Second, although the relational critique presented here uses examples most familiar to me, those of the affirmative action hiring of women in academic settings, it can be used to illustrate the effects of affirmative action measures for other groups and in other areas.

The Traditional Understanding of Role Modeling

The value of role modeling as understood in the literature on affirmative action is that it provides a consequentialist argument for affirmative action. Charges of unjust discrimination are answered by showing that role models play a positive role in achieving substantive equality of opportunity for two reasons. In the first kind of argument, many defenders of affirmative action focus on the imitative function of role modeling as an explanation for the causal connections between members' encountering others in their group in positions from which they were traditionally excluded and them pursuing the same career paths; thereby having the beneficial consequence of increasing the numbers of members of disadvantaged groups in places where they are underrepresented. Rhode, for example, writes, "[a]lthough positive effects are difficult to quantify, social science research suggests that role models have helped expand women's aspirations" (Rhode 1989, 188). Once we uncover the real reasons for the imitative success of role models, however, the scope and value of the role model begin to expand.

In the second kind of argument, a role model is taken to provide more than a way to increase numbers. Under this reasoning, identifying members of disadvantaged groups for preferential treatment should not be understood as reverse discrimination or even as justified discrimination. Rather, affirmative action hiring is nondiscriminatory because a closer affinity and sympathy among same-group members makes being a member of a disadvantaged group a qualification for certain positions.[20] To grasp how this argument works, let us examine a particular version of it as it applies to the affirmative action hiring of women in philosophy.

In a direct response to Sumner's rejection of the second kind of argument for role modeling, a rejection based on his concern about merely revising the concept "discrimination," Pamela Courtenay Hall argues, "equity hiring is a matter of 'responsive hiring' rather than a matter of justified discrimination in such workplaces as philosophy departments—'responsive hiring' because it is hiring that is responsive to long-ignored though clearly identifiable responsibilities and needs" (Courtenay Hall 1992, 235). She defends the hiring of women in philosophy departments as a needed response not only because it increases the number of women in philosophy, but also because women have perspectives that can challenge traditional modes of doing philosophy, contribute to new ways of understanding what philosophy is, and provide new theories that begin with the long-excluded experiences of women.[21] We can already note that these contributions could be made in any discipline.

Courtenay Hall argues that being a woman is a qualification for a teaching job "not because of mere linkage to the generic goal of employment equity, but rather, because it is more deeply an attribute needed for the job that is to be done" (Courtenay Hall 1992, 246). Women as role models provide an atmosphere sympathetic to women's experiences and conducive to women's self-development. Being able to identify with others and feel welcome in areas traditionally dominated by advantaged white males are phenomena whose value should not be underestimated.[22] Christine Overall points out that as a defense of affirmative action, however, this argument for role modeling raises the following pertinent questions: "why are sensitive and interested males not adequate? Why is a shared interest in and talent for history, let us say, or biology or philosophy, not enough to make a man a good role model for women students?" (Overall 1987a, 180).

Michael Martin attempts to answer this kind of question by explaining that while men *can* fill these roles, "women are more likely to be able to teach such a course than men are: they have the insight to do so, not because of some innate ability, but because of their raised consciousness and a special interest brought about in large part by the women's movement" (Martin 1973, 328). He concludes, "[w]omen students need women professors as models, not male professors sensitive to women's problems" (Martin 1973, 331). Courtenay Hall provides a similar answer by pointing out that "given that what is central to feminist philosophy (if anything is) is its starting point in the experiences of women, to look to a male philosopher to provide a standpoint in feminist philosophy would seem to be missing the point" (Courtenay Hall 1992, 238). Finally, Overall provides two possible answers to her own questions. "[T]he presence of a male as a would-be model fails to fulfil the advertising function which seems so crucial to role models. That is, his presence does not provide evidence to women students that they are welcome in the field and will not be discriminated against. Secondly, it is more difficult to identify with an individual of the other sex than with one of one's own sex. The absence of a common background and experience may make the sharing of perspectives of the male role model and his female students difficult" (Overall 1987a, 180).[23]

These reasons return us to the two arguments for role modeling with which I began this section: the imitative effect of role modeling increases numbers, and in sharing experiences with female emulators, role models make gender a qualification. Yet there are still problems with the answers given by Martin, Courtenay Hall, and Overall to the question "why women role models?" Not only do the answers fail to capture certain vital aspects of role modeling, but they also raise other questions. The argument that women have a particular perspective or shared experiences fails because it universalizes talk for and about all women. With respect to an argument for affirmative action, questions are then raised about whether women who do not share these experiences or have this perspective should be hired. Should candidates be screened for their affiliation with the groups to which they are members? Should the selection of candidates be based on traditional stereotypes about what members of those groups are like? How are we to treat people whose disadvantages result from the intersection of their membership in a number of groups? We need to take a closer look at how role models function when they are placed in contexts from which they were traditionally excluded. The common view of the concept of the role model hinders an understanding of role models as moral persons in interactive relationships.

Expanding the Role of Role Models

Overall explains that arguments in favor of role modeling are made "without much consideration of the implications of the concept, and of the web of assumptions of which it forms a part" (Overall 1987a, 179), a "web of assumptions" that has both isolating and damaging effects on those placed in the role of the model. The isolating effects come from raised expectations that a token role model can solve problems of underrepresentation. The damaging effects come from pressures on role models to assimilate into current structures. In summing up her concerns, Overall warns, "feminists should think very carefully about advocating the presence of women as role models, if their presence merely turns out to reinforce existing educational and corporate values, and conventional strategies for personal advancement. The rationale for providing female role models should not be just to help women students conform more readily to traditional pathways to traditionally defined success" (Overall 1987a, 183).

As I understand it, Overall is not arguing that women should not be role models, but criticizing the way the concept of the role model is understood.[24] Too often the role model is forced into contexts in which her role is understood to be that of the token representative who will "take care" of those like her. Moreover, "[t]he role model metaphor encourages us to think of the person who is the model as being distinct and isolated from her role as a model . . . instead of as a real person with hopes, needs, struggles, and fears like their own" (Overall 1987a, 184). The understanding of the concept encourages a distancing from the person, a person who is viewed as having been hired because she or he is a member of a disadvantaged group. These concerns are instances of the trappings of the second horn of the dilemma of difference: further stigmatization, disadvantage, and marginalization.

These are genuine worries, ones that emerge from the expectations and assumptions of those who are positioned to judge the capabilities and performance of those who are let into the spheres of influence and power. The assumption is that "the admission of a few women to carefully controlled places, so that they can serve as 'role models'—those cardboard and ephemeral constructs" (Code 1991, 263) can satisfy demands for the greater representation of women while maintaining a status quo of oppressive structures. As Code observes, this way of understanding the function of role models "offers minimal revolutionary promise" (Code 1991, 263).

As I take it, the key to answering Overall's worries about the concept "role model" and to retaining the idea that there is something vital and valuable in what role models do is to turn our attention to the "real person with hopes, needs, struggles, and fears." In capturing what it is like to be in a role and treated or viewed in that way, we can begin to reshape our understanding of role modeling. We can learn about the radical potential of role modeling by shifting from perceiving role models as filling a need for the presence of group members with similar experiences to viewing them as beings whose actions and interactions in relationships contribute to new and valuable ways of knowing and of relating to others. When we apply relational insights to the inter-

active relationships that take place between role models and emulators, for example, we discover that the role model will often be
a much more radical presence than is usually thought.

Shifting our focus to the "real person" highlights the fact that
people serving as role models are not "cardboard and ephemeral
constructs"; they are living beings in interactive relationships. To
capture this point about the personhood and agency of role models, Code calls for a change in concept: "I refer intentionally to
character models rather than *role* models in order to emphasise the
ontological significance of this point. . . . The point is to show
that, unlike roles, these ways of being are not to be assumed and
cast aside casually and randomly. Character models are living instances of possible ways of being, for a society" (Code 1986, 58,
her emphasis). As "living instances of possible ways of being,"
character models have an impact not captured in arguments for
role modeling that understand role models as effective ways for
achieving proportional representation.[25] Further, those who assume that role models want or need to assimilate to succeed miss
the more complex nature and effects of role modeling. Code's
concept of the character model comes closer to describing what
role models do and are, but it does not yet capture the full impact
and implications of the effects of role modeling.

"Character model" still has connotations of separateness and
fixity that do not quite capture the significance and importance of
interactive relationships. Further, the concept of character model
invites moral evaluation. Characters can be observed, described,
and judged by others to be good, bad, or flawed—models to be
emulated or ignored. When MacIntyre, for example, discusses
our entry into society as characters in a narrative, into "roles into
which we have been drafted" (MacIntyre 1981, 201), he has in
mind that we come to learn the roles and play the characters set
for us by the tradition into which we are born. This is not the
picture of the relational self that I have presented.

Affirmative action policies place moral persons, not fixed character roles, into interactive relationships with the dominant and
powerful. They are moral agents who through their own complex network of relationships are unique persons as well as members of disadvantaged groups who share self-concepts and
identities with other members. As members of disadvantaged
groups they can name and claim their constructed difference as

part of the emancipatory struggle toward reconstructing the perceptions and stereotypes of those identities. As unique persons formed in and through a complex of multiple relationships in various contexts they bring a plurality of perspectives into liberal contexts that endorse inclusion, but practice assimilation. For these reasons, role models, who have particular perspectives that they bring into their interactive relationships with others, may be more appropriately referred to as "subjects of difference."

Role modeling is not only about the imitative and supportive functions that role models have on members of their group or groups, it is also about the effects they have on all those with whom they interact and relate. The interactive behavior of the role model shows that the causal connections between the number of role models and emulators are not simple or unidirectional. In describing the interactions between teachers and students, for example, Overall captures the significance of these personal and dyadic relationships for changes to self-concepts. "[W]hat must be stressed is . . . the potential for mutual relationships between role models and those for whom they constitute an example. The mentor can learn from her pupil. Furthermore, the pupil can learn to trust in her own competence . . . and in the reliability of her female peers" (Overall 1987a, 185). I want to expand this account of interactive relationships even further by emphasizing the effects of the presence of role models in broad relational contexts in which they interact with the dominant and powerful. We shall discover that this is one way to extend the reach of subjects of difference from academic settings to many other areas.

A suggestive example will show that placing that dyadic relationship between teacher and pupil, in which each is affected by the relationship and self-concepts and understandings change, into the broader social and political context of currently valued and entrenched structures has the potential for changing those structures. Suppose that the teacher uses examples of women to illustrate points she is making in her lectures. It is not difficult to grasp the potential effects on the student: she tells other students about the teacher, the examples, the fact that this teaching method is rare, or her enthusiasm for learning new perspectives on a traditional discipline. The student may bring this up in class or may communicate to the teacher the impact of these different classroom experiences on her. The teacher may learn that this teaching method is rare, that it makes a difference to some of her students, or that it excludes other students. The example shows how the initial impact of the teacher on the student can form the trust and respect that Overall discusses, but it also extends the potential effects from the relationships to other issues and social contexts. Room is made for raising issues of power and authority in the classroom and of exclusion and marginalization with respect to the material and to others. Room is also made for bringing these issues into students' homes, into parents' workplaces, and into political constituencies. From such a simple example, we can extract various potential effects of one-to-one relationships, relationships that draw in a complex network in which many more than two people change and are changed.

A relational approach emphasizes that the interdependence and interactions of people have an impact on our understanding of ourselves and others. Viewing interactive relationships as formative of identity and self-concepts emphasizes the ontological significance of relationships and forces us to understand role models more as subjects of difference than as "cardboard constructs." Members of disadvantaged groups are not playing roles; and those who are affected by them are not merely modeling those roles. They are persons in a network of relationships, and they confront the stereotypes of them by being in the social and political contexts from which they were excluded in the past. The difficulties confronting solitary members of disadvantaged groups should not be underestimated, however. Fear and isolation may make it impossible to do anything more than fill the expectations of those in power and control. Yet, even here, small openings for change can be created. The example of the multiple effects of the network of relationships arising from the initial impact of the dyadic relationship between teacher and student shows how this can work. Other teachers are placed to reflect on their teaching methods and their effects on students. Other students are forced to critically examine assumptions about particular disciplines or about fellow students.

We can use the model of the complex network of relationships in which we interact with others to answer the other set of questions raised at the end of the last section about whether affirmative action policies should identify candidates who genuinely represent the group to which they belong. Part of the answer returns us to the concept of the orientation to other and the greater likeli-hood that members of disadvantaged groups will be more atten-tive to issues raised about their difference.[26] Because members of disadvantaged groups need to pay attention to relationships that adversely affect them, their greater awareness of shared experi-ences and common patterns can serve as a source of knowledge about personhood and social relations. Another part of the answer is found in the fact that our situatedness in a complex and ever-changing network of relationships makes the idea of fixed and static identities difficult to maintain. There is no set of characteris-tics that captures what it is to be a member of a particular group or set of groups. The idea that members ought to be hired to represent some identifiable set of interests of their group(s) is un-tenable.

Social contexts, particular circumstances, and personal relation-ships all influence levels of disadvantage, commitment to social causes, and identification with same-group members. These fac-tors explain how and why some members of disadvantaged groups manage to assimilate all too well and ultimately deny that their difference has been or is relevant to the way they are treated. Finally, even though we are far from reaching this state of affairs, we need to acknowledge that in contexts where affirmative action is legitimated through legislation, where these measures are in place in many areas, and where there are steady increases in the representation of members of disadvantaged groups, it will be-come more difficult to argue that men, for example, cannot effec-tively represent or be sympathetic about women's issues or that women represent a united front.[27] The long-term effects of genu-ine interaction in a network of complex and ever-changing rela-tionships would manifest themselves in the promotion of equal concern and respect for everyone and a respect for human diver-sity and ways of being. The effects may even bring about the proliferation of relationships that are sources of strength, personal growth, and moral development. But we are far from reaching this state of affairs, and members of disadvantaged groups continue to provide important perspectives on the structures of power, per-spectives that can and do reveal inequalities and injustices that continue to go unnoticed.

There are glimpses of some changes in our social context. The account in the previous chapter of the intertwinings of the different approaches of care and justice supports the idea that the "traditional sexual division of labor in public and private spheres is breaking down for many women and some men" (Ferguson 1987, 353). In interactive contexts, as Ferguson points out, "many adult women who engage in similar social practices with adult men, e.g. as business or professional colleagues, may also share with them the so-called masculine voice of moral reasoning. And men influenced enough by feminist women to attempt coparenting may develop a feminine voice of moral reasoning due to this practice" (Ferguson 1987, 351). While this discussion focuses on the limited case of how women can change both themselves and men through new interactive contexts and practices, the basic point of the political potential contained in interactive relationships between oppressors and those who are oppressed can be extended to include the possibility of change both to the perceptions and self-concepts of any disadvantaged group and to structures other than the family as we know it.

The discussion in the previous chapter shows that it is not only a matter of men and women having or trading the "voices" of care and justice but of allowing perspectives of people from many and multiple groups to inform us about what justice needs and care demands. Understood in this way, justice and care intersect in ways that can change policies and transform structures. We can imagine a number of implications for our understanding of care and justice, for example, if we lived in a context in which policies and legislation encouraged rather than deterred same-sex couples from raising children. Caring for children to whom one may not have biological connections would challenge not only traditional notions of the family but the prime value our society places on having and caring only or mainly for one's own biological offspring. As many feminists point out, access to new reproductive technologies tends to be restricted to white, middle-class, heterosexuals.[28] These policies not only reflect current structures and values, they prevent new possibilities from coming into being.

We shall discover in the next section that the full force of my argument that affirmative action measures are more subversive than is generally thought, that they hold the promise of "displacing entrenched thought structures," can be captured by taking the perspectives of subjects of difference as a starting point for thinking about the treatment of members of disadvantaged groups. This strategy of valuing perspectives is central to a relational approach and to finding a way to escape the pitfalls of the dilemma of difference. Minow, for example, writes, "[a]n alternative route to breaking free of the difference dilemma is to take seriously the perspective of those who have not been the norm in the past. From their own perspective, women, members of minority groups, and disabled people may not be abnormal; they may instead introduce more varied and more inclusive definitions of what is normal" (Minow 1990a, 95). When this idea is applied to the particular case of the affirmative action hiring of women in academic settings, we learn that affirmative action contributes to providing conditions for treating all people with equal concern and respect. Affirmative action legitimates inclusion of the different into current structures of influence and power, enables the questioning and reshaping of oppressive structures, and makes it possible for the powerful to respect the less powerful.

Using Relational Insights to Defend Affirmative Action

Affirmative action measures are generally viewed from the perspective of the powerful, who are in the position of granting special treatment and access to positions of power for those they view as different. From this perspective, the danger of further stigmatization of the disadvantaged becomes very real. Members of disadvantaged groups are allowed in and expected to perform within a structure in which hierarchies and power differentials are accepted and respected. Assuming a neutral and objective perspective from which to judge others perpetuates inequalities for those viewed as different. Taking the perspective of the dominant and powerful as the standard of comparison for assessing all perspectives has several ramifications: it makes it difficult to question existing structures that exclude some members whose differences continue to matter; it places the emphasis on increasing numbers as the means and the measure of achieving substantive equality of opportunity rather than focusing on understanding and including difference; and it misses the more subversive and radical elements of affirmative action measures.

To grasp the pernicious effects of assuming that there is a neutral perspective for judging others, take the least controversial type

of affirmative action, tie-breaking. Suppose an all-male department in a university has a history of selecting men in cases in
which male and female candidates are equally qualified. They reason that the male would be more seriously committed to research
because he will not take time off to have or care for children.[29]
Further, because they only interact with males in the workplace,
they also fear that a woman will not fit in and be "one of the
boys." They worry, for example, that she will be offended by
their "humor" about women, that she will be one of those "up-
tight" women who takes sexist comments too seriously. Suppose
that under pressure to hire women, they now select a woman in
a tie-breaking case. The point is that she is hired in a context in
which she is already perceived as having certain liabilities: she
may take time off to have children or she may not like their sexist
humor.

Given these background assumptions about child care, and fears
about what her difference will mean for their all-male workplace,
it is not unreasonable to speculate that if she decides to have children or responds negatively to a sexist comment she will merely
reinforce perceptions of these as liabilities. In the all-male department, perceptions of childbearing and child rearing as activities
that get in the way of academic responsibilities not only reinforce
stereotypes; they also make it difficult to restructure the workplace to integrate or accommodate caring for children or to perceive child-care responsibilities as an important and valuable
social activity. Entrenched assumptions about child-care responsibilities may also limit career advancement opportunities for the
woman who decides to have children. All of the consequences
and effects noted thus far emerge from the way her identity is
constructed around perceptions about what her difference means
for the all-male department. We need to examine how things
look from her perspective to highlight other consequences that
are detrimental to her self-respect and self-image and that perpetuate inequalities not discussed in liberal theories of equality.

From her perspective, the world is not as it seems to her colleagues. She knows that child-care responsibilities need not be
viewed as limitations on self-development and the realization of
goals. She knows that excluding child care responsibilities from
what is considered to be "work" perpetuates perceptions and stereotypes of women's work as less-valuable and important. She

knows that sexist humor and sexual harassment are not harmless activities but have an impact on self-image and self-confidence when one is the object of these activities. She recognizes all of the ways in which the effects of the construction of her difference, her identity, limit her opportunities to pursue her interests, projects, and goals. When she is told that she should "loosen up" about sexist comments, she may feel that she really cannot fit in unless she becomes silent on these issues. Valuable opportunities to learn new ways of understanding sexism or sexual harassment from her perspective as a woman who experiences these things differently are then closed off.

When the dominant and powerful claim to know what her difference means for the workplace and claim to understand what things are like for her, possibilities for challenging settled ways of thinking about equality and justice and for imagining new structures that address the inequalities she experiences are foreclosed. This discussion of issues with respect to child care and sexism in the workplace is fairly familiar to us now, but think of the complex of different factors with respect to perceptions, assumptions, and expectations that would suddenly appear if the new colleague introduced her lesbian partner to the department. Think too of the commonalities and the differences with respect to the sorts of inequalities experienced by women with different sexual orientations. Taking difference seriously means being able to conceive of and be open to the positive contributions that can be made by those whose perspectives are different from the dominant and powerful.

In much of the literature, the prevalent response to the problems faced by role models is to fall back on arguments about the importance of achieving a "critical mass" of representatives from disadvantaged groups. Overall, for example, rightly points out that "in practice, the presence of an individual, sole woman is not enough to effect change in an organization" (Overall 1987a, 184–185) and adds that "what we should be seeking, as feminists, is the infiltration of massive numbers of women into existing organizations . . . the transformation of those organizations, and the production of new structures. What is important is not just the presence of individuals, but the shoring up of the sex ratio so that women constitute a large percentage of every organization's personnel" (Overall 1987a, 184–185). Increasing numbers is an important goal. As we discovered in the previous chapter, having a context in which one is not isolated in male-dominated structures is vital for developing critical perspectives for understanding and fighting oppression. Within oppressive structures, these critical perspectives expand our understanding of difference and of the potentially radical impact that subjects of difference can have on policies and structures. New perspectives can change workplace structures that view the genuine inclusion of difference as violations of the injunction to treat equals equally. Only when the perspectives of the disadvantaged are included in current structures can conditions for equality obtain.

If we examine the relational dynamics of interactions in the workplace when affirmative action measures are implemented or enforced, we realize that we are already undergoing a restructuring in which the inclusion of difference has had and will continue to have an impact.[30] Subjects of difference have an impact not only on other members of the same group but also on members of other groups. Most importantly, they can and do have an impact on the perceptions that the advantaged have of the traditionally disadvantaged members of society. That impact is felt when stereotypes, formerly entrenched and intransigent, are questioned, and ways of understanding those labeled and viewed as different are challenged and changed. For example, the presence of the woman in the all-male department who encounters a "chilly climate,"[31] if she lives her difference, forces her male colleagues to confront sexist stereotypes and perceptions; the ways in which they have constructed and understood what the difference of gender means. I would not want to underestimate the difficulty subjects of difference have in changing perceptions of difference when they are the lone representatives of the groups of which they are members. Isolation and marginalization may mean that relationships with the dominant and powerful result in further damage to self-concepts, autonomy, moral development, and levels of self-respect. Further, without a strong affirmative action hiring policy, a solitary representative has great difficulty being taken seriously. But I would also not want to underestimate the subversive impact of role modeling in its potential to radically transform relationships and workplace structures. Confrontations with stereotypes are more likely in contexts in which the advantaged have to interact, communicate, and live with those labeled as different.

The radical implications of role modeling also place an onus on subjects of difference to live lives that make a difference. There is a sense in which all members of disadvantaged groups become politicized agents. bell hooks emphasizes that responsibility when she writes, "[t]hough I am not at all into the term 'role model,' I know that having many young black women looking at me, not just at my work, but at how I'm living my life—my habits of being, and seeing me as an example, as someone charting the journey, has made me work harder to get my life together. Knowing that they are watching me, seeing what's going on with my psyche, my inner well-being, has changed my priorities. I am less self-indulgent" (hooks 1990, 229). I would add that the responsibility is heightened with the realization that subjects of difference challenge stereotypes and perceptions of difference and make possible the reconstruction and reconstitution of difference, the promotion of equal concern and respect for all people, and the enhancement of respect for human diversity and ways of being.

Members of disadvantaged groups contribute not only by being models for members of the same group to imitate, not only because they have histories and experiences shared by same group members, but also because they have experiences and perspectives that can change entrenched social practices and political contexts, the practices and contexts that support the view of difference as inferior and as the basis for unequal treatment. The perspectives and experiences of the disadvantaged become privileged vantage points in the sense that they are "living instances of possible ways of being" (Code 1986, 58). Taking seriously the ways in which identities are structured in relational contexts means that affirmative action measures cannot be understood as merely making the status quo of competition for hierarchical positions more fair. Relational theory demonstrates the impact that affirmative action has on changing the very institutional structures that entrench and perpetuate inequalities. A respect for difference requires that we take the diverse perspectives of those whose difference continues to be an obstacle to their self-realization and development into account in our reflections about workplace structures and policies. A commitment to equality requires a sustained support of affirmative action as one way of implementing the second principle of respect for human diversity and ways of being.

Relational theory begins with the ontological significance of relationships and shows how relationships structure identities, create dynamics of power and control, and become interactive sites of struggle, confrontation, and change. In formulating policies that are sensitive to improving the conditions of members of disadvantaged groups, equality theorists need to acknowledge the implications of the primacy of relationships to an understanding of equality. Identifying, understanding, and dealing with difference are perspective-laden. Differences are defined relationally and are given significance through social practices and in political contexts. This means that the significance given to differences can be challenged and the perspectives of the different can offer this challenge. By making explicit the challenge that subjects of difference present to existing structures, we strengthen the case for affirmative action.

Drawing Conclusions and Looking Ahead: Relinquishing Equality of Opportunity?

Equality theorists begin with the idea of people as moral equals and formulate theories that specify the conditions needed for treating all people with equal concern and respect. Throughout, I have retained both the idea of people as moral equals and the fundamental commitment to equal concern and respect for all people, but reconceived each of them. At the base of what makes us equal is a conception of moral personhood as an ongoing process of engagement with others in a network of relationships shaped by social practices and political contexts. A relational approach replaces starting points for theorizing about equality and justice. Instead of taking the task to be that of determining what moral equals need to flourish and develop as individual and independent entities, relational theory asks what moral equals situated, embedded, and interacting in relationships of interdependency need to flourish and develop. We now understand that making the inherent sociality and interdependence of human beings the starting point for theorizing about conditions for treating people with equal concern and respect changes our understanding of people and of what is needed to achieve equality.

In this work, I have concentrated on liberal theory for two reasons. First, it has had an enormous impact on our understanding of equality and it continues to play a vital role in formulating accounts of how societies need to be structured to ensure equal treatment. Second, when we apply relational insights to our particular political context of liberalism, we uncover assumptions underlying this framework of institutional structures and thereby expand our understanding of equality and justice. But with what may now seem to some to be a harsh critical examination of liberal theory in hand, we can now examine what was left as an open question in the concluding section of Chapter 4: whether the liberal ideal of equality of opportunity remains an appropriate goal at all. In an initial attempt to provide a description of the kind of equality that fits my relational account, I suggested that we need considerable equality of resources in order to achieve genuine equality of opportunity broadly conceived.

The discussion of affirmative action, an issue closely associated with liberal structures of competition and merit, suggests that relational theory moves us away from equality of opportunity as it is cast in a liberal framework. Applying relational theory to the issue of affirmative action highlights the inequalities that remain in our social practices and political structures; inequalities that determine life prospects on the basis of meritocratic structures that accept and assume particular values and goals. By questioning the established norms, standards, and rules that structure the kinds of opportunities that are available and who has them, relational theory challenges the very structures that fix opportunities even in the seemingly opportunity rich area of the workplace. Relational theory calls for a critical examination of the exclusionary effects of current workplace designs, hierarchical structures, understandings of what constitutes talent and ability, and criteria of merit and qualifications on those who have been and continue to be disadvantaged.

We discovered that few substantive equality theorists who defend affirmative action question existing structures when they fix their focus on the goal of substantive equality of opportunity and use data on representation as the measure for the achievement of this goal. Unless workplace structures are challenged, affirmative action measures may succeed only in perpetuating a status quo in which assimilation is the aim and different contributions and perspectives that challenge existing structures and ways of thinking are unwelcome and resisted. I have argued that people who are members of disadvantaged groups offer valuable perspectives on those structures. The relational interpretation of the role played by members of disadvantaged groups when affirmative action policies are in place and strengthened demonstrates that the framework can be restructured from within when these perspectives are validated and valued. It also demonstrates that the project of equalizing starting positions and ensuring genuine equality of opportunity, broadly conceived as the opportunity to pursue interests, projects, and goals, is a much more difficult goal than liberals have thus far imagined. In fact, relational theory suggests that attentiveness to the inequalities revealed by a genuine consideration of perspectives could have dramatic social and attitudinal effects and change our understanding of all the various conceptions of equality, that of opportunity, of wealth, of resources, of well-being, of life prospects, of capabilities, and of results.

The kind of equality that is required by relational theory might be described as "equality of respect," a conception that attends to the perspectives of diverse people in the particularities of social practices and political contexts that shape people's needs, circumstances, conditions, and opportunities. Such a conception does not reject cherished notions of autonomy, moral agency, justice, impartiality, rights, welfare, and opportunity but rather reinterprets them as capacities and goals that are shaped in and through a network of complex and ever-changing relationships in which each of us is situated. An analysis of inequalities in these terms shows that an account of opportunities requires much more than liberals have recognized in their attention to distributing resources of material goods. As Sen's capabilities approach has so convincingly captured, the particular needs and diverse capacities of many people generate kinds of inequalities that are not addressed by attending only to opportunities or income levels.

Sen defends an equality of capability conception: a focus on the freedom to achieve valuable functionings, or well-being more generally, rather than on equal opportunities as such or equal resources. Because a relational approach focuses on the network of relationships within which actual people and their circumstances get shaped by concrete social practices and political contexts, an equality of respect conception is positioned to provide crucial information about the needs and capabilities of diverse others and about what is required for eliminating the inequalities they experience. I suggest than an equality of respect conception can do more than this by identifying other sorts of inequalities missed by theorists so far. Relational theory can tell us in what ways and what sorts of relationships at personal and public levels are detrimental to autonomy, moral agency, and equal opportunity. It shows what is needed to allow people to break free of oppressive relationships and to conceptualize new possibilities for promoting self-determining capacities and for enhancing the moral development and growth of all citizens.

The interests, projects, and goals of people who are members of disadvantaged groups continue to be devalued and this devaluation continues to have effects that circumscribe one's activities, limit opportunities, and reduce one's freedom to meet basic needs and develop capacities. If we take seriously the commitment to equal concern and respect for all people, then the kinds of inequalities that are generated in and through the relationships we find ourselves in at personal and public levels need to be addressed. Some of the inequalities that have not been apparent to equality theorists emerge for people who are in relationships of state dependency, power, and oppression. In these relationships between the powerful and the powerless, the oppressors and those who are oppressed, differences make their mark and continue to determine life prospects. Being identified as different has detrimental effects on opportunities in this very general sense.

The relational theory of equality I have defended has two foundational principles that have their source in classical liberal arguments but are reconceived in terms of the starting point of relationships: we ought to treat everyone with equal concern and respect, and we ought to respect human diversity and ways of being. Relational theory highlights diversity by illuminating the variety and complexity of relationships and the diverse shaping of them in social practices and political contexts. What the theory cannot provide are general conditions for satisfying equality of respect in all contexts or for all time. These conditions can only be settled dialogically in concrete contexts by taking account of the perspectives of everyone involved under conditions that promote a presentation of diverse views and that enforce mechanisms for giving and assessing justifications for current and proposed policies. I have applied this theory to our liberal structures to unfold the shortcomings of liberal theory and to suggest ways of working from within the current structures to change policies and practices. The project ends by looking ahead and envisioning the possibility of exploring the implications of the relational approach to equality presented here to other political contexts.

Endnotes

Chapter 1

1. This insight about the significance of social relations is reiterated in a recent work on Marxist theory by Christine Sypnowich: "the individual's needs, wants, and even his very personality are the product of interaction with other individuals in a community" (Sypnowich 1990, 89). Numerous theorists such as Hegel, Habermas, Buber, Bradley, Hume, and communitarians recognize the fundamental importance of social relations and explore the significance of this for epistemological and metaphysical issues as well as moral and political theory.

Chapter 2

1. My discussion of Wittgenstein's theory of meaning will be limited to a bare outline: what is needed to elucidate how a concept like equality is used. I provide a fuller account of his theory in *Paradigms: The Later Wittgenstein's View of Meaning* (Koggel 1981).

2. In explaining how a child learns a language, Quine defends the idea of a basic human capacity to notice similarities and differences. "If the child is to be amenable to such training, however, what he must have is a prior tendency to weight qualitative differences unequally. He must, so to speak, sense more resemblance between some stimulations than between others" (Quine 1960, 83).

3. The use of "she" in this context is meant to be jarring. Wittgenstein would never have thought of the builders as women, and readers fall into the same assumptions about the builders being male. If the use of "she" surprises, this too should tell us something about language.

I put women in this context of the builders' community throughout as a way of startling people out of their expectations and assumptions.

4. These remarks on background conditions for rule-following contain insights central to Wittgenstein's *On Certainty*. Consider, for example, what the following set of comments reveals about background conditions of certainty and predictability. "The game of doubting itself presupposes certainty" (Wittgenstein 1969, §115). "The child learns to believe a host of things. I.e. it learns to act according to these beliefs. Bit by bit there forms a system of what is believed, and in that system some things stand unshakeably fast and some are more or less liable to shift" (Wittgenstein 1969, §144). "In order to make a mistake, a man must already judge in conformity with mankind" (Wittgenstein 1969, §156). "The child learns by believing the adult. Doubt comes *after* belief" (Wittgenstein 1969, §160, his emphasis).

5. The following remark from Wittgenstein shows the complexity of speech acts: "we do the most various things with our sentences. Think of exclamations alone, with their completely different functions.

Water! Away! Ow! Help! Fine! No!
Are you inclined still to call these words 'names of objects'?" (Wittgenstein 1953, §27).

6. Monk describes the goal of his book as attempting to bridge the gap in Wittgenstein scholarship between "those who study his work in isolation from his life and those who find his life fascinating but his work unintelligible" (Monk 1991, xvii–xviii).

7. Teresa Iglesias makes a similar point about the human subject being essentially a moral subject and argues that the Wittgenstein of the *Tractatus* held this view in his comments about the import of ethics as contained in what could be shown and not said (Iglesias 1988–1990, 146–154).

8. Nussbaum examines Aristotle's criticisms of Platonism and refers us to her own work in support of this interpretation of Aristotle (Nussbaum 1995, 68).

9. Terminology used by F. H. Bradley in "My Station and Its Duties," a chapter of *Ethical Studies* (Bradley 1927).

10. Hacking's account of how only people are affected by classifications and descriptions of them is controversial and could arguably be extended to nonhuman species. For example, classifying rats and describing them as carriers of diseases does affect how rats are treated.

11. I thank Susan Babbitt for pointing out that Hacking's model of the two vectors of influence leaves out of account those aspects of change that emerge first in the moral imagination of those who present radical challenges to an entrenched status quo of oppression. Among

other things, her book *Impossible Dreams* explores the topic of moral imagination (Babbitt 1995a).

Chapter 3

1. In a footnote to an otherwise highly critical analysis of the different voice, Joan Williams agrees that the ethic of care is not Gilligan's main contribution. "Gilligan's primary contribution was to articulate a modern challenge to 'male norms' " (Williams 1989, 802).

2. Will Kymlicka makes a similar point when he writes "[w]e need to know *in advance* what we can rely on, and what we are responsible for, if we are to make long-term plans" (Kymlicka 1990, 280, his emphasis).

3. The reference to the word "persons" is taken from §24 of the B.N.A. Act, *S.C.R. [Supreme Court Reports]* 276 (1928).

4. Peter Westen describes classical liberal arguments in ways that fit the account I have given of their underlying logic. "For centuries, moral philosophers, arguing that all human beings are prescriptively equal, have searched for a descriptive standard by which humans are in fact equal. For the Stoics, the descriptive standard was the possession of reason; for the Epicureans, it was the capacity to experience happiness; for Christians, it was knowledge of good and evil; for Hobbes, it was the capacity to kill and be killed; for Kant, it was rationality; for John Rawls, it is 'moral personality,' a capacity to make plans and give justice; and for others, it is the state of being 'conscious beings who necessarily have intentions and purposes and see what they are doing in a certain light' " (Westen 1990, 122–123).

5. In *Ethics and the Limits of Philosophy*, Bernard Williams presents the argument in this way:

> Since I necessarily want my basic freedom, I must be opposed to courses of action that would remove it. Hence I cannot agree to any arrangement of things by which others would have the right to remove my basic freedom. So when I reflect on what arrangement of things I basically need, I see that I must claim a *right* to my basic freedom. In effect, I must lay it down as a rule for others that they respect my freedom. I claim this right solely because I am a rational agent with purposes. But if this fact alone is the basis of my claim, then a similar fact must equally be the basis of such a claim by others. If, as I suppose, I legitimately and appropriately think that they should respect my freedom, then I must recognize that they legitimately and appropriately think that I should respect their freedom. In moving from my need for freedom to "they ought not to inter-

fere with me," I must equally move from their need to "I ought not to interfere with them." (Williams 1985, 59–60, his emphasis).

6. Andrew Brook provides an interesting use of Sidgwick's principle of "mere numerical difference makes no moral difference" in his defense of why we can be said to have obligations to future generations (Brook 1992, 364–365).

7. The following remark is a favorite of mine and captures Wittgenstein's point that many questions raised by philosophers only make sense within the language games of philosophical enquiry. "I am sitting with a philosopher in the garden; he says again and again 'I know that that's a tree', pointing to a tree that is near us. Someone else arrives and hears this, and I tell him: 'This fellow isn't insane. We are only doing philosophy' " (Wittgenstein 1969, §467).

8. There is an extensive feminist literature that analyzes classic liberal texts: for example, Pateman (1988, 1989); Eisenstein (1981); Whitbeck (1973); and Gutmann (1980). Two collections of essays, one edited by Mahowald (1983) and one by Lange and Clark (1979), contain samples both from classical liberals explicitly describing women's irrationality as the justification for excluding them as members of the political sphere and feminist critiques of traditional philosophical texts.

9. Genevieve Lloyd examines the concept of rationality in traditional philosophy and its role in explaining women's inferiority and justifying women's exclusion (Lloyd 1986; 1989). Morwenna Griffiths and Joanna Hodge look at the exclusion of the emotional and of the bodily from traditional philosophical discourse (Griffiths 1988; Hodge 1988). And as we will discover, Gilligan outlines how traditional theories of moral development exclude and denigrate the virtues associated with caring for others.

10. I think that this depiction of her own work sheds light on what appears to be Gilligan's puzzling response to critics who raise objections about her methodology and the evidence for a different voice it yields. In a 1986 forum on *In a Different Voice*, Gilligan replies to a series of critical articles about her methodology in the following way: "[t]o claim that there is a voice different from those which psychologists have represented, I need only one example—one voice whose coherence is not recognized within existing interpretive schemes. To claim that common themes recur in women's conceptions of self and morality, I need a series of illustrations" (Gilligan 1986b, 327–328). Gilligan views criticisms about her methodology to be instances of the very tendencies she wants us to resist: using current research methods as the standard from which to judge her method of listening to and interpreting women's stories.

11. In "Reconstructing Sexual Equality," Christine Littleton seems

to agree that features of language are important to Gilligan's account when she writes, "while Carol Gilligan's *In a Different Voice* does not deal explicitly with language, it is aptly titled" (Littleton 1987, 1281). She does not, however, explain what she means by this comment.

12. Gilligan writes, "[f]or Jake, the equation of moral judgment with the logic of justice reasoning encourages him to take the position that anyone disagreeing with his judgment has 'the wrong set of priorities' " (Gilligan 1986b, 329).

13. A similar point is captured by Gilligan when she writes, "we know ourselves as separate only insofar as we live in connection with others, and we experience relationships only insofar as we differentiate self from other" (Gilligan 1982, 63).

Chapter 4

1. Nielsen writes concerning "the fundamental belief in the *moral* equality of persons" that it "is a deeply entrenched belief widely, but not quite universally, shared (at least in theory) across the political spectrum. It is as much a part of Nozick's moral repertoire as Cohen's" (Nielsen 1985, 307, his emphasis). Dworkin gives a similar account of how the requirement to treat people with equal concern and respect is held in common by various political theorists (Dworkin 1978, 180).

2. For a similar argument about the need to clarify the concept of equality of opportunity because by itself it is an "incomplete predicate," consult Onora O'Neill (1973).

3. Lesley Jacobs defines formal equality as the requirement "that everyone have the same legal rights of access to all advantaged social positions and offices and that these positions and offices be open to talents in the sense that they are to be distributed to those able and willing to strive for them" (Jacobs 1994, 64).

4. In an interesting and important work on Kant's ethics, Lilian Yahng presents a convincing case for rejecting an interpretation of Kant as only being concerned with formulating universal rules that apply without exception. By focusing on the second and third formulations of the categorical imperative rather than the much discussed first, she interprets Kant's work on "treating people as ends and never as mere means" and "a kingdom of ends" in a way that makes Kant's theory much more sympathetic to a defense of positive rights than is apparent in Nozick's account or is usually thought (Yahng 1997).

5. Amy Gutmann elects to call her defense of a "more equal distribution of goods, services, and opportunities" "liberal egalitarianism" (Gutmann 1980, 2). Nielsen also favors the term "liberal egalitarians" and

uses it to describe Rawls's and Dworkin's conceptions of equality (Nielsen 1985, vii).

6. Kymlicka calls his defense of substantive theory "modern liberalism," as exemplified in theory "from J. S. Mill through to Rawls and Dworkin" (Kymlicka 1989, 10).

7. Onora O'Neill uses the phrase "substantive equality of opportunity" to characterize liberals who focus on the fairness of the competition (O'Neill 1973). There is also Trakman (1994), Finley (1986, 192), and Rhode (1989, 275).

Chapter 5

1. L. W. Sumner understands Rawls's answer to the question of why the principles are morally binding to be that "the principles which rational individuals would agree on under fair conditions are themselves fair" (Sumner 1987, 159).

2. An argument similar to Okin's about putting oneself into each person's place is given by Thomas Nagel in *The Possibility of Altruism* (Nagel 1970, 138–142).

3. Kai Nielsen articulates this argument in terms that the pragmatists, Pierce and Dewey, used to criticize the method of Cartesian doubting. Such isolated critical thinking assumes a social context. "[I]f we have no place to start as social creatures with a battery of beliefs, we cannot even start" (Nielsen 1994b, 525).

4. Interestingly, in some of Okin's most recent work she develops the idea of a dialogical approach. *Justice, Gender, and the Family* incorporated empathy, but still within the model of the solitary reasoner able to move in and out of the original position and in and out of particular places. In a paper Okin gave at the Canadian Philosophical Association Meetings in 1994, she outlined Benhabib's expansion of Habermas's communicative ethics as a promising model for engaging in more accurate and adequate thinking about difference (Okin 1994). While Benhabib takes the model of communicative ethics to be a reason to reject the methodology of the original position, Okin thinks that it can still be usefully employed in and applied to the original position.

5. Benhabib takes such communication to be a rejection of empathy "for it does not mean emotionally assuming or accepting the point of view of the other" (Benhabib 1992, 137). Benhabib characterizes empathy the way I characterize sympathy: as "the capacity to 'feel with, to feel together' " (Benhabib 1992, 168). I distinguish empathy from sympathy in terms of empathy's cognitive aspects of reasoning through and about what other perspectives are like.

6. For other clear and detailed discussions by Nielsen of wide reflective equilibrium, there is also Nielsen (1994a, 100, 117–127).

7. Theoretical works on needs and capability assessments are appearing with greater frequency. Examples include a collection of essays by Martha Nussbaum and Amartya Sen called *The Quality of Life* (Nussbaum and Sen 1993) and by Nussbaum and Glover called *Women, Culture, and Development* (Nussbaum and Glover 1995). Recent work by Joan Tronto (Tronto 1993, 140–155) considers Nussbaum's account of needs and capabilities as a promising start for developing a standard for assessing inequalities and disadvantages similar to the kind of account Sen offers.

8. In recent work, Okin argues that an analysis of women's inequality is less affected by considerations of race, culture, and class, for example, than some feminists have argued. Okin presents evidence to support her case that "the problems of women of different races and cultures are in many respects 'similar to those of white, western women but moreso' " (Okin 1995, 277). I do not think she makes the case, but that is another project.

9. I am indebted to Jean Harvey for pointing out these passages in Rawls. In her paper, "Justice and Basic Rights," Harvey uses Rawls's account of envy to undermine his assumption that it is unreasonable for the less-advantaged to envy the well-off because this just worsens their own situation. For Harvey's argument and my response to it, consult Harvey (1997) and Koggel (1997).

10. In assessing his own work and critics' reactions to it in the introduction to *Political Liberalism*, Rawls writes, "I believe also, though I do not try to show in these lectures, that the alleged difficulties in discussing problems of gender and the family can be overcome" (Rawls 1993, xxxix). However, he undermines confidence that he fully understands the difficulties when in one place he writes, "I do assume that in some form the family is just" and in another, "[t]he same equality of the Declaration of Independence which Lincoln invoked to condemn slavery can be invoked to condemn the inequality and oppression of women" (Rawls 1993, xxxix). Articulating a commitment to moral equality is a necessary, but not a sufficient, step for addressing historically entrenched inequality and oppression.

Chapter 6

1. As an example of feminists who depict all liberal theory as operating with individualistic conceptions of the self, Kymlicka cites Jaggar's description of liberalism in *Feminist Politics and Human Nature* (Kymlicka

1989, 14–15). From what we have learned about Nielsen's and Cohen's critiques of Nozick's defense of pure formal equality, Kymlicka is wrong to characterize socialists as assuming all liberal theory is excessively individualistic.

2. Sandel's wavering on the issue of too thin or too thick emerges from different takes on Rawls's insistence that natural and social endowments are morally arbitrary and do not attach to individuals in any constitutive sense. He views the interpretation of the Rawlsian self as thick to be one that Rawls explicitly disavows (Sandel 1982, 80; 150) but argues that it emerges from Rawls's own comments about natural talents as a "common" or "collective" or "social" asset to be used for the "common advantage" (Rawls 1971, 101; 179; 107) and from comments in the latter half of *A Theory of Justice*, where Rawls talks about the importance of "social union," "shared final end of all the members," and "the tie of community" (Rawls 1971, 526; 527; 529; 565).

3. Another place where Sandel offers a voluntarist interpretation is in the following description of friendship: "[f]riendship becomes a way of knowing as well as liking. Uncertain which path to take, I consult a friend who knows me well, and together we deliberate, offering and assessing by turns competing descriptions of the person I am, and of the alternatives I face as they bear on my identity. To take seriously such deliberation is to allow that my friend may grasp something I have missed, may offer a more adequate account of the way my identity is engaged in the alternatives before me. . . . To deliberate with friends is to admit this possibility, which presupposes in turn a more richly-constituted self than deontology allows" (Sandel 1982, 181).

4. Sandel uses the concepts "voluntarist" and "cognitivist" throughout *Liberalism and the Limits of Justice* and defines them in these terms: "if I am a being with ends, there are at least two ways I might 'come by' them: one is by choice, the other by discovery, by 'finding them out'. The first sense of 'coming by' we might call the voluntarist dimension of agency, the second sense the cognitive dimension. Each kind of agency can be seen as repairing a different kind of dispossession" (Sandel 1982, 58).

5. As Charles Mills puts it, "[n]ostalgia for the past comes more easily for those who can identify with its ruling groups—not women, marginalized in the Athenian household, not workers, unapologetically exploited by pre-union capitalism and excluded from the franchise through property qualifications, and certainly not blacks, the naturally servile barbarian Other to Western Civilization" (Mills 1994, 7).

6. Marilyn Friedman provides a very good analysis of communitarianism in *What Are Friends For?*, a summary of which is captured in the following: "First, the communitarian's metaphysical conception of an

inherently social self has little usefulness for normative analysis. . . . Second, communitarian theory pays insufficient regard to the illegitimate moral claims that communities make on their members, linked, for example, to hierarchies of domination and subordination. Third, the specific communities of family, neighborhood, and nation so commonly invoked by communitarians are troubling paradigms of social relationships and communal life" (Friedman 1993, 237).

7. Ann Ferguson describes these aspects of what she calls the "difference theory of the self" as emerging from psychoanalytic object-relations theory. "Girls have an immediate role model for what it is to be female. . . . Consequently the girl defines a sense of self that is relational or incorporative (i.e. I am like mom in these ways). . . . Gender identity for the boy comes out differently. Society teaches him that to be male is not to be female, and due to the relative or complete absence of his father he lacks a male role model as immediate for him as is the mother for the little girl. Thus he learns to define himself oppositionally instead of relationally (I am not-mother, I am not-female)" (Ferguson 1987, 347). For a full account of object-relations theory, see Chodorow (1978; 1986).

8. Examples of this literature are found in collections of essays such as *Women and Moral Theory*, edited by Eva Feder Kittay and Diana T. Meyers, *An Ethic of Care: Feminist and Interdisciplinary Perspectives*, edited by Mary Jeanne Larrabee, and *Feminist Ethics*, edited by Claudia Card. Some of these essays criticize and some develop Gilligan's ethic of care. Larrabee's collection, for example, comments on several aspects of Gilligan's research, from the accuracy of the statistical data, to the implications for traditional moral theory, to the role of care in feminist theory. A refreshing analysis and application of the ethic of care to traditional notions of the self, standard moral reasoning, the division of moral philosophy into practical issues and theory, and epistemological questions is Rita Manning's *Speaking from the Heart* (Manning 1992).

9. Joan Tronto remarks, "[t]he equation of Gilligan's work with women's morality is a cultural phenomenon, and not of Gilligan's making" (Tronto 1987, 241). Kathy Davis's article "Toward a Feminist Rhetoric" explores answers to some pertinent questions about the phenomenon of the Gilligan debate itself. "[W]hy has the Gilligan controversy been so popular? Why did Gilligan's claim for a female ethic of care incite such interest in the first place and more to the point, why does it continue to remain a 'hot item' on the feminist agenda despite such massive criticism?" (Davis 1992, 220). She takes Gilligan's studies to be an example of successful theories that "literally *force* the audience to respond. In addition to being provocative, such theories are ambiguous enough to enable different groups of scholars to support them as well as

to require synthesis for the benefit of students and colleagues" (Davis 1992, 221, her emphasis).

10. Jean Grimshaw describes the constant change and lack of fixity of personhood in these terms: "[t]he self is *always* a more or less precarious and conflicted construction of, and compromise between, conflicting and not always conscious desires and experiences, which are born out of the ambivalences and contradictions in human experience and relationships with others" (Grimshaw 1988, 103–104, her emphasis).

11. Hume's moral theory is noteworthy for attempting to explain how emotions function in moral behavior and decision-making within social contexts. He explains that sympathy works best to motivate us to act when those close to us are the objects of pains and pleasures (Hume 1740, 488). He later expands the capacity to sympathize with individual others to whole communities, by explaining sympathy's utility in social relations. "[I]t will suffice to remark . . . that no qualities are more entitled to the general good-will and approbation of mankind than beneficence and humanity, friendship and gratitude, natural affection and public spirit, or whatever proceeds from a tender sympathy with others, and a generous concern for our kind and species" (Hume 1751, 178). Annette Baier's work builds on Humean insights about sympathy and care (Baier 1987a).

12. What I say here about close relationships nested in a network of relationships is meant to answer worries that Sue Campbell has expressed. She argued that experiencing grief over the death of a loved one has a greater impact on self-concepts than the death of a stranger has. She took this example to be a problem for an account that takes a "world of relationships" to be constitutive of self-concepts and identity. I thank her for clarifying my thinking on this and many other points.

13. Lorraine Code (1987a, 357–382), Susan Sherwin (1992, 50), and many of the articles in Claudia Card's *Feminist Ethics* critically analyze the inadequacy of the mother–child relationship as a model for feminist ethics.

14. Some feminists view friendships as more promising models for self-realization and agency because they represent interdependent and interactive relationships with equals. Examples include Annette Baier's account of "second persons" (Baier 1985a), Lorraine Code's development of Baier's account in terms of friendships between adults (Code 1987a; 1991), and Marilyn Friedman's work on the importance of equal relations to self-concepts and agency in *What Are Friends For?* (Friedman 1993).

15. In addition to Allen's account of privacy, the same collection of readings, *Beyond Domination*, contains interesting discussions of women, the private sphere, and the need for privacy by Gould (1983b) and Nicholson (1983b).

16. Eva Feder Kittay uses the word "doulia" to capture the idea of caring for "those who become needy by virtue of tending to those in need" and calls for an extension of the notion to the public domain (Kittay 1997, 233–234). I examine other aspects of Kittay's work on dependency in Chapter 7.

17. For a discussion of the issue of Gilligan's advocacy of care, consult work by Annette Baier, Lawrence Blum, Owen Flanagan and Kathryn Jackson, John Broughton, Joan Tronto, Marilyn Friedman, Seyla Benhabib, and Barbara Houston. I side with the interpretation of Gilligan as providing a critical analysis of care, evidence for which is in her account of the reasoning that takes place at the third level of an ethic of care. At this stage, Gilligan describes women who respond to and struggle with perceptions of their proper role and function prevalent in the broader social context and who reject damaging and uncritical care for others. She describes level three reasoning in terms of women's achievement of *reflective* self-consciousness and of a *critical perspective* on the "dynamics of relationships" (Gilligan 1982, 74). In other words, she identifies women's traditional roles and feminine virtues as sources of inequalities that ought to be addressed and views the actions that women take in response to their conditions of inequality as indicative of developed moral reasoning.

18. Critics such as Marilyn Friedman point out that Gilligan fails "to acknowledge the potential for *violence and harm* in human interrelationships and human community. . . . The complex reality of social life encompasses the human potential for helping, caring for, and nurturing others *as well as* the potential for harming, exploiting, and oppressing others" (Friedman 1987, 104, her emphasis).

19. Some of the Supreme Court judges drew from statistical evidence that the law was variously interpreted and unevenly applied from region to region to conclude that procedural equality was being violated (Supreme Court of Canada 1988, 473–478). These were also the findings of the government's Badgley Committee set up in 1976 to study how the abortion law worked in practice (Canada. Committee on the Operation of the Abortion Law 1977).

20. Consult John Broughton's "Women's Rationality and Men's Virtues" for a different kind of interpretation of the very same responses given by Gilligan's subjects (Broughton 1983, 597–642).

21. Important discussions of feminist theory's neglect of issues such as race, culture, sexual orientation, and disability are appearing with greater frequency. There is, for example, work by Lugones (1987; 1991); Lorde (1984); Collins (1990); Harris (1990); Kline (1989); Nzegwu (1995); and Crenshaw (1989).

22. An example of how a recognition of different factors affects our

analysis of social practices and resultant inequalities is given by Marlee Kline, who argues that some feminist accounts of motherhood do not coincide with black women's experiences of either motherhood or work. "The traditional ideological division between motherhood and employment that has been applied to white women has not applied in the same way to Black women, who have traditionally been perceived simultaneously as workers and mothers" (Kline 1989, 374).

23. In *Talking Back: Thinking Feminist, Thinking Black*, hooks discusses the importance of considering the interconnectedness of the multiple factors of sex, race, and class as a more adequate account of women's oppression than that provided by theorists such as Gilligan. An examination of her numerous publications shows how hooks herself sometimes falls into the tendency to universalize and assume perspectives when she privileges certain kinds of oppression over others.

24. For an interesting analysis of persons whose identities and interests are tied up with those on whom they are dependent, check Susan Babbitt's discussion of the "deferential wife" in "Feminism and Objective Interests: The Role of Transformational Experiences in Rational Deliberation" (Babbitt 1993).

25. Giving the care perspective a broader application coheres and coincides with adjustments by both Kohlberg and Gilligan in their work since 1982. Kohlberg's work shows movement in the direction of validating the care perspective (Kohlberg et al. 1983, 121–141). There, he claims that even in his early work he attributed women's lower scores on his scale of moral development to differences in education and found similarities between scores for women and for working-class males (Kohlberg et al. 1983, 122). Gilligan and her supporters have moved in the direction of loosening the correspondence between justice as the voice of men and care as the voice of women (Gilligan 1988, xxxiii–xxxviii; Gilligan and Attanucci 1988, 82–85).

26. Joan Tronto explains that "[o]bject-relations theory cannot stand as the explanation for gender differences in morality if we accept the evidence reported by Stack and others that men do care as well. In this way, the biases of race, class, and ethnicity are exposed among a variety of dimensions, and reach back to the underlying supports for Gilligan's theory being read so overwhelmingly as a gender difference" (Tronto 1993, 85).

27. Lawrence Houston concurs when he writes, "in African moral development, most of the focus is on social conduct rather than on individual behavior" (Houston 1990, 121).

28. Jean Baker Miller captures the simple point underlying the orientation to other: "anyone in a subordinate position must learn to be attuned to the vicissitudes of mood, pleasure, and displeasure of the

dominant group" (Miller 1986, 39). So too does Allan Bloom in a different context when he writes, "[c]hildren tend to be rather better observers of adults' characters than adults are of children's, because children are so dependent on adults that it is very much in their interest to discover the weaknesses of their elders" (Bloom 1987, 315).

29. At the very beginning of *Feminist Theory: From Margin to Center*, bell hooks captures nicely a central insight about the value of different perspectives. "Living as we did—on the edge—we developed a particular way of seeing reality. We looked both from the outside in and from the inside out. We focused our attention on the center as well as on the margin. We understood both. . . . Our survival depended on an ongoing public awareness of the separation between margin and center and an ongoing private acknowledgment that we were a necessary, vital part of that whole" (hooks 1984, i). Feminist epistemology builds on these insights by arguing for the importance of experiences and perspectives in an account of what we can know. Consult, for example, Sandra Harding (1986; 1989; 1990; 1991); Nancy Hartsock (1983); Alison Jaggar (1983a, 351–394); Lorraine Code (1987a; 1987b; 1988a; 1988b; 1991); Anne Seller (1988); Linda Alcoff and Elizabeth Potter (1993); and Linda Alcoff (1988).

30. Marilyn Frye has an excellent analysis of oppression in *The Politics of Reality* (Frye 1983, 1–16). For an important analysis of the difference between social groups whose members experience oppression and aggregates or associations whose members do not, consult Iris Young's discussion in *Justice and the Politics of Difference* (Young 1990, 40–48).

Chapter 7

1. Dworkin defines the right to equal treatment as "the right to an equal distribution of some opportunity or resource or burden" (Dworkin 1978, 227) and gives as an example the right that gives each person one and only one vote. Other appropriate examples are the negative liberty rights defended by libertarians. Dworkin defines the right to treatment as an equal as "the right, not to receive the same distribution of some burden or benefit, but to be treated with the same respect and concern as anyone else." It is the right to have one's interests "treated as fully and sympathetically as the interests of any others" (Dworkin 1978, 227).

2. The *Sears* case has been discussed extensively in the feminist literature. Examples are Williams (1989); Minow (1987; 1990b); and Scott (1990).

3. Davis provides a sample drawn from the literature of how close a

link there is between discrediting Gilligan's research and expressing moral and political concerns about it. "The Gilligan debate provides myriad instances of critics going to great lengths to establish that a specifically female ethic of care rests on methodological or theoretical quicksand, only to do an about-face in their closing paragraphs where true colors are tellingly revealed and a host of decidedly unscientific fears expressed: Gilligan opens up the possibility of 'the cult of true womanhood' (Luria 1986), radical feminist separatism (Walker 1983), acceptance of male irresponsibility in moral matters (Code 1983), or support of the status quo of female subordination (Auerbach et al. 1985)" (Davis 1992, 225).

4. Manning describes her response to *In a Different Voice* as being "jolted out of [her] dogmatic slumber" (Manning 1992, 1). In an intriguing response to Gilligan's descriptions of care, Robin West typifies the "shock of recognition" reaction:

> When I read Carol Gilligan's book for the first time several years ago, I had an unequivocal shock of recognition. What she is saying, I thought then and still think, is important, transformative, empowering, exciting, enlivening, and, most fundamentally, it is simply *true*. It is true of me, and was true of my mother, and is true of my sisters. She has described the way I think, what I value, what I fear, how I have grown, and how I hope to grow. And she has described the moral lives of the women I know as well. Her book captures what I know and have always known but have never been able to claim as my own moral vision, and what parts of that vision I share with women generally (West 1988, 55–56, her emphasis).

West then goes on to explain that she had similar reactions of recognition to reading Andrea Dworkin's descriptions of women's experiences of victimization.

5. The list of feminists who have explored the tension in feminist theory between those who assert and those who deny difference is extensive. For example, there is an important article on the debate by Linda Alcoff called "Cultural Feminism versus Poststructuralism: The Identity Crisis in Feminist Theory" (Alcoff 1988). Consult also Bacchi (1990), Fuss (1989), Jaggar (1990), Littleton (1987), Offen (1988), Scott (1990), Sypnowich (1993a, 1993b), West (1988), Williams (1989), and the collection of essays edited by Hirsch and Keller (1990).

6. Kathryn Pauly Morgan describes the context in which women's identities are constructed for them by others as "moral madness." "We are first told that there is a moral domain in which we achieve excellence. Then we are told that we can only achieve excellence in that domain. Then we are told that this domain is not a domain in which

morality operates in its most exemplary way—if at all. And finally we are blamed for living our moral lives in that domain while being told that we can do no other. This must generate moral confusion if not outright madness" (Morgan 1987, 212). The source of "madness" is the constant and unavoidable struggle with the social construction of difference.

7. Thornton writes, "[w]hat has happened in recent feminist thought is that *liberation* has entered alongside *equality* as the coordinating concept of the programme for women's advancement" (Thornton 1986, 96, her emphasis). She argues that feminists "must look beyond equality to liberation" and that "liberationism fully accepts the genders as they are as the starting point of feminism" (Thornton 1986, 98). She argues that in contrast, "sex equality, or the removal of women's disqualification, does nothing in itself to explore new societal forms which build on the distinctive gender characteristics of women" (Thornton 1986, 98).

8. A point perhaps at odds with Audre Lorde's belief that "the master's tools will never dismantle the master's house" (Lorde 1984, 110–113).

9. Hawkesworth points out that feminists have advanced a number of important insights and contributions all within the framework of reasoned argument.

> They have labored long and hard to apply tools of logic and induction to the circumstances of women's lives. They have raised an epistemological challenge to men's claim to "know" women's "nature" and to "know" what is in women's best interests. They have argued forcefully that women should be considered 'human' rather than a species apart. They have demonstrated that the values of freedom, equality, independence, knowledge, opportunity, self-determination so highly prized by men hold the same attraction for women. They have proven that the obstacles to women's full participation in social, political, economic, and intellectual life are humanly created and imposed and hence amenable to human alteration. They have argued on the grounds of justice, progress, individualism, and social utility that society be structured in accordance with the 'principles of perfect equality, admitting no power or privilege on the one side, nor disability on the other.' (Hawkesworth 1990, 119).

10. Linda Krieger defends Gilligan's interpretation of justice as purely formal and assumes that this is a correct depiction of all liberal theory in her examination of how the issue of pregnancy is a difference that cannot fit into the strict formal equality conception (Krieger 1987).

11. Many, including Kohlberg, take the ethic of justice to be exem-

plified in Kant's moral theory. Yahng argues that this interpretation of Kant can only be maintained when all the weight is placed on the first formulation of the categorical imperative, a formula for determining universal moral rules by abstracting from particular contexts and moral agents. When attention turns to Kant's discussion of "treating people as ends and never merely as means" and of the "kingdom of ends," it is far from clear that Kant can be used as the base for Kohlberg's account of developed moral reasoning (Yahng 1997). More importantly with respect to care ethics, Kant's moral theory may not be so very different from care's concern for others.

12. In a defense of Kohlberg's ethic of justice, Gertrud Nunner-Winkler argues that the Heinz dilemma, as Kohlberg presents it, requires a contextual response. She points out that unlike perfect duties or negative rights that allow for no exceptions and can be obeyed without "taking note of situational specifics," imperfect duties "require situation-specific knowledge, for they demand contextually situated decisions in regard to when and where to act and in regard to whom" (Nunner-Winkler 1984, 146). Lawrence Blum develops this idea further by arguing that the ability to apply principles is dependent on the capacity to care for individuals. "[W]hat it takes to bring such principles to bear on individual situations involves qualities of character and sensibilities which are themselves moral, and which go beyond the straightforward process of consulting a principle and then conforming one's will and action to it" (Blum 1988, 59).

13. Kymlicka expresses the point in this way: "the whole contrast between responsibilities and rights threatens to collapse" (Kymlicka 1990, 275).

14. Kymlicka argues that caring for others assumes a commitment to and belief in the equal worth of all individuals (Kymlicka 1990, 275–276). Broughton makes a similar point: "Gilligan and her subjects seem to presuppose something like 'the right of all to respect as a person,' 'the right to be treated sympathetically and as an equal,' and 'the duty to respect and not to hurt others.' . . . [I]t is difficult to see in what way she is not . . . recommending more or less binding rights and duties or perhaps even 'principles' of personal welfare and benevolent concern" (Broughton 1983, 122).

15. "Just Caring" is also used by Rita Manning as the title of chapter 4 of her book, *Speaking from the Heart*, (Manning 1992) and of an article in *Hypatia*. Manning argues for a greater role for the ethic of care by demonstrating that while principle-based ethics give us minimum standards for moral behavior, care goes beyond this in giving us rules for positive moral responses to others.

16. Kittay's work on the one-sided dependency of persons with dis-

abilities and of the elderly extends dependency considerations beyond those of early childhood. She focuses on dependency as "a feature of our human condition" and examines cases of "utter dependency" (Kittay 1997, 220) to illuminate the implications of this "less tractable form of relationality" for political theory (Meyers 1997, 11). I extend the notion of dependency even further to cover public relationships of state and institutional dependency and focus on the *interdependency* of people to examine the implications of all sorts of relationships for equality analysis.

17. Tronto also emphasizes interdependence when she writes, "it is part of the human condition that our autonomy occurs only after a long period of dependence, and that in many regards, we remain dependent upon others throughout our lives. . . . Since people are sometimes autonomous, sometimes dependent, sometimes providing care for those who are dependent, humans are best described as interdependent. Thinking of people as interdependent allows us to understand both autonomous and involved elements of life" (Tronto 1993, 162). And although Gilligan leaves the idea undeveloped in her work, she depicts care as "evolv[ing] around a *central* insight, that self and other are interdependent" (Gilligan 1982, 74, my emphasis).

18. Kittay has been developing an interesting and important analysis of Rawls and, in particular, of Rawls's later work in what she refers to as a "dependency critique," some of which appeared in a paper she read at Queen's University in 1993 (Kittay 1993).

19. Drydyk uses Ruddick's notion of maternal thinking in the context of global ethics. He uses the knowledge of care and neglect that maternal thinking generates to provide a critique of Eurocentrism and to argue that we have a moral obligation to extend equal concern and respect toward people in any society (Drydyk 1995).

20. In a fairly uncharacteristic interpretation of what Gilligan means by complementarity, Elizabeth Schneider captures what I believe is Gilligan's essential argument: "[s]he suggests that if you include both voices, you will transform the very nature of the conversation; the discourse is no longer either simply about justice or simply about caring; rather it is about bringing them together to transform the domain" (Schneider 1986, 517).

21. Wittgenstein discusses the phenomenon of "seeing as" and shifting perspectives in a number of places in Part II of the *Philosophical Investigations* (Wittgenstein 1953).

22. This is one reason some critics understand Gilligan as propounding a *feminine* and not a *feminist* ethic. As Sherwin points out, it is the dual project of describing phenomena of oppression and prescribing the means for eliminating oppression that distinguishes the two. "Feminist ethics is different from feminine ethics. It derives from the explicitly

political perspective of feminism, wherein the oppression of women is seen to be morally and politically unacceptable. Hence it involves more than recognition of women's actual experiences and moral practices; it incorporates a critique of the specific practices that constitute their oppression" (Sherwin 1992, 49).

23. The list of feminist writers who take consciousness-raising to be a vital contribution to feminist theory is extensive. Elizabeth Schneider, for example, gives consciousness-raising a primary role. "In conscious-ness-raising groups, learning starts with the individual and personal (the private), moves to the general and social (the public), and then reflects back on itself. . . . Consciousness-raising as feminist method is a form of praxis because it transcends the theory and practice dichotomy" (Schnei-der 1986, 511). Catharine MacKinnon describes it as *the* methodology of feminist theory (MacKinnon 1982, 1983). Also consult Seller (1988, 179); Griffiths (1988, 146–147); Sherwin (1989, 19); Bartlett (1990, 556–557); and Code (1991, 292).

24. Susan Sherwin discusses women's experiences as a component essential to feminist theory: "the methodology of feminism is the meth-odology of women's thought: consciousness-raising begins with per-sonal experience, focusing on the details of experience, and then collectively moves to a broader analysis. . . . [F]eminists seek to concen-trate on women's own experience" (Sherwin 1989, 27).

25. Jaggar defends women-centered communities as creating a space "free from male intrusion. In this space, women can nurture each other and themselves. They can begin to practice their own values and be-come clearer about them by doing so. They can develop the skills and the strengths forbidden to women under patriarchy" (Jaggar 1983a, 270). Frye expands separatist strategies to include various kinds of separa-tion from male-defined and male-dominated relationships, institutions, and practices: "[b]reaking up or avoiding close relationships or working relationships; forbidding someone to enter your house; excluding some-one from your company, or from your meeting; withdrawal from partic-ipation in some activity or institution, or avoidance of participation; avoidance of communications and influence from certain quarters (not listening to music with sexist lyrics, not watching tv); withholding com-mitment or support; rejection of or rudeness toward obnoxious individ-uals" (Frye 1983, 97). While I would not want to undermine the positive effects that separatist strategies can achieve, I think that the idea of a network of relationships emphasizes the difficulties of escaping "a world of relationships."

26. An example of very good discussion of Rawls's later work is Kit-tay's dependency critique. Kittay evaluates such Rawlsian notions in *Political Liberalism* as "well-ordered society," "self-originating sources of

valid claims," "free and equal citizens," and "fully cooperating members of society" to show that the considerations of those who are dependent and those who care for dependents are not represented by the liberal self or in the liberal society that Rawls describes (Kittay 1997).

27. Rawls writes, "[s]ince we start within the tradition of democratic thought, we also think of citizens as free and equal persons. The basic intuitive idea is that in virtue of what we may call their moral powers, and the powers of reason, thought, and judgment connected with those powers, we say that persons are free. And in virtue of their having these powers to the requisite degree to be fully cooperating members of society, we say that persons are equal" (Rawls 1985, 233).

28. In *Political Liberalism* Rawls denies that changes to his theory are the result of communitarian objections. "The changes in the later essays are sometimes said to be replies to criticisms raised by communitarians and others. I don't believe there is a basis for saying this" (Rawls 1993, xvii). This is an interesting disclaimer. But, if his revisions are not in response to communitarians, they are clarifications of the scope of his theory made in light of communitarian objections.

29. In "Foundations of Liberal Equality," Dworkin presents a very important critique of Rawls on tolerance and an interesting liberal defense of it in terms that articulate the ethical convictions that are foundational to liberalism (Dworkin 1995).

30. J. S. Andrews provides an interesting discussion of the difference between Rawls's political liberalism and more comprehensive liberal substantive theories such as Dworkin's. Andrews develops an argument for multicultural civic education as a public and political matter (it fosters the capacity for a sense of justice). Andrews uses Rawls's own endorsement of toleration to argue that political issues of justice and moral issues of how to live a good life are not so easily separable and that justice requires attention to the moral education of citizens (Andrews 1994).

31. Patricia Williams outlines the subversive impact of using rights discourse. "The vocabulary of rights speaks to an establishment that values the guise of stability, and from whom social change for the better must come (whether it is given, taken, or smuggled). Change argued for in the sheep's clothing of stability ('rights') can be effective, even as it destabilizes certain other establishment values" (Williams 1991, 149).

32. Jean Harvey is developing an interesting account of the need to incorporate an account of these sorts of rights in a theory of justice. She calls for a conception of social justice that moves away from strict attention to distributional issues and provides an account of a set of basic rights and obligations that have "more to do with *relationships and interactions* than to do with the distribution of assets" (Harvey 1997, 6, her emphasis).

33. I have borrowed from Minow's work on the relationality of difference. There are other critics working on this topic. Lucinda Finley also describes her work as a "new approach to differences that sees them as relational and thus accepts them in a nonhierarchical, nonpejorative way" (Finley 1986, 204).

34. A relational approach can be applied to current policies in addition to affirmative action as well as generate new ones. Minow's work is significant in both respects. Another application that tests the merits of a specific policy is found in Kittay's "Taking Dependency Seriously: Social Cooperation, The Family Medical Leave Act, and Gender Equality Considered in Light of the Social Organization of Dependency Work" (Kittay 1995).

Chapter 8

1. Jan Narveson's libertarian account is an exception to the acceptance of the right to nondiscrimination. He formulates an extreme version of mere formal equality and argues that even antidiscrimination legislation is an unjust interference with the freedom of private sector employers to associate with whomever they choose regardless of their reasons (Narveson 1991; 1995, 249).

2. Dworkin argues that these examples of American Supreme Court rulings on affirmative action illustrate the distinction between the right to equal treatment and the right to treatment as an equal. The right to equal treatment requires that everyone have the same right to the assignment of law school places, no matter what their differences. The right to treatment as an equal, on the other hand, allows special treatment to be given to those who have been and continue to be disadvantaged because of their difference (Dworkin 1978, 227).

3. The literature on affirmative action has many examples of arguments on both sides of the issue concerning whether or not compensation to all members of disadvantaged groups can be justified. On the side of those who defend strict compensation to individuals and not groups, consult Goldman (1975a; 1975b; 1977); Newton (1973); Blackstone (1975); Sher (1975; 1977); Gross (1975); Simon (1974; 1978a; 1978b; 1979); Levin (1980; 1981); and Lee (1985). On the side of those who defend compensation to groups, consult Jaggar's reply to Goldman's objections (1977); Brooks (1983); Boxill (1978); Nickel (1974a; 1974b); and America (1986). Judith Jarvis Thomson argues that all individuals who are members of disadvantaged groups suffer the detrimental effects of "lack of self-confidence, and lack of self-respect" through discrimination (Thomson 1973, 381) and that this justifies compensating all mem-

bers of disadvantaged groups. A similar argument is provided by Minas (1977).

4. Considering justice in terms of compensation for discriminatory actions also raises questions about the burden placed on innocent white males. Here again, the literature provides arguments on both sides of the issue. Examples of those who defend the burdens placed on all white males include Pluhar (1981); Fried (1973); and Thomson (1973). Examples of those who do not think the burden on white males can be justified include Carr (1982); Groarke (1983; 1990); Brooks (1983); and Gross (1975).

5. Hawkesworth views the retributive and compensatory models of justice as "grounded in individualist assumptions that undermine cross-generational claims of justice for groups" (Hawkesworth 1990, 107). She adds "[t]hat women have suffered discrimination at determinate points in history can be proven; but identifying the particular men responsible for that situation is often far more difficult. The model of compensation underlying this conception of justice requires identification of specific parties in specific instances. Absent such identification, no rectification is possible. Thus, the retributive conception of justice cannot support feminist claims for compensation to contemporary women for a legacy of historical injustices" (Hawkesworth 1990, 107).

6. Judith Jarvis Thomson argues that "the nature of the wrongs done is such as to make jobs the best and most suitable form of compensation. What blacks and women were denied was full membership in the community; and nothing can more appropriately make amends for that wrong than precisely what will make them feel they now finally have it" (Thomson 1973, 383).

7. Work by Beauchamp (1979); Wasserstrom (1976; 1978); Thalberg (1972; 1973); Nagel (1989); and Vanterpool (1989) argue in favor of utilitarian justifications for affirmative action as justified discrimination.

8. There is unnecessary confusion about underrepresentation and underutilization in the literature. Judy Wubnig, for example, misrepresents proponents of affirmative action as arguing for proportional representation for all members of all groups in all positions with no regard for qualifications. She argues that proponents of affirmative action would support measures that ensured that because women represent half the population, positions such as basketball players, musicians, mathematicians, and so on should have 50–50 representation by women and men (Wubnig 1976, 36–38). Mary Hawkesworth clarifies the confusion by distinguishing underutilization from underrepresentation. "Underutilization involves a comparison of the number of women in particular career positions with the number of women in the labor force who possess all the relevant qualifications for the job. Studies of underutiliza-

tion compare, for example, the number of women faculty hired in specific disciplines with the number of women Ph.D.s in that discipline who are on the job market in a given year. What investigations of underutilization seek to explain is not the dearth of women professionals or women in skilled craft positions per se, but the dearth of women in these fields given the availability of qualified women candidates" (Hawkesworth 1990, 53). A similar discussion of underutilization is provided in Ezorsky (1977).

9. In addition to Sumner's account, there is an extensive literature defending affirmative action as a means of leveling out the effects of biased perceptions: Warren (1977); Purdy (1984); Minas (1977); Wendell (1980); and Nicholson (1983a).

10. Diana Majury goes so far as to suggest that "[p]ragmatically, at least in Canada, women have no choice but to address equality-based arguments; at the very least, we have to be ready to respond to arguments framed in terms of equality" (Majury 1987, 265). She adds that the *Charter* "should put an end to, or perhaps foreclose, any discussion of whether or not Canadian women should advocate or support an equality-based approach to issues" (Majury 1987, 265–266).

11. The report by the Canadian Advisory Council on the Status of Women (1989) reviews the effects of the equality provisions three years after implementation. The report discusses the background negotiations leading up to the equality provisions, the legislation, and the court cases relevant to Section 15. For similar discussions, consult Day (1987); Gibson (1986); Eberts (1985a; 1985b); Bankier (1985); Lahey (1987; 1989); Smith (1986); and Bayefsky (1987).

12. In the margin to Section 15(2) the phrase "affirmative action" is used to identify the measures. Similar distinctions and provisions for affirmative action measures are also present in the Canadian Human Rights Code and in many provincial human rights codes.

13. Kymlicka turns to the *Charter* to provide an interesting analogy between arguments in favour of affirmative action and those in favor of minority rights:

> The relationship between Section 15.1 and Section 35 can be seen as analogous to the relationship between 15.1 and 15.2, which provides for affirmative action to promote the position of disadvantaged groups. Just as the provision for affirmative action can be seen as spelling out the basic right to equality guaranteed in 15.1, given the special circumstances of those disadvantaged groups, so the guarantee of aboriginal rights can be seen as spelling out what it means to treat aboriginal people as equals, given their special circumstances. The requirement to compensate for unequal circumstances, through

affirmative action and minority rights, is not in conflict with the demand that everyone have equal protection of the law. Rather, it helps instruct judges how to interpret that fundamental requirement (Kymlicka 1989, 190–191).

The references are to Sections 15 and 35 of the *Charter.* Section 35 defines the "Rights of the Aboriginal Peoples of Canada." Kymlicka defends minority rights as positive measures, in addition to affirmative action, for dealing with entrenched and intransigent inequalities.

14. *Action Travail des Femmes v. Canadian National Railway Company Co. et al. Dominion Law Reports* 40 D.L.R. (4th), 1987.

15. Many assume that affirmative action is just "demeaning to the favoured person or group" (Hunter 1986, 202). Similar discussions are in Lee (1985) and Bloom (1987, 96). In a tongue-in-cheek reply to this kind of argument, Rhode gives the following anecdote: "[m]any members of underrepresented groups find it demeaning to be denied affirmative action on the ground that they will experience it as demeaning. Barbara Babcock, an Assistant Attorney General in the Carter administration, made a similar point. When asked how she felt about gaining her position because she was a woman, Babcock responded, 'It feels better than being rejected for the position because you're a woman.' " (Rhode 1989, 187–188). Rhode adds, "omitted from many critics' calculations are the consequences of living with the discrimination that equal-opportunity approaches fail to address. Whether conscious or unconscious, such discrimination exacts a heavy toll" (Rhode 1989, 188). Other discussions attacking the assumption of stigmatization are provided by Massey (1981) and Vanterpool (1989).

16. Minow provides a more extensive examination of the particular problems that pregnancy and child care present for liberal conceptions in "Adjudicating Differences" (Minow 1990b).

17. Linda Nicholson casts doubt on the notion that criteria for determining merit are objective by showing that biased perceptions of the talents and capacities of children who are members of disadvantaged groups result in streamlining these children in educational institutions long before they even get to the job market (Nicholson 1983a; Morgan 1983).

18. In commenting on how little gets changed when the norms remain in place, Sandra Harding writes, "[a] meritocracy, by structuring society so that a re-examination of the goals and favored means of achieving them is done only by those who are already powerful and thereby have an interest in remaining powerful, hampers the legitimate and necessary critical examination by all the members of the society of the nature and functioning of the society" (Harding 1978/1979, 218).

19. J. E. Bickenbach outlines an ecological or interactive approach to disability that takes into account "the essential role played by environmental factors (social, attitudinal, physical) in the creation of the various dimensions of disability" (Bickenbach 1997, 287). More extensive work in this area is provided in Bickenbach (1993).

20. Michael Davis argues that affirmative action is not discriminatory and that race, in the United States, is a qualification for jobs (Davis 1983).

21. For discussions of what women can contribute in the way of different perspectives and methodologies to a discipline, there is work by Boddington (1988); Moulton (1989); and Sherwin (1987).

22. My own experiences as a lecturer in introductory philosophy courses testify to the importance of female students' being able to observe that others "like them" can do philosophy. Female students repeatedly tell me that having a female instructor makes a difference. When I press them to tell me why, they say that most of their philosophy courses make them feel unwelcome because the syllabus is dominated by male authors, there is an aggressiveness in the way that philosophical debates are conducted that makes them feel uncomfortable, and there is a sometimes not so subtle rejection of their comments when they attempt to introduce female contributors into the discussion. These reasons are elements of systemic discrimination and are more difficult to identify and address than overt and blatant discrimination. In a 1991 report by the Canadian Philosophical Association on the notorious underrepresentation of women in philosophy, the authors not only give data of underrepresentation but provide reasons for it that correspond closely to the kind of reasons given by Courtenay Hall and my female students (Baker et al. 1991). The data are corroborated by Statistics Canada, whose figures for female faculty show that philosophy runs a close second to religion as the discipline in the arts and social sciences with the fewest number of women (Statistics Canada. *Teachers in Universities*, 81–241; *Universities: Enrolment and Degrees*, 81–204). Consult also the report by Symons and Page (1984) for statistical data on university hiring and promotion. A controversial interpretation of the data is offered by Irvine (1996), who argues that relative to their numbers in the pool of applicants, women have been preferentially hired in universities for the last three decades. Articles by Burns (1994) and Sumner (1996) reinterpret the data and challenge Irvine's approach.

23. Code provides a possible explanation for why the "sharing of perspectives of the male role model and his female students" may be difficult. "[A] sense of cognitive dissonance constrains their aspirations when women *always* have to define their cognitive standards according to possibilities only rarely available to people like themselves. People

learn about their possibilities, initially, from observing what people 'like them' (whatever the extension of that phrase) can do" (Code 1991, 187, her emphasis).

24. There is an interesting discussion by Jeanne Speizer, who argues that the concept of role model, being fairly new, needs further definition and study and not quick conclusions about the effects on numbers of the presence of role models in institutions (Speizer 1981).

25. Rhode calls the focus on greater proportional representation "a 'body count' approach to affirmative action" (Rhode 1989, 189). Yet, when it comes to defending affirmative action, she herself justifies it in terms of increasing numbers.

26. In an uncompromising argument in favor of strong affirmative action policies that will give women an equal representation in public offices, Hawkesworth argues that "[w]hat could reasonably be expected is that women in office would be sensitive to forms of disadvantage that uniquely affect women and that they would take such problems seriously. Thus, sex parity in office would function as a procedural mechanism designed to ensure that the relevance of sex in any particular policy instance would remain an open question" (Hawkesworth 1990, 184).

27. In the context of her argument for equal representation of women in public office, Hawkesworth writes, "[b]ecause individual women are as different from one another as they are from men, it would be a mistake to expect a univocal stance from women in office. Because the pressures upon legislators from constituents, lobbyists, political parties, colleagues, committee responsibilities, personal loyalties, and individual expertise and conscience all play a role in determining officials' policy stances, it would be absurd to expect women in office to form a unified and invariant voting bloc" (Hawkesworth 1990, 183).

28. As one example of feminist work on the topic of restrictions with respect to who has access to New Reproductive Technologies, consult Christine Overall (1987b, 166–190).

29. Mary Anne Warren labels some of these unarticulated perceptions "secondary sexism" (Warren 1977, 11). It needs to be noted that a lot happens before the candidates are determined to be equally qualified. More overt perceptions such as that her philosophical interests are not mainstream or that she is less aggressive in philosophical debates or that she is too aggressive about feminism are factors that may prevent her from ever getting as far as the tie-breaking situation.

30. Some of these changes are evident in my own experiences in the university setting. When I was an M.A. student over a decade ago, experiences of sexist humor, sexual harassment, and marginalization in the classroom were, more often than not, internalized as personal problems and taken as indications of having provoked the comments or

harassment and of not measuring up intellectually. With so few other women students and faculty, these issues were just not discussed. Changes began with an increase in women's representation at the faculty and student level. Women started speaking about their experiences and discovered that other women shared those experiences. More than a decade later, I notice in female students a heightened awareness about what counts as discrimination and of the subtle forms it can take. And along with some resentments and bitterness about changes, I also notice male faculty who can and do take account of women's experiences as valid entry points to a better understanding of difference.

31. For discussions of the effects of a chilly climate, consult Backhouse (1990); Finn (1989); and Caplan (1993).

Bibliography

Addelson, Kathryn Pyne. (1991). *Impure Thoughts: Essays on Philosophy, Feminism & Ethics*. Philadelphia: Temple University Press.

Adler, Jonathan E. (1987). "Moral Development and the Personal Point of View." In *Women and Moral Theory*, ed. Eva Feder Kittay and Diana T. Meyers. Totowa, N.J.: Rowman & Littlefield.

————— (1989). "Particularity, Gilligan and the Two-Levels View: A Reply." *Ethics* 100 (October):149–156.

Alcoff, Linda. (1988). "Cultural Feminism versus Poststructuralism: The Identity Crisis in Feminist Theory." *Signs* 13, no. 3:405–436.

Alcoff, Linda, and Elizabeth Potter, eds. (1993). *Feminist Epistemologies*. New York: Routledge.

Allen, Anita L. (1983). "Women and Their Privacy: What is at Stake?" In *Beyond Domination: New Perspectives on Women and Philosophy*, ed. Carol C. Gould. Totowa, N.J.: Rowman & Allanheld.

America, Richard F. (1986). "Affirmative Action and Redistributive Ethics." *Journal of Business Ethics* 5 (February):73–77.

Andrews, J. S. (1994). "Liberal Equality and the Justification of Multicultural, Civic Education." *The Canadian Journal of Law and Jurisprudence* VII (1):111–126.

Aristotle. *Politics*, trans. Benjamin Jowett. In *The Basic Works of Aristotle*, ed. Richard McKeon. New York: Random House, 1941.

Auerbach, Judy, Linda Blum, Vicki Smith, and Christine Williams. (1985). "On Gilligan's *In a Different Voice*." *Feminist Studies* 11 (1):149–161.

Axelsen, Diana. (1977/1978). "With All Deliberate Delay: On Justifying Preferential Policies in Education and Employment." *Philosophical Forum (Boston)* 9 (Winter/Spring):264–288.

Babbitt, Susan. (1992). "Feminists and Nature: A Defence of Essentialism." Paper read at C-SWIP Annual Conference, York University.

———— (1993). "Feminism and Objective Interests: The Role of Trans-formation Experiences in Rational Deliberation." In *Feminist Episte-mologies*, ed. Linda Alcoff and Elizabeth Potter. New York: Routledge.

———— (1995a). *Impossible Dreams: Rationality, Integrity, and Moral Imagi-nation*. Boulder, Colo.: Westview Press.

———— (1995b). "Political Philosophy and the Challenge of the Per-sonal: From Narcissism to Radical Critique." *Philosophical Studies* 77:293–318.

Bacchi, Carol Lee. (1990). *Same Difference: Feminism and Sexual Differ-ence*. Sydney: Allen & Unwin.

Backhouse, Constance. (1990). "Women Faculty at the University of Western Ontario: Reflections on the Employment Equity Award." *Canadian Journal of Women and the Law* 4, no. 1:36–65.

Baier, Annette C. (1985a). *Postures of the Mind: Essays on Mind and Mor-als*. Minneapolis: University of Minnesota Press.

———— (1985b). "What Do Women Want in a Moral Theory?" *Nous* 19:53–63.

———— (1987a). "Hume, the Women's Moral Theorist?" In *Women and Moral Theory*, ed. Eva Feder Kittay and Diana T. Meyers. Totowa, N.J.: Rowman & Littlefield.

———— (1987b). "The Need for More Than Justice." In *Science, Moral-ity & Feminist Theory*, ed. Marsha Hanen and Kai Nielsen. Calgary: The University of Calgary Press.

———— (1991). "Whom Can Women Trust?" In *Feminist Ethics*, ed. Claudia Card. Lawrence, Kans.: University Press of Kansas.

Baker, Brenda, Josiane Boulad-Ayoub, Lorraine Code, Michael Mc-Donald, Kathleen Okruhlik, Susan Sherwin and Wayne Sumner. (1991). *Report to the Canadian Philosophical Association from the Commit-tee to Study Hiring Policies Affecting Women*. Ottawa: Canadian Philo-sophical Association.

Bankier, Jennifer K. (1985). "Equality, Affirmative Action, and the Charter: Reconciling 'Inconsistent' Sections." *Canadian Journal of Women and the Law* 1:134–152.

Barry, Brian. (1973). *A Liberal Theory of Justice: A Critical Examination of the Principal Doctrines in* A Theory of Justice *by John Rawls*. Oxford: Clarendon Press.

Bartky, Sandra Lee. (1990). *Femininity and Domination: Studies in the Phe-nomenological of Oppression*. New York: Routledge.

Bartlett, Katharine T. (1990). "Feminist Legal Methods." In *Feminist Legal Theory: Foundations*, ed. D. Kelly Weisberg. Philadelphia: Tem-ple University Press, 1993.

Baumrind, Diana. (1986). "Sex Differences in Moral Reasoning: Re-sponse to Walker's (1984) Conclusion that There are None." In *An*

Ethic of Care: Feminist and Interdisciplinary Perspectives, ed. Mary J. Larrabee. New York: Routledge, 1993.

Bayefsky, Anne F. (1986). "Orientation of Section 15 of the Canadian Charter." In *Litigating the Values of a Nation*, ed. Joseph Weiler and Robin Elliot. Toronto: Carswell.

—— (1987). "Defining Equality Rights under the Charter." In *Equality and Judicial Neutrality*, ed. Kathleen E. Mahoney and Sheilah L. Martin. Toronto: Carswell.

Beauchamp, Tom L. (1979). "Blackstone and the Problem of Reverse Discrimination." *Social Theory and Practice* 5 (Spring):227–238.

Benhabib, Seyla. (1987a). "The Generalized and the Concrete Other: The Kohlberg-Gilligan Controversy and Moral Theory." In *Women and Moral Theory*, ed. Eva Feder Kittay and Diana T. Meyers. Totowa, N.J.: Rowman & Littlefield.

—— (1987b). "Introduction: Beyond the Politics of Gender." In *Feminism As Critique: On the Politics of Gender*, ed. Seyla Benhabib and Drucilla Cornell. Minneapolis: University of Minnesota Press.

—— (1992). *Situating the Self: Gender, Community and Postmodernism in Contemporary Ethics*. New York: Routledge.

—— (1995). "Cultural Complexity, Moral Interdependence, and the Global Dialogical Community." In *Women, Culture and Development: A Study of Human Capabilities*, ed. Martha Nussbaum and Jonathan Glover. Oxford: Clarendon Press.

Benhabib, Seyla, and Drucilla Cornell, eds. (1987). *Feminism as Critique: On the Politics of Gender*. Minneapolis: University of Minnesota Press.

Benjamin, Jessica. (1983). "In a Different Voice: Psychological Theory and Women's Development Review." *Signs: Journal of Women in Culture and Society* 9, no. 2:297–298.

Bickenbach, Jerome E. (1993). *Physical Disability and Social Policy*. Toronto: University of Toronto Press.

—— (1997). "Disability and Equality." In *Contemporary Moral Issues*, 4th edition, ed. Wesley Cragg and Christine Koggel. Toronto: McGraw-Hill Ryerson.

Blackstone, William T. (1975). "Reverse Discrimination and Compensatory Justice." *Social Theory and Practice* 3, no. 3:253–288.

Blackstone, William, and Robert Heslep, eds. (1977). *Social Justice and Preferential Treatment*. Athens: University of Georgia Press.

Bloom, Allan. (1987). *The Closing of the American Mind*. New York: Simon and Schuster.

Blum, Lawrence A. (1988). "Gilligan and Kohlberg: Implications for Moral Theory." In *An Ethic of Care: Feminist and Interdisciplinary Perspectives*, ed. Mary Jeanne Larrabee. New York: Routledge, 1993.

Blum, Lawrence, Marcia Homiak, Judy Housman, and Naomi Scheman. (1976). "Altruism and Women's Oppression." In *Women and Philosophy: Toward a Theory of Liberation*, ed. Carol C. Gould and Marx W. Wartofsky. New York: G. P. Putnam's Sons.

Boddington, Paula Ruth. (1988). "The Issue of Women's Philosophy." In *Feminist Perspectives in Philosophy*, ed. Morwenna Griffiths and Margaret Whitford. Bloomington: Indiana University Press.

Bordo, Susan. (1990). "Feminism, Postmodernism, and Gender-Scepticism." In *Feminism/Postmodernism*, ed. Linda J. Nicholson. New York: Routledge.

Boxill, Bernard R. (1978). "The Morality of Preferential Hiring." *Philosophy & Public Affairs* 7, no. 3:246–268.

Brabeck, Mary. (1983). "Moral Judgment: Theory and Research on Differences Between Males and Females." In *An Ethic of Care: Feminist and Interdisciplinary Perspectives*, ed. Mary Jeanne Larrabee. New York: Routledge, 1993.

Bradley, F. H. (1927). *Ethical Studies*. Oxford: Clarendon Press.

Brook, Andrew. (1992). "Obligations to Future Generations: A Case Study." In *Contemporary Moral Issues*, 3rd edition, ed. Wesley Cragg. Toronto: McGraw-Hill Ryerson.

Brooks, D. H. M. (1983). "Why Reverse Discrimination Is Especially Wrong." *Journal of Value Inquiry* 17:305–312.

Broughton, John M. (1983). "Women's Rationality and Men's Virtues: A Critique of Gender Dualism in Gilligan's Theory of Moral Development." In *An Ethic of Care: Feminist and Interdisciplinary Perspectives*, ed. Mary Jeanne Larrabee. New York: Routledge, 1993.

Burns, Steven. (1994). "The Canadian Philosophical Association Decision on Employment Equity." *Deutsche Zeitschrift für Philosophie*, 42 (3): 523–529. Published in German translation.

Butler, Judith. (1990). "Gender Trouble, Feminist Theory, and Psychoanalytic Discourse." In *Feminism/Postmodernism*, ed. Linda J. Nicholson. New York: Routledge.

Cain, Patricia A. (1990). "Feminism and the Limits of Equality." In *Feminist Legal Theory: Foundations*, ed. D. Kelly Weisberg. Philadelphia: Temple University Press, 1993.

Canada. Committee on the Operation of the Abortion Law. (1977). *Report*. Ottawa: Supply and Services Canada.

Canada. Federal Court of Appeal. (1985). *Canadian National Railway Company v. Canadian Human Rights Commission et al.* 1 F.C. 101.

Canada. Royal Commission on Equality in Employment. (1983). *Research Studies of the Commission on Equality in Employment*. Ottawa: Supply and Services Canada.

——— (1984). *Report of the Commission on Equality in Employment*. Ottawa: Supply and Services Canada.

Canadian Advisory Council on the Status of Women. (1989). *Canadian Charter Equality Rights for Women: One Step Forward or Two Steps Back?* Ottawa: Canadian Advisory Council on the Status of Women.

Caplan, Paula J. (1993). *Lifting a Ton of Feathers: A Woman's Guide for Surviving in the Academic World.* Toronto: University of Toronto Press.

Card, Claudia. (1990). "Caring and Evil." *Hypatia* 5, no. 1:100–108.

Card, Claudia, ed. (1991). *Feminist Ethics.* Lawrence, Kans.: University Press of Kansas.

Carr, C. R. (1982). "Unfair Sacrifice-Reply to Pluhar's 'Preferential Hiring and Unjust Sacrifice.'" *Philosophical Forum (Boston)* 14, no. 1:94–97.

Chegwidden, Paula, and Wendy Katz. (1983). "American and Canadian Perspectives on Affirmative Action: A Response to the Fraser Institute." *Journal of Business Ethics* 2:191–202.

Chodorow, Nancy Julia. (1978). *The Reproduction of Mothering.* Berkeley: University of California Press.

———— (1986). "Toward a Relational Individualism: The Mediation of Self Through Psychoanalysis." In *Reconstructing Individualism: Autonomy, Individuality, and the Self in Western Thought,* ed. Thomas C. Heller, Morton Sosna, and David E. Wellbery. Stanford: Stanford University Press.

Code, Lorraine. (1983). "Responsibility and the Epistemic Community: Woman's Place." *Social Research* 50, no. 3:537–555.

———— (1986). "Simple Equality Is Not Enough." *Australasian Journal of Philosophy,* Supplement to v. 64 (June):48–65.

———— (1987a). "Second Persons." In *Science, Morality & Feminist Theory,* ed. Marsha Hanen and Kai Nielsen. Calgary: The University of Calgary Press.

———— (1987b). "The Tyranny of Stereotypes." In *Women: Isolation and Bonding: The Ecology of Gender,* ed. Kathleen Storrie. Toronto: Methuen.

———— (1988a). "Credibility: A Double Standard." In *Feminist Perspectives: Philosophical Essays on Method and Morals,* ed. Lorraine Code, Sheila Mullett, and Christine Overall. Toronto: University of Toronto Press.

———— (1988b). "Experience, Knowledge and Responsibility." In *Feminist Perspectives in Philosophy,* ed. M. Griffiths and M. Whitford. Bloomington: Indiana University Press.

———— (1991). *What Can She Know? Feminist Theory and the Construction of Knowledge.* Ithaca: Cornell University Press.

Code, Lorraine, Sheila Mullett, and Christine Overall, eds. (1988). *Feminist Perspectives: Philosophical Essays on Method and Morals.* Toronto: University of Toronto Press.

Code, Lorraine, Maureen Ford, Kathleen Martindale, Susan Sherwin, and Debra Shogan. (1991). *Is Feminist Ethics Possible?* Ottawa: CRIAW/ICREF.

Cohen, G. A. (1978). "Robert Nozick and Wilt Chamberlain: How Patterns Preserve Liberty." In *Justice and Economic Distribution*, ed. John Arthur and William H. Shaw. Englewood Cliffs, N.J.: Prentice-Hall.

———— (1995). "Incentives, Inequality, and Community." In *Equal Freedom: Selected Tanner Lectures on Human Values*, ed. Stephen Darwall. Ann Arbor: University of Michigan Press.

Collins, Patricia Hill. (1990). *Black Feminist Thought: Knowledge, Consciousness, and the Politics of Empowerment*. Boston: Unwin Hyman.

Courtenay Hall, Pamela. (1992). "From Justified Discrimination to Responsive Hiring: The Role Model Argument and Female Equity Hiring in Philosophy." In *Contemporary Moral Issues*, 3rd edition, ed. Wesley Cragg. Toronto: McGraw-Hill Ryerson.

Crenshaw, Kimberle. (1989). "Demarginalizing the Intersection of Race and Sex: A Black Feminist Critique of Antidiscrimination Doctrine, Feminist Theory and Antiracist Politics." In *Feminist Legal Theory: Foundations*, ed. D. Kelly Weisberg. Philadelphia: Temple University Press, 1993.

Darity, William. (1987). "Equal Opportunity, Equal Results and Social Hierarchy." *Praxis International* 7 (July):174–185.

Davis, Kathy. (1992). "Toward a Feminist Rhetoric: The Gilligan Debate Revisited." *Women's Studies International Forum* 15, no. 2: 219–231.

Davis, Michael. (1981). "Racial Quotas, Weights, and Real Possibilities: A Moral for Moral Theory." *Social Theory and Practice* 7 (Spring):49–84.

———— (1983). "Race as Merit." *Mind* 92 (July):347–367.

Day, Shelagh. (1987). "Impediments to Achieving Equality." In *Equality and Judicial Neutrality*, ed. Kathleen E. Mahoney and Sheilah L. Martin. Toronto: Carswell.

De Lauretis, Teresa. (1990). "Upping the Anti (sic) in Feminist Theory." In *Conflicts in Feminism*, ed. Marianne Hirsch and Evelyn Fox Keller. New York: Routledge.

Dill, Bonnie Thornton. (1987). "The Dialectics of Black Womanhood." In *Feminism and Methodology: Social Science Issues*, ed. Sandra Harding. Bloomington: Indiana University Press.

Di Stefano, Christine. (1990). "Dilemmas of Difference: Feminism, Modernity, and Postmodernism." In *Feminism/Postmodernism*, ed. Linda J. Nicholson. New York: Routledge.

Drydyk, Jay. (1995). "Discourse Ethics and Eurocentrism." Unpublished paper.

Dworkin, Ronald. (1978). *Taking Rights Seriously.* London: Duckworth.

———— (1981a). "What is Equality? Part 1: Equality of Welfare." *Philosophy & Public Affairs* 10, no. 3:185–246.

———— (1981b). "What is Equality? Part 2: Equality of Resources." *Philosophy & Public Affairs* 10, no. 4:283–345.

———— (1995). "Foundations of Liberal Equality." In *Equal Freedom: Selected Tanner Lectures on Human Values,* ed. Stephen Darwall. Ann Arbor: University of Michigan Press.

Eberts, Mary. (1985a). "Gender Based Discrimination and Section 15." In *Equality: Section 15 and Charter Procedures.* Toronto: Law Society of Upper Canada, Continuing Legal Education.

———— (1985b). "Sex-based Discrimination and the Charter." In *Equality Rights and the Canadian Charter of Rights and Freedoms,* ed. Anne F. Bayefsky and Mary Eberts. Toronto: Carswell.

Eichler, Margrit. (1988). "The Elusive Idea-Defining Equality." *Canadian Human Rights Yearbook* 5:167–188.

Eisenstein, Zillah R. (1981). *The Radical Future of Liberal Feminism.* New York: Longman.

———— (1984). *Feminism and Sexual Equality: Crisis in Liberal America.* New York: Monthly Review Press.

Engelmann, Paul. (1967). *Letters from Ludwig Wittgenstein with a Memoir.* Oxford: Blackwell.

Ezorsky, Gertrude. (1974). "It's Mine." *Philosophy & Public Affairs* 3, no. 3:321–330.

———— (1977). "Hiring Women Faculty." *Philosophy & Public Affairs* 7, no. 1:82–91.

———— (1981). "On Refined Utilitarianism." *Journal of Philosophy* 78 (March):156–159.

———— (1991). *Racism and Justice: The Case for Affirmative Action.* Ithaca: Cornell University Press.

Faust, Beatrice. (1980). *Women, Sex & Pornography.* London: Melbourne House.

Ferguson, Ann. (1987). "A Feminist Aspect Theory of the Self." In *Science, Morality & Feminist Theory,* ed. Marsha Hanen and Kai Nielsen. Calgary: The University of Calgary Press.

Finley, Lucinda M. (1986). "Transcending Equality Theory: A Way Out of the Maternity and the Workplace Debate." In *Feminist Legal Theory: Foundations,* ed. D. Kelly Weisberg. Philadelphia: Temple University Press, 1993.

Finn, Geraldine. (1989). "On the Oppression of Women in Philosophy—or Whatever Happened to Objectivity?" In *Feminism: From Pressure to Politics,* ed. Angela Miles and Geraldine Finn. Montreal: Black Rose Books.

Flanagan, Owen, and Kathryn Jackson. (1987). "Justice, Care, and Gender: the Kohlberg-Gilligan Debate Revisited." *Ethics* 97:622–637.

Flax, Jane. (1990). "Postmodernism and Gender Relations in Feminist Theory." In *Feminism/Postmodernism*, ed. Linda J. Nicholson. New York: Routledge.

Flew, Antony. (1989). *Equality in Liberty and Justice*. London: Routledge.

Fox-Genovese, Elizabeth. (1985/1986). "Women's Rights, Affirmative Action, and the Myth of Individualism." *George Washington Law Review* 54:338–374.

Fraser Institute. (1982). *Discrimination, Affirmative Action and Equal Opportunity*. Vancouver: Fraser Institute.

Fried, Marlene Gerber. (1973). "In Defense of Preferential Hiring." *Philosophical Forum (Boston)* 5, no. 2:309–319.

——— (1979). "The Invisibility of Oppression." *Philosophical Forum (Boston)* 11 (Fall):18–29.

Friedman, Marilyn. (1985). "Abraham, Socrates, and Heinz: Where are the Women? (Care and Context in Moral Reasoning)." In *Moral Dilemmas: Philosophical and Psychological Issues in the Development of Moral Reasoning*, ed. Carol Gibb Harding. Chicago: Precedent Publishing, Inc.

——— (1987). "Beyond Caring: The De-moralization of Gender." In *Science, Morality & Feminist Theory*, ed. Marsha Hanen and Kai Nielsen. Calgary: The University of Calgary Press.

——— (1991). "The Social Self and the Partiality Debates." In *Feminist Ethics*, ed. Claudia Card. Lawrence, Kans.: University Press of Kansas.

——— (1993). *What Are Friends For?: Feminist Perspectives on Personal Relationships and Moral Theory*. Ithaca: Cornell University Press.

Frye, Marilyn. (1983). *The Politics of Reality: Essays in Feminist Theory*. Freedom, Calif.: The Crossing Press.

——— (1985). "History and Responsibility." *Women's International Studies Forum* 8, no. 3:215–217.

Fullinwider, Robert K. (1975). "Preferential Hiring and Compensation." *Social Theory and Practice* 3 (Spring):307–320.

——— (1980). *The Reverse Discrimination Controversy*. Totowa, N.J.: Rowman & Littlefield.

Fuss, Diana. (1989). *Essentially Speaking: Feminism, Nature & Difference*. New York: Routledge.

Garry, Ann, and Marilyn Pearsall, eds. (1989). *Women, Knowledge, and Reality: Explorations in Feminist Philosophy*. Boston: Unwin Hyman.

Gatens, Moira. (1991). *Feminism and Philosophy: Perspectives on Difference and Equality*. Bloomington: Indiana University Press.

Gibson, Dale. (1986). "Accentuating the Positive and Eliminating the Negative: Remedies for Inequality Under the Canadian Charter." In

Righting the Balance: Canada's New Equality Rights, ed. Lynn Smith. Saskatoon: The Canadian Human Rights Reporter.

Gilligan, Carol. (1982). *In a Different Voice: Psychological Theory and Women's Development*. Cambridge, Mass.: Harvard University Press.

——— (1986a). "Remapping the Moral Domain: New Images of the Self in Relationship." In *Reconstructing Individualism: Autonomy, Individuality, and the Self in Western Thought*, ed. Thomas C. Heller, Morton Sosna, and David E. Wellbery. Stanford: Stanford University Press.

——— (1986b). "Reply to Critics." *Signs: Journal of Women in Culture and Society* 11, no. 2:324–333.

——— (1987a). "Moral Orientation and Moral Development." In *Women and Moral Theory*, ed. Eva Feder Kittay and Diana T. Meyers. Totowa, N.J.: Rowman & Littlefield.

——— (1987b). "Woman's Place in Man's Life Cycle." In *Feminism and Methodology: Social Science Issues*, ed. Sandra Harding. Bloomington: Indiana University Press.

——— (1988). "Adolescent Development Reconsidered." In *Mapping the Moral Domain: A Contribution of Women's Thinking to Psychological Theory and Education*, ed. Carol Gilligan et al. Cambridge, Mass.: Harvard University Press.

——— (1993). "Letter to Readers, 1993." In *In a Different Voice: Psychological Theory and Women's Development*. Cambridge, Mass.: Harvard University Press.

Gilligan, Carol, and Jane Attanucci. (1988). "Two Moral Orientations." In *Mapping the Moral Domain: A Contribution of Women's Thinking to Psychological Theory and Education*, ed. Carol Gilligan et al. Cambridge, Mass.: Harvard University Press.

Ginzberg, Ruth. (1991). "Philosophy Is Not a Luxury." In *Feminist Ethics*, ed. Claudia Card. Lawrence, Kans.: University Press of Kansas.

Goldman, Alan H. (1975a). "Limits to the Justification of Reverse Discrimination." *Social Theory and Practice* 3, no. 2:289–306.

——— (1975b). "Reparations to Individuals or Groups?" *Analysis* 35, no. 5:168–170.

——— (1976). "Affirmative Action." *Philosophy & Public Affairs* 5, no. 2:178–195.

——— (1977). "Reply to Jaggar's 'Relaxing the Limits on Preferential Treatment.'" *Social Theory and Practice* 4, no. 2:235–237.

——— (1979). *Justice and Reverse Discrimination*. Princeton, N.J.: Princeton University Press.

——— (1987). "The Justification of Equal Opportunity." *Social Philosophy and Policy* 5, no. 1:88–103.

Gould, Carol C., ed. (1983a). *Beyond Domination: New Perspectives on Women and Philosophy*. Totowa, N.J.: Rowman & Allanheld.

————— (1983b). "Private Rights and Public Virtues: Women, the Family, and Democracy." In *Beyond Domination: New Perspectives on Women and Philosophy*, ed. Carol C. Gould. Totowa, N.J.: Rowman & Allanheld.

Gould, Carol C., and Marx W. Wartofsky, eds. (1976). *Women and Philosophy: Toward a Theory of Liberation*. New York: G. P. Putnam's Sons.

Grant, Judith. (1987). "I Feel Therefore I Am: A Critique of Female Experience as the Basis for a Feminist Epistemology." *Women & Politics* 7, no. 3:99–113.

Green, Karen. (1986). "Rawls, Women and the Priority of Liberty." *Australasian Journal of Philosophy*, Supplement to v. 64 (June):26–36.

Greeno, Catherine G., and Eleanor E. Maccoby. (1986). "How Different is the 'Different Voice'?" *Signs: Journal of Women in Culture and Society* 11, no, 2:310–316.

Griffith, William B. (1994). "Equality and Egalitarianism: Framing the Contemporary Debate." *The Canadian Journal of Law and Jurisprudence* VII, no. 1:5–26.

Griffiths, Morwenna. (1988). "Feminism, Feelings and Philosophy." In *Feminist Perspectives in Philosophy*, ed. Morwenna Griffiths and Margaret Whitford. Bloomington: Indiana University Press.

Griffiths, Morwenna, and Margaret Whitford, eds. (1988). *Feminist Perspectives in Philosophy*. Bloomington: Indiana University Press.

Grimshaw, Jean. (1988). "Autonomy and Identity in Feminist Thinking." In *Feminist Perspectives in Philosophy*, ed. Morwenna Griffiths and Margaret Whitford. Bloomington: Indiana University Press.

Groarke, Leo. (1983). "Beyond Affirmative Action." *Atlantis* 9, no. 1:13–24.

————— (1990). "Affirmative Action as a Form of Restitution." *Journal of Business Ethics* 9, no. 3:207–213.

————— (1996). "What's in a Number? Consequentialism and Employment Equity." *Dialogue* 35, no. 2:359–373.

Gross, Barry R. (1975). "Is Turn about Fair Play?" *Journal of Critical Analysis* 5, no. 4:126–135.

————— (1987). "Real Equality of Opportunity." *Social Philosophy and Policy* 5, no. 1:120–142.

Gross, Elizabeth. (1986). "Conclusion: What Is Feminist Theory?" In *Feminist Challenges: Social and Political Theory*, ed. Carole Pateman and Elizabeth Gross. Boston: Northeastern University Press.

Grosz, Elizabeth. (1990). "Philosophy." In *Feminist Knowledge: Critique and Construct*, ed. Sneja Gunew. London: Routledge.

Gutmann, Amy. (1980). *Liberal Equality*. Cambridge: Cambridge University Press.

————— (1985). "Communitarian Critics of Liberalism." *Philosophy & Public Affairs* 14, no. 3:308–322.

Hacking, Ian. (1986). "Making Up People." In *Reconstructing Individualism: Autonomy, Individuality, and the Self in Western Thought*, ed. Thomas C. Heller, Morton Sosna, and David E. Wellbery. Stanford: Stanford University Press.

Halperin, David M. (1989). "Sex Before Sexuality: Pederasty, Politics, and Power in Classical Athens." In *Hidden from History: Reclaiming the Gay and Lesbian Past*, ed. Martin Duberman et al. New York: New American Library.

Hanen, Marsha. (1987). "Introduction: Toward Integration." In *Science, Morality & Feminist Theory*. Calgary: The University of Calgary Press.

———— (1988). "Feminism, Objectivity, and Legal Truth." In *Feminist Perspectives: Philosophical Essays on Method and Morals*, ed. Lorraine Code, Sheila Mullett, and Christine Overall. Toronto: University of Toronto Press.

Hanen, Marsha, and Kai Nielsen, ed. (1987). *Science, Morality & Feminist Theory*. Calgary: The University of Calgary Press.

Haraway, Donna. (1988). "Situated Knowledges: The Science Question in Feminism and the Privilege of Partial Perspective." *Feminist Studies* 14, no. 3:575–599.

Harding, Sandra. (1976). "Feminism: Reform or Revolution." In *Women and Philosophy: Toward a Theory of Liberation*, ed. Carol C. Gould and Marx W. Wartofsky. New York: G. P. Putnam's Sons.

———— (1978/1979). "Is the Equality of Opportunity Principle Democratic?" *Philosophical Forum (Boston)* 10 (Winter/Summer):206–223.

———— (1986). "The Instability of the Analytical Categories of Feminist Theory." In *Feminist Theory in Practice and Process*, ed. Micheline R. Malson et al. Chicago: University of Chicago Press, 1989.

———— (1987a). "The Curious Coincidence of Feminine and African Moralities: Challenges for Feminist Theory." In *Women and Moral Theory*, ed. Eva Feder Kittay and Diana T. Meyers. Totowa, N.J.: Rowman & Littlefield.

———— (1987b). "Epistemological Questions." In *Feminism and Methodology: Social Science Issues*, ed. Sandra Harding. Bloomington: Indiana University Press.

———— (1989). "Feminist Justificatory Strategies." In *Women, Knowledge, and Reality: Explorations in Feminist Philosophy*, ed. Ann Garry and Marilyn Pearsall. Boston: Unwin Hyman.

———— (1990). "Feminism, Science, and the Anti-Enlightenment Critique." In *Feminism/Postmodernism*, ed. Linda J. Nicholson. New York: Routledge.

———— (1991). *Whose Science? Whose Knowledge? Thinking from Women's Lives*. Ithaca: Cornell University Press.

Harding, Sandra, ed. (1987). *Feminism and Methodology: Social Science Issues*. Bloomington: Indiana University Press.

Harris, Angela P. (1990). "Race and Essentialism in Feminist Legal Theory." In *Feminist Legal Theory: Foundations*, ed. D. Kelly Weisberg. Philadelphia: Temple University Press, 1993.

Hartmann, Heidi. (1987). "The Family as the Locus of Gender, Class, and Political Struggle." In *Feminism and Methodology: Social Science Issues*, ed. Sandra Harding. Bloomington: Indiana University Press.

——— (1992). "The Unhappy Marriage of Marxism and Feminism: Towards a More Progressive Union." In *Feminist Philosophies*, ed. Janet A. Kourany, James P. Sterba, and Rosemarie Tong. Englewood Cliffs, N.J.: Prentice-Hall.

Hartsock, Nancy C. M. (1983). "The Feminist Standpoint: Developing a Ground for a Specifically Feminist Historical Materialism." In *Discovering Reality: Feminist Perspectives on Epistemology, Metaphysics, Methodology, and Philosophy of Science*, ed. Sandra Harding and Merrill B. Hintikka. Boston: D. Reidel Publishing Co.

Harvey, Jean. (1997). "Justice and Basic Rights." Paper read at the Learned Societies Congress, St. John's, Newfoundland.

Hawkesworth, Mary E. (1984). "The Affirmative Action Debate and Conflicting Conceptions of Individuality." In *Business Ethics in Canada*, 2nd ed., ed. Deborah C. Poff and Wilfrid J. Waluchow. Scarborough, Ont.: Prentice-Hall Canada, 1991.

——— (1989). "Knowers, Knowing, Known: Feminist Theory and Claims of Truth." In *Feminist Theory in Practice and Process*, ed. Micheline R. Malson et al. Chicago: University of Chicago Press.

——— (1990). *Beyond Oppression: Feminist Theory and Political Strategy*. New York: Continuum.

Hekman, Susan J. (1995). *Moral Voices, Moral Selves: Carol Gilligan and Feminist Moral Theory*. Cambridge: Polity Press.

Held, Virginia. (1973). "Reasonable Progress and Self-Respect." *The Monist* 57, no. 1:12–27.

——— (1976). "Marx, Sex, and the Transformation of Society." In *Women and Philosophy: Toward a Theory of Liberation*, ed. Carol C. Gould and Marx W. Wartofsky. New York: G. P. Putnam's Sons.

——— (1987a). "Feminism and Moral Theory." In *Women and Moral Theory*, ed. Eva Feder Kittay and Diana T. Meyers. Totowa, N.J.: Rowman & Littlefield.

——— (1987b). "Non-contractual Society: A Feminist View." In *Science, Morality & Feminist Theory*, ed. Marsha Hanen and Kai Nielsen. Calgary: The University of Calgary Press.

——— (1993). *Feminist Morality: Transforming Culture, Society, and Politics*. Chicago: The University of Chicago Press.

Hill, Thomas E. Jr. (1991). "The Message of Affirmative Action." *Social Philosophy and Policy* 8, no. 2: 108–129.

Hirsch, Marianne, and Evelyn Fox Keller, eds. (1990). *Conflicts in Feminism*. New York: Routledge.

Hoagland, Sarah Lucia. (1990). "Some Concerns about Nel Noddings' Caring." *Hypatia* 5, no. 1:109–114.

———— (1991). "Some Thoughts about 'Caring.'" In *Feminist Ethics*, ed. Claudia Card. Lawrence, Kans.: University Press of Kansas.

Hobbes, Thomas. (1941). "Philosophical Rudiments Concerning Government and Society." In *The Collected Works of Thomas Hobbes*, Vol. II, ed. Sir W. Molesworth. London: Routledge / Thoemmes Press, 1992.

Hodge, Joanna. (1988). "Subject, Body and the Exclusion of Women from Philosophy." In *Feminist Perspectives in Philosophy*, ed. Morwenna Griffiths and Margaret Whitford. Bloomington: Indiana University Press.

hooks, bell. (1984). *Feminist Theory: From Margin to Center*. Boston: South End Press.

———— (1988). *Talking Back: Thinking Feminist, Thinking Black*. Toronto: Between the Lines.

———— (1990). *Yearning: Race, Gender, and Cultural Politics*. Toronto: Between the Lines.

Houston, Barbara. (1987). "Rescuing Womanly Virtues: Some Dangers of Moral Reclamation." In *Science, Morality & Feminist Theory*, ed. Marsha Hanen and Kai Nielsen. Calgary: The University of Calgary Press.

———— (1988). "Gilligan and the Politics of a Distinctive Women's Morality." In *Feminist Perspectives: Philosophical Essays on Method and Morals*, ed. Lorraine Code, Sheila Mullett, and Christine Overall. Toronto: University of Toronto Press.

———— (1990). "Caring and Exploitation." *Hypatia* 5, no. 1:115–119.

Houston, Lawrence N. (1990). *Psychological Principles and the Black Experience*. Lanham, Md.: University Press of America.

Hughes, Judith. (1988). "The Philosopher's Child." In *Feminist Perspectives in Philosophy*, ed. Morwenna Griffiths and Margaret Whitford. Bloomington: Indiana University Press.

Hume, David. (1740). *A Treatise of Human Nature*, ed. L. A. Selby-Bigge. Oxford: Clarendon Press, 1888.

———— (1751). *Enquiries Concerning Human Understanding and Concerning the Principles of Morals*, ed. L. A. Selby-Bigge. Oxford: Clarendon Press, 1902.

Hunter, Ian. (1976). "Human Rights Legislation in Canada: Its Origin, Development and Implementation." *University of Western Ontario Law Review* 15:17–22.

———— (1985). "When Human Rights Become Wrongs." *University of Western Ontario Law Review* 23, no. 2:197–204.

Iglesias, Teresa. (1988–1990). "Russell and the Ethical Concern of Wittgenstein's *Tractatus.*" *Philosophical Studies*, XXXII:141–155.

Irvine, A. D. (1996). "Jack & Jill & Employment Equity." *Dialogue* 35, no. 2:255–292.

Jacobs, Lesley A. (1994). "Equal Opportunity and Gender Disadvantage." *The Canadian Journal of Law and Jurisprudence* VII, no. 1:61–71.

Jaggar, Alison M. (1977). "Relaxing the Limits on Preferential Treatment." *Social Theory and Practice* 4, no. 2:227–235.

——— (1983a). *Feminist Politics and Human Nature*. Totowa, N.J.: Rowman & Littlefield.

——— (1983b). "Human Biology in Feminist Theory: Sexual Equality Reconsidered." In *Beyond Domination: New Perspectives on Women and Philosophy*, ed. Carol C. Gould. Totowa, N.J.: Rowman & Allanheld.

——— (1987). "Sex Inequality and Bias in Sex Differences Research." In *Science, Morality & Feminist Theory*, ed. Marsha Hanen and Kai Nielsen. Calgary: The University of Calgary Press.

——— (1989). "Feminist Ethics: Some Issues for the Nineties." *Journal of Social Philosophy* 20, no. 1–2:91–107.

——— (1990). "Sexual Difference and Sexual Equality." In *Theoretical Perspectives on Sexual Difference*, ed. Deborah L. Rhode. New Haven: Yale University Press.

——— (1991). "Feminist Ethics: Projects, Problems, Prospects." In *Feminist Ethics*, ed. Claudia Card. Lawrence, Kans.: University Press of Kansas.

Kant, Immanuel. (1785). *Grounding for the Metaphysics of Morals*, trans. James W. Ellington. Indianapolis: Hackett Publishing, 1981.

——— (1797). On a Supposed Right to Tell Lies from Benevolent Motives. In *Kant's Critique of Practical Reason and Other Works on the Theory of Ethics*, trans. T. K. Abbott. London: Longmans, Green & Co., 1927.

Katzenstein, Mary Fainsod, and David D. Laitin. (1987). "Politics, Feminism, and the Ethics of Caring." In *Women and Moral Theory*, ed. Eva Feder Kittay and Diana T. Meyers. Totowa, N.J.: Rowman & Littlefield.

Keller, Evelyn Fox, and Helene Moglen. (1987). "Competition and Feminism: Conflicts for Academic Women." *Signs: Journal of Women in Culture and Society* 12, no. 3:493–511.

Kerber, Linda K. (1986). "Some Cautionary Words for Historians." *Signs: Journal of Women in Culture and Society* 11, no. 2:304–310.

Kessler-Harris, Alice. (1988). "The Just Price, the Free Market, and the Value of Women." *Feminist Studies* 14, no. 2:235–250.

Kittay, Eva Feder. (1993). "Equality, Rawls, and the Dependency Critique." Paper read at Department of Philosophy Colloquium Series, Queen's University.

———— (1995). "Taking Dependency Seriously: Social Cooperation, The Family Medical Leave Act, and Gender Equality Considered in Light of the Social Organization of Dependency Work." *Hypatia* 10, no. 1:8–29.

———— (1997). "Human Dependency and Rawlsian Equality." In *Feminists Rethink the Self*, ed. Diana Tietjens Meyers. Boulder, Colo.: Westview Press.

Kittay, Eva Feder, and Diana T. Meyers, eds. (1987). *Women and Moral Theory*. Totowa, N.J.: Rowman & Littlefield.

Kline, Marlee. (1989). "Race, Racism, and Feminist Legal Theory." In *Feminist Legal Theory: Foundations*, ed. D. Kelly Weisberg. Philadelphia: Temple University Press, 1993.

Koggel, Christine. (1981). *Paradigms: The Later Wittgenstein's View of Meaning*. Thesis (M.A.) Carleton University. Ottawa: National Library Microfiche.

———— (1994). "A Feminist View of Equality and Its Implications for Affirmative Action." *The Canadian Journal of Law and Jurisprudence* VII, no. 1:43–59.

———— (1997). "Commentary on 'Justice and Basic Rights.'" Paper read at the Learned Societies Congress, St. John's, Newfoundland.

Kohlberg, Lawrence, Charles Levine, and Alexandra Hewer. (1983). *Moral Stages: A Current Formulation and a Response to Critics*. Basel, Switzerland: S. Karger.

Krieger, Linda J. (1987). "Through a Glass Darkly: Paradigms of Equality and the Search for a Woman's Jurisprudence." *Hypatia* 2, no. 1:45–61.

Kripke, Saul A. (1982). *Wittgenstein on Rules and Private Language: An Elementary Exposition*. Cambridge, Mass.: Harvard University Press.

Kymlicka, Will. (1989). *Liberalism, Community, and Culture*. Oxford: Clarendon Press.

———— (1990). *Contemporary Political Philosophy*. Oxford: Clarendon Press.

Lacoste, Louise. (1983). "The Trivialization of the Notion of Equality." In *Discovering Reality: Feminist Perspectives on Epistemology, Metaphysics, Methodology, and Philosophy of Science*, ed. Sandra Harding and Merrill B. Hintikka. Boston: D. Reidel Publishing Co.

Ladner, Joyce A. (1987). "Introduction to Tomorrow: The Black Woman." In *Feminism and Methodology: Social Science Issues*, ed. Sandra Harding. Bloomington: Indiana University Press.

Lahey, Kathleen A. (1987). "Feminist Theories of (In)equality." In *Equality and Judicial Neutrality*, ed. Kathleen E. Mahoney and Sheilah L. Martin. Toronto: Carswell.

———— (1989). "Celebration and Struggle: Feminism and Law." In

Feminism: From Pressure to Politics, ed. Angela Miles and Geraldine Finn. Montreal: Black Rose Books.

Lange, Lynda, and Lorenne Clark, ed. (1979). *The Sexism of Social and Political Theory: Women and Reproduction from Plato to Nietzsche*. Toronto: University of Toronto Press.

Larrabee, Mary Jeanne, ed. (1993a). *An Ethic of Care: Feminist and Interdisciplinary Perspectives*. New York: Routledge.

———— (1993b). "Gender and Moral Development: A Challenge for Feminist Theory." In *An Ethic of Care: Feminist and Interdisciplinary Perspectives*, ed. Mary Jeanne Larrabee. New York: Routledge.

Lee, Sander H. (1985). "Reverse Discrimination and Social Justice." *Philosophy Research Archives* 11 (March):155–168.

Lepofsky, M. David, and Jerome E. Bickenbach. (1985). "Equality Rights and the Physically Handicapped." In *Equality Rights and the Canadian Charter of Rights and Freedoms*, ed. Anne F. Bayefsky and Mary Eberts. Toronto: Carswell.

Levin, Michael E. (1980). "Reverse Discrimination, Shackled Runners, and Personal Identity." *Philosophical Studies* 37 (Fall):139–149.

———— (1981). "Is Racial Discrimination Special?" *Journal of Value Inquiry* 15:225–234.

———— (1982). "Opportunity-Right." *Philosophical Quarterly* 32 (October):361.

Littleton, Christine A. (1987). "Reconstructing Sexual Equality." *California Law Review* 75, no. 12:1279–1337.

Lloyd, Genevieve. (1986). "Selfhood, War and Masculinity." In *Feminist Challenges: Social and Political Theory*, ed. Carole Pateman and Elizabeth Gross. Boston: Northeastern University Press.

———— (1989). "The Man of Reason." In *Women, Knowledge, and Reality: Explorations in Feminist Philosophy*, ed. Ann Garry and Marilyn Pearsall. Boston: Unwin Hyman.

Locke, John. (1690). Selections from the *Essay Concerning Human Understanding*. In *From Descartes to Locke*, ed. T. V. Smith and Marjorie Grene. Chicago: The University of Chicago Press, 1940.

Lorde, Audre. (1984). *Sister Outsider: Essays and Speeches*. Freedom, Calif.: The Crossing Press.

Lugones, Maria C. (1987). "Playfulness, 'World'-travelling, and Loving Perception." *Hypatia* 2, no. 2:3–19.

———— (1991). "On the Logic of Pluralist Feminism." In *Feminist Ethics*, ed. Claudia Card. Lawrence, Kans.: University Press of Kansas.

Luria, Zella. (1986). "A Methodological Critique." *Signs: Journal of Women in Culture and Society* 11, no. 2:316–321.

MacIntyre, Alasdair. (1981). *After Virtue: A Study in Moral Theory*. London: Duckworth.

———— (1988). *Whose Justice? Which Rationality?* Notre Dame, Ind.: University of Notre Dame Press.

MacKinnon, Catharine A. (1979). *Sexual Harassment of Working Women.* New Haven: Yale University Press.

———— (1982). "Feminism, Marxism, Method, and the State: An Agenda for Theory." *Signs: Journal of Women in Culture and Society* 7, no. 3:515–544.

———— (1983). "Feminism, Marxism, Method, and the State: Toward Feminist Jurisprudence." *Signs: Journal of Women in Culture and Society* 8, no. 4:635–658.

———— (1987). *Feminism Unmodified.* Cambridge, Mass.: Harvard University Press.

———— (1990). "Legal Perspectives on Sexual Difference." In *Theoretical Perspectives on Sexual Difference*, ed. Deborah L. Rhode. New Haven: Yale University Press.

Macleod, Alistair M. (1983). "Equality of Opportunity." In *Moral Issues*, ed. Jan Narveson. Toronto: Oxford University Press.

Mahowald, Mary Briody, ed. (1983). *Philosophy of Woman: An Anthology of Classic and Current Concepts*, 2nd ed. Indianapolis: Hackett Publishing Company.

Majury, Diana. (1987). "Strategizing in Equality." In *Feminist Legal Theory: Foundations*, ed. D. Kelly Weisberg. Philadelphia: Temple University Press, 1993.

Manning, Rita. (1992). *Speaking from the Heart: A Feminist Perspective on Ethics.* Lanham, Md.: Rowman & Littlefield.

Martin, Michael. (1973). "Pedagogical Arguments for Preferential Hiring and Tenuring of Women Teachers in the University." *Philosophical Forum (Boston)* 5, no. 2:325–333.

Marx, Karl. (1845). "Theses on Feuerbach." In *Karl Marx: Early Writings*, Trans. Rodney Livingstone and Gregor Benton. New York: Vintage Books, 1975.

Massey, Stephen J. (1981). "Rethinking Affirmative Action." *Social Theory and Practice* 7, no. 1:21–47.

Matsuda, Mari J. (1986). "Liberal Jurisprudence and Abstracted Visions of Human Nature: A Feminist Critique of Rawls's Theory of Justice." In *Feminist Legal Theory: Foundations*, ed. D. Kelly Weisberg. Philadelphia: Temple University Press, 1993.

Meyers, Diana T. (1987). "The Socialized Individual and Individual Autonomy: An Intersection between Philosophy and Psychology." In *Women and Moral Theory*, ed. Eva Feder Kittay and Diana T. Meyers. Totowa, N.J.: Rowman & Littlefield.

———— (1989). *Self, Society, and Personal Choice.* New York: Columbia University Press.

———— (1997). "Introduction." In *Feminists Rethink the Self*, ed. Diana T. Meyers. Boulder, Colo.: Westview Press.

Miller, Jean Baker. (1986). *Toward a New Psychology of Women*, 2nd ed. Boston: Beacon Press.

Mills, Charles W. (1994). "Carnal Knowledges: Beyond Rawls and Sandel." Paper read at University of Western Ontario's Philosophy Department conference "A Question of Values: New Canadian Perspectives in Ethics and Political Philosophy."

Minas, Anne C. (1977). "How Reverse Discrimination Compensates Women." *Ethics* 88 (October):74–79.

Minow, Martha. (1987). "The Supreme Court 1986 Term—Foreword: Justice Engendered." *Harvard Law Review* 101, no. 10:10–95.

———— (1990a). *Making All the Difference: Inclusion, Exclusion and American Law*. Ithaca: Cornell University Press.

———— (1990b). "Adjudicating Differences: Conflicts among Feminist Lawyers." In *Conflicts in Feminism*, ed. Marianne Hirsch and Evelyn Fox Keller. New York: Routledge.

Monk, Ray. (1991). *Ludwig Wittgenstein: The Duty of Genius*. London: Vintage.

Moody-Adams, Michele M. (1991). "Gender and the Complexity of Moral Voices." In *Feminist Ethics*, ed. Claudia Card. Lawrence, Kans.: University Press of Kansas.

Morgan, Kathryn Pauly. (1983). "Response to Nicholson's 'Affirmative action, Education, and Social Class.' " *Philosophy of Education: Proceedings* 39:243–247.

———— (1987). "Women and Moral Madness." In *Science, Morality & Feminist Theory*, ed. Marsha Hanen and Kai Nielsen. Calgary: University of Calgary Press.

Moulton, Janice. (1989). "A Paradigm of Philosophy: The Adversary Method." In *Women, Knowledge, and Reality: Explorations in Feminist Philosophy*, ed. Ann Garry and Marilyn Pearsall. Boston: Unwin Hyman.

Mullett, Sheila. (1987). "Only Connect: The Place of Self-knowledge in Ethics." In *Science, Morality & Feminist Theory*, ed. Marsha Hanen and Kai Nielsen. Calgary: The University of Calgary Press.

———— (1988). "Shifting Perspective: A New Approach to Ethics." In *Feminist Perspectives: Philosophical Essays on Method and Morals*, ed. Lorraine Code, Sheila Mullett, and Christine Overall. Toronto: University of Toronto Press.

Nagel, Thomas. (1970). *The Possibility of Altruism*. Princeton: Princeton University Press.

———— (1989). "A Defense of Affirmative Action." In *Moral Choices: Ethical Theories and Problems*, ed. Joseph Grčić. St. Paul, Minn.: West Publishing Company.

—— (1991). *Equality and Partiality*. New York: Oxford University Press.

Narveson, Jan. (1985). "Equality vs. Liberty: Advantage, Liberty." *Social Philosophy & Policy* 2, no. 1:33–60.

—— (1991). "Have We a Right to Non-Discrimination?" In *Business Ethics in Canada*, 2nd edition, ed. Deborah C. Poff and Wilfred J. Waluchow. Scarborough, Ont.: Prentice-Hall Canada.

—— (1995). *Moral Matters*. Peterborough: Broadview Press.

Nedelsky, Jennifer. (1989). "Reconceiving Autonomy." *Yale Journal of Law and Feminism* 1, no. 7:7–36.

—— (1993). "Reconceiving Rights as Relationship." *Review of Constitutional Studies* 1, no. 1:1–26.

Nelson, Lynn Hankinson. (1994). "Critical Notice of Lorraine Code *What Can She Know? Feminist Theory and the Construction of Knowledge*." *Canadian Journal of Philosophy* 24, no. 2:295–326.

Newton, Lisa. (1973). "Reverse Discrimination as Unjustified." *Ethics* 83, no. 4:308–312.

Nicholson, Linda J. (1983a). "Affirmative Action, Education, and Social Class." *Philosophy of Education: Proceedings* 39:233–242.

—— (1983b). "Feminist Theory: The Private and the Public." In *Beyond Domination: New Perspectives on Women and Philosophy*, ed. Carol C. Gould. Totowa, N.J.: Rowman & Allanheld.

—— (1983c). "Women, Morality, and History." In *An Ethic of Care: Feminist and Interdisciplinary Perspectives*, ed. Mary Jeanne Larrabee. New York: Routledge, 1993.

Nicholson, Linda J., ed. (1990). *Feminism/Postmodernism*. New York: Routledge.

Nickel, James W. (1974a). "Classification by Race in Compensatory Programs." *Ethics* 84 (January):146–150.

—— (1974b). "Should Reparations Be to Individuals or to Groups?" *Analysis* 34, no. 5:154–160.

Nielsen, Kai. (1985). *Equality and Liberty: A Defense of Radical Egalitarianism*. Totowa, N.J.: Rowman & Allanheld.

—— (1987). "Afterword: Feminist Theory—Some Twistings and Turnings." In *Science, Morality & Feminist Theory*, ed. Marsha Hanen and Kai Nielsen. Calgary: The University of Calgary Press.

—— (1989). "Equality of Condition and Self-Ownership." In *Ethics and Basic Rights*, ed. Guy Lafrance. Ottawa: The University of Ottawa Press.

—— (1994a). "How to Proceed in Social Philosophy: Contextualist Justice and Wide Reflective Equilibrium." *Queen's Law Journal* 20, no. 1:89–137.

—— (1994b). "Justice as a Kind of Impartiality." *Laval théologique et philosophie* 50, no. 3:511–529.

Noddings, Nel. (1984). *Caring: A Feminine Approach to Ethics and Moral Education*. Berkeley: University of California Press.

——— (1990). "A Response." *Hypatia* 5, no. 1:120–126.

Nozick, Robert. (1974). *Anarchy, State, and Utopia*. New York: Basic Books, Inc.

Nunner-Winkler, Gertrud. (1984). "Two Moralities? A Critical Discussion of an Ethic of Care and Responsibility Versus an Ethic of Rights and Justice." In *An Ethic of Care: Feminist and Interdisciplinary Perspectives*, ed. Mary Jeanne Larrabee. New York: Routledge, 1993.

Nussbaum, Martha. (1995). "Introduction." In *Women, Culture and Development: A Study of Human Capabilities*, ed. Martha Nussbaum and Jonathan Glover. Oxford: Clarendon Press.

Nussbaum, Martha, and Amartya Sen, eds. (1993). *The Quality of Life*. Oxford: Clarendon Press.

Nussbaum, Martha, and Jonathan Glover, eds. (1995). *Women, Culture and Development: A Study of Human Capabilities*. Oxford: Clarendon Press.

Nzegwu, Nkiru. (1995). "Recovering Igbo Traditions: A Case for Indigenous Women's Organizations in Development." In *Women, Culture and Development: A Study of Human Capabilities*, ed. Martha Nussbaum and Jonathan Glover. Oxford: Clarendon Press.

Offen, Karen. (1988). "Defining Feminism: A Comparative Historical Approach." *Signs: Journal of Women in Culture and Society* 14, no. 1:119–157.

Okin, Susan Moller. (1982). "Women and the Making of the Sentimental Family." *Philosophy & Public Affairs* 11, no. 1:65–88.

——— (1989). *Justice, Gender, and the Family*. New York: Basic Books.

——— (1994). "Gender and Relativism." Paper read at Learned Societies Conference, Canadian Philosophical Association Meetings, The University of Calgary.

——— (1995). "Inequalities between the Sexes in Different Cultural Contexts." In *Women, Culture and Development: A Study of Human Capabilities*, ed. Martha Nussbaum and Jonathan Glover. Oxford: Clarendon Press.

O'Neill, Onora. (1973). "How Do We Know when Opportunities Are Equal?" *Philosophical Forum (Boston)* 5, no. 2:334–346.

Overall, Christine. (1987a). "Role Models: A Critique." In *Women: Isolation and Bonding: The Ecology of Gender*, ed. Kathleen Storrie. Toronto: Methuen.

——— (1987b). *Ethics and Human Reproduction: A Feminist Analysis*. Boston: Unwin Hyman.

——— (1988). "Feminism, Ontology, and 'Other Minds.' " In *Feminist Perspectives: Philosophical Essays on Method and Morals*, ed. Lorraine

Code, Sheila Mullett, and Christine Overall. Toronto: University of Toronto Press.

———— (1992). *Role Muddles: The Stereotyping of Feminists.* Ottawa: CRIAW/ICREF.

Pateman, Carole (1987). "Introduction: The Theoretical Subversiveness of Feminism." In *Feminist Challenges: Social and Political Theory,* ed. Carole Pateman and Elizabeth Gross. Boston: Northeastern University Press.

———— (1988). *The Sexual Contract.* Stanford: Stanford University Press.

———— (1989). *The Disorder of Women: Democracy, Feminism and Political Theory.* Stanford, Calif.: Stanford University Press.

Pateman, Carole, and Elizabeth Gross, ed. (1986). *Feminist Challenges: Social and Political Theory.* Boston: Northeastern University Press.

Pierce, Christine. (1991). "Postmodernism and Other Skepticisms." In *Feminist Ethics,* ed. Claudia Card. Lawrence, Kans.: University Press of Kansas.

Pluhar, Evelyn B. (1981). "Preferential Hiring and Unjust Sacrifice." *Philosophical Forum (Boston)* 12, no. 3:214–224.

Puka, Bill. (1990). "The Liberation of Caring: A Different Voice for Gilligan's 'Different Voice.' " In *An Ethic of Care: Feminist and Interdisciplinary Perspectives,* ed. Mary Jeanne Larrabee. New York: Routledge, 1993.

Purdy, Laura M. (1984). "In Defense of Hiring Apparently Less Qualified Women." *Journal of Social Philosophy* 15 (Summer):26–33.

Putnam, Ruth Anna. (1995). "Why Not a Feminist Theory of Justice?" In *Women, Culture and Development: A Study of Human Capabilities,* ed. Martha Nussbaum and Jonathan Glover. Oxford: Clarendon Press.

Quine, Willard V. O. (1960). *Word & Object.* Cambridge, Mass.: M.I.T. Press.

Rawls, John. (1971). *A Theory of Justice.* Cambridge, Mass.: Harvard University Press.

———— (1985). "Justice as Fairness: Political Not Metaphysical." *Philosophy & Public Affairs* 14, no. 3:227–251.

———— (1993). *Political Liberalism.* New York: Columbia University Press.

Rhode, Deborah L. (1989). *Justice and Gender: Sex Discrimination and the Law.* Cambridge, Mass.: Harvard University Press.

———— (1990). "Definitions of Difference." In *Theoretical Perspectives on Sexual Difference,* ed. Deborah L. Rhode. New Haven: Yale University Press.

Rioux, Marcia H. (1994). "Towards a Concept of Equality of Well-being: Overcoming the Social and Legal Construction of Inequality." *The Canadian Journal of Law and Jurisprudence* VII, no. 1:127–147.

Rosenblum, Nancy L. (1989). "Pluralism and Self-Defense." In *Liberalism and the Moral Life*, ed. Nancy L. Rosenblum. Cambridge, Mass.: Harvard University Press.

Rosenfeld, Michel. (1991). *Affirmative Action and Justice: A Philosophical and Constitutional Inquiry.* New Haven: Yale University Press.

Rousseau, Jean Jacques. (1760). *Emile.* Trans. Barbara Foxley. London: Dent, 1911.

Ruddick, Sara. (1984). "Preservative Love and Military Destruction." In *Mothering: Essays in Feminist Theory*, ed. Joyce Trebilcot. Totowa, N.J.: Rowman and Allenheld.

———— (1989). *Maternal Thinking: Towards a Politics of Peace.* London: The Women's Press.

Sandel, Michael J. (1982). *Liberalism and the Limits of Justice.* Cambridge: Cambridge University Press.

———— (1984). "Morality and the Liberal Ideal." *New Republic* 190 (May 7):15–17.

———— (1987). "The Political Theory of the Procedural Republic." In *Rule of Law: Ideal or Ideology?* ed. Allan C. Hutchinson and Patrick Monahan. Toronto: Carswell.

Sasseen, Robert F. (1976). "Affirmative Action and the Principle of Equality." *Studies in Philosophy and Education* 9 (Spring):275–295.

Scales, Ann C. (1986). "The Emergence of Feminist Jurisprudence: An Essay." *The Yale Law Journal*, 95:1373–1403.

Schneider, Elizabeth M. (1986). "The Dialectic of Rights and Politics: Perspectives from the Women's Movement." In *Feminist Legal Theory: Foundations*, ed. D. Kelly Weisberg. Philadelphia: Temple University Press, 1993.

Schwarzenbach, Sibyl. (1987). "Rawls and Ownership: The Forgotten Category of Reproductive Labor." In *Science, Morality & Feminist Theory*, ed. Marsha Hanen and Kai Nielsen. Calgary: The University of Calgary Press.

Scott, Joan W. (1990). "Deconstructing Equality-Versus-Difference: Or, the Uses of Poststructuralist Theory for Feminism." In *Conflicts in Feminism*, ed. Marianne Hirsch and Evelyn Fox Keller. New York: Routledge.

Seller, Anne. (1988). "Realism Versus Relativism: Towards a Politically Adequate Epistemology." In *Feminist Perspectives in Philosophy*, ed. Morwenna Griffiths and Margaret Whitford. Bloomington: Indiana University Press.

Sen, Amartya. (1992). *Inequality Reexamined.* Cambridge, Mass.: Harvard University Press.

———— (1995a). "Equality of What?" In *Equal Freedom: Selected Tanner Lectures on Human Values*, ed. Stephen Darwall. Ann Arbor: University of Michigan Press.

——— (1995b). "Gender Inequality and Theories of Justice." In *Women, Culture and Development: A Study of Human Capabilities*, ed. Martha Nussbaum and Jonathan Glover. Oxford: Clarendon Press.

Sher, George. (1975). "Justifying Reverse Discrimination in Employment." *Philosophy & Public Affairs* 4, no. 2:159–170.

——— (1977). "Groups and Justice." *Ethics* 87 (January):174–181.

Sherwin, Susan. (1987). "Feminist Ethics and in Vitro Fertilization." In *Science, Morality & Feminist Theory*, ed. Marsha Hanen and Kai Nielsen. Calgary: The University of Calgary Press.

——— (1989). "Philosophical Methodology and Feminist Methodology: Are They Compatible?" In *Women, Knowledge, and Reality: Explorations in Feminist Philosophy*, ed. Ann Garry and Marilyn Pearsall. Boston: Unwin Hyman.

——— (1992). *No Longer Patient: Feminist Ethics and Health Care.* Philadelphia: Temple University Press.

Sidgwick, Henry. (1966). *The Methods of Ethics.* New York: Dover Publications.

Simon, Robert L. (1974). "Preferential Hiring: A Reply to Judith Jarvis Thompson." *Philosophy & Public Affairs* 3, no. 3:312–320.

——— (1978a). "Preferential Treatment: For Groups or for Individuals?" *National Forum* 58 (Winter):7–9.

——— (1978b). "Statistical Justifications of Discrimination." *Analysis* 38, no. 1:37–42.

——— (1979). "Individual Rights and 'Benign' Discrimination." *Ethics* 90 (October):88–97.

Singer, Linda. (1987). "Value, Power and Gender: Do We Need a Different Voice?" In *Power, Gender, Values*, ed. Judith Genova. Edmonton: Academic Printing & Publishing.

Smith, Lynn. (1986). "A New Paradigm for Equality Rights." In *Righting the Balance: Canada's New Equality Rights*, ed. Lynn Smith. Saskatoon: The Canadian Human Rights Reporter.

Speizer, Jeanne J. (1981). "Role Models, Mentors, and Sponsors: The Elusive Concepts." *Signs: Journal of Women in Culture and Society* 6, no. 4:692–712.

Stack, Carol B. (1986). "The Culture of Gender: Women and Men of Color." *Signs: Journal of Women in Culture and Society* 11, no. 2:321–324.

Statistics Canada. *Teachers in Universities*, Catalogue no. 81–241. Ottawa: Minister of Supply & Services.

——— *Universities: Enrolment and Degrees*, Catalogue no. 81–204. Ottawa: Minister of Supply & Services.

Sumner, L. W. (1987). "Positive Sexism." *Social Philosophy and Policy* 5, no. 1:204–222.

———— (1989). *The Moral Foundation of Rights.* Oxford: Clarendon Press.

———— (1996). "Why the Numbers Count." *Dialogue* 35, no. 2:375–385.

Supreme Court of Canada. (1987). *Action Travail des Femmes v. Canadian National Railway Co. et al. Dominion Law Reports,* 40 D.L.R. (4th).

———— (1988). *Morgentaler, Smoling and Scott v. The Queen. Dominion Law Reports,* 44 D.L.R. (4th).

Symons, Thomas H. B. and James E. Page. (1984). *Some Questions of Balance: Human Resources, Higher Education and Canadian Studies.* Ottawa: Association of Universities and Colleges of Canada.

Sypnowich, Christine. (1990). *The Concept of Socialist Law.* Oxford: Clarendon Press.

———— (1993a). "Some Disquiet about 'Difference.' " *Praxis International* 13, no, 2:99–112.

———— (1993b). "Justice, Community, and the Antinomies of Feminist Theory." *Political Theory* 21, no. 3:484–506.

Taylor, Charles. (1989). "Cross-Purposes: The Liberal-Communitarian Debate." In *Liberalism and the Moral Life,* ed. Nancy Rosenblum. Cambridge, Mass.: Harvard University Press.

Thalberg, Irving. (1972). "Justifications of Institutional Racism." *Philosophical Forum (Boston)* 3, no. 2:243–264.

———— (1973). "Reverse Discrimination and the Future." *Philosophical Forum (Boston)* 5, no. 2:294–308.

Thomas, Laurence. (1994). "Truth, Liberalism, and Equality: A Review Essay of Ezorsky's *Racism and Justice.*" *APA Newsletters* 93, no. 1: 133–139.

Thompson, Janna. (1986). "Women and Political Rationality." In *Feminist Challenges: Social and Political Theory,* ed. Carole Pateman and Elizabeth Gross. Boston: Northeastern University Press.

Thomson, Judith Jarvis. (1973). "Preferential Hiring." *Philosophy & Public Affairs* 2, no. 4:364–384.

Thornton, Merle. (1986). "Sex Equality Is not Enough for Feminism." In *Feminist Challenges: Social and Political Theory,* ed. Carole Pateman and Elizabeth Gross. Boston: Northeastern University Press.

Tong, Rosemarie. (1989). *Feminist Thought: A Comprehensive Introduction.* Boulder, Colo.: Westview Press.

Trakman, Leon E. (1994). "Substantive Equality in Constitutional Jurisprudence: Meaning within Meaning." *The Canadian Journal of Law and Jurisprudence* VII, no. 1:27–42.

Tronto, Joan C. (1987). "Beyond Gender Difference to a Theory of Care." In *An Ethic of Care: Feminist and Interdisciplinary Perspectives,* ed. Mary Jeanne Larrabee. New York: Routledge, 1993.

———— (1993). *Moral Boundaries: A Political Argument for an Ethic of Care.* New York: Routledge.

Valverde, Mariana. (1987). *Sex, Power and Pleasure.* Baltimore: New Society Publishers.

Vanterpool, Rudolph V. (1989). "Affirmative Action Revisited: Justice and Public Policy Considerations." *Public Affairs Quarterly* 3, no. 4 (October):47–59.

Vetterling, Mary K. (1973). "Some Common Sense Notes on Preferential Hiring." *Philosophical Forum (Boston)* 5, no. 2:320–324.

Vizkelety, Beatrice. (1990). "Affirmative Action, Equality and the Courts: Comparing *Action Travail des Femmes v. CN* and *Apsit and the Manitoba Rice Farmers Association v. The Manitoba Human Rights Commission.*" *Canadian Journal of Women and the Law* 4:287–310.

Walker, James C. (1983). "In a Diffident Voice: Cryptoseparatist Analysis of Female Moral Development." *Social Research* 50, no. 3:665–695.

Walker, Lawrence J. (1984). "Sex Differences in the Development of Moral Reasoning: A Critical Review." In *An Ethic of Care: Feminist and Interdisciplinary Perspectives,* ed. Mary Jeanne Larrabee. New York: Routledge, 1993.

Walzer, Michael. (1983). *Spheres of Justice: A Defense of Pluralism and Equality.* New York: Basic Books, Inc., Publishers.

Warren, Mary Anne. (1977). "Secondary Sexism and Quota Hiring." *Philosophy & Public Affairs* 6, no. 3:240–261.

Wasserstrom, Richard. (1976). "The University and the Case for Preferential Treatment." *American Philosophical Quarterly* 13 (April):165–170.

———— (1978). "A Defense of Programs of Preferential Treatment." *National Forum,* 58, no. 1:15–18.

Weinzweig, Marjorie. (1987). "Pregnancy Leave, Comparable Worth, and Concepts of Equality." *Hypatia* 2, no. 1:71–101.

Weisberg, D. Kelly. (ed.) (1993). *Feminist Legal Theory: Foundations.* Philadelphia: Temple University Press.

Wendell, Susan. (1980). "Discrimination, Sex Prejudice and Affirmative Action." *Atlantis* 6, no. 1:40–50.

———— (1987). "A (Qualified) Defense of Liberal Feminism." *Hypatia* 2, no. 2:65–93.

West, Robin. (1988). "Jurisprudence and Gender." *The University of Chicago Law Review* 55, no. 6:1–72.

Westen, Peter. (1982). "The Empty Idea of Equality." *Harvard Law Review* 95, no. 3:537–596.

———— (1985). "The Concept of Equal Opportunity." *Ethics* 95 (July):837–850.

———— (1990). *Speaking of Equality: An Analysis of the Rhetorical Force of 'Equality' in Moral and Legal Discourse.* Princeton: Princeton University Press.

Whitbeck, Caroline. (1973). "Theories of Sex Difference." *Philosophical Forum (Boston)* 5, no. 2:54–80.

————— (1983). "A Different Reality: Feminist Ontology." In *Women, Knowledge, and Reality: Explorations in Feminist Philosophy*, ed. Ann Garry and Marilyn Pearsall. Boston: Unwin Hyman, 1989.

Williams, Bernard. (1985). *Ethics and The Limits of Philosophy*. Cambridge, Mass.: Harvard University Press.

Williams, Joan C. (1989). "Deconstructing Gender." *Michigan Law Review* 87, no. 4:797–845.

Williams, Patricia J. (1991). *The Alchemy of Race and Rights*. Cambridge, Mass.: Harvard University Press.

Wittgenstein, Ludwig. (1953). *Philosophical Investigations*, Trans. G. E. M. Anscombe. Oxford: Basil Blackwell, 1976.

————— (1958). *The Blue and Brown Books*. Oxford: Basil Blackwell, 1964.

————— (1961). *Tractatus Logico-Philosophicus*. London: Routledge & Kegan Paul.

————— (1969). *On Certainty*, ed. G. E. M. Anscombe and G. H. von Wright. New York: Harper Torchbooks.

Wubnig, Judy. (1976). "The Merit Criterion of Employment: An Examination of Some Current Arguments against Its Use." *The Humanist* (September/October):36–39.

Yahng, Lilian. (1997). *Focus Imaginarius: Rational Being in the Kingdom of Ends*. Thesis (Senior). Bryn Mawr College.

Young, Iris Marion. (1987). "Impartiality and the Civic Public: Some Implications of Feminist Critiques of Moral and Political Theory." In *Feminism as Critique: On the Politics of Gender*, ed. Seyla Benhabib and Drucilla Cornell. Minneapolis: University of Minnesota Press.

————— (1990). *Justice and the Politics of Difference*. Princeton: Princeton University Press.

Young-Bruehl, Elisabeth. (1987). "The Education of Women as Philosophers." *Signs: Journal of Women in Culture and Society* 12, no. 2:207–221.

Index

299

About the Author

Christine Koggel is assistant professor of philosophy at Bryn Mawr College. She has a doctorate from Queen's University in Kingston, where she held a Social Sciences and Humanities Research Council of Canada Doctoral Fellowship. She was also awarded a S.S.H.R.C.C. Postdoctoral Fellowship, which was taken up at York and Queen's. She has coedited *Contemporary Moral Issues* (1997) and is currently editing *Moral Issues in Global Perspective*.